James Edwin Thorold Rogers

Cobden and Modern Political Opinion

Essays on Certain Political Topics

James Edwin Thorold Rogers

Cobden and Modern Political Opinion
Essays on Certain Political Topics

ISBN/EAN: 9783741190797

Manufactured in Europe, USA, Canada, Australia, Japa

Cover: Foto ©Suzi / pixelio.de

Manufactured and distributed by brebook publishing software (www.brebook.com)

James Edwin Thorold Rogers

Cobden and Modern Political Opinion

COBDEN

AND

MODERN POLITICAL OPINION.

COBDEN

AND

MODERN POLITICAL OPINION.

ESSAYS ON CERTAIN POLITICAL TOPICS.

BY

JAMES E. THOROLD ROGERS.

London
MACMILLAN AND CO.
1873

[All rights reserved.]

OXFORD:
BY E. B. GARDNER, E. PICKARD HALL, AND J. H. STACY,
PRINTERS TO THE UNIVERSITY.

PREFACE.

The following pages are an attempt to define the place which Cobden holds in the political and economical history of this country, and to explain the attitude which he took on most of the leading topics of his time. Some of these topics are accomplished facts; others are still debateable questions, though they are in process of settlement, and, as I believe, in the direction which he indicated. I have a further purpose in this publication; that of adding my contribution to the memory of the wisest and most farsighted statesman whom this country, fertile as it has been in great men, has produced. And I wish also to state my own convictions, gathered mainly from my long and familiar intercourse with Cobden, on certain public questions.

A near connexion between his family and mine brought about that I knew Cobden intimately from my youth. They who had similar advantages will bear me out when I say that Cobden was ready to speak upon every topic of public interest, and that his knowledge of facts was as remarkable as the clearness with which he interpreted the moral or political significance of events. A diligent reader and an acute observer, he was possessed in the highest degree of that inductive faculty which enables a few men to grasp great principles, and of that logical precision which endows a few more with the power of determining the true relations of any public event. With those who believe that the highest political sagacity consists in negotiating the terms of a compromise, the precision and breadth of Cobden's opinions is always mistaken for narrowness. This is the charge which the Trimmer always alleges against the man of strong and deep convictions. It is probable that the advocate of compromises performs a very useful function in the economy of political action, but he has no field for his operations unless rival opinions are also advocated with energy. It is certain that every contest between privilege and freedom produces its Halifax, who is distrusted by both parties, but who generally contrives to secure the advantages of the situation.

I have attempted to illustrate, as far as the materials before me allow, the position which Cobden took on the several subjects treated of in the following pages. These materials consist of his writings and speeches. The former were collected and published soon after his death by Mrs. Cobden, the latter were edited under the joint superintendence of my friend Mr. Bright and myself. A third source of information is his correspondence, which was exceedingly copious. A selection of this correspondence is happily in course of publication. Cobden was among the best of letter writers, for he wrote with the greatest fluency, clearness, and vivacity. A letter of his gave one all the impressions of an animated conversation.

I have relied to an extent which it is obviously impossible to define on the many conversations which I had with him on the various topics discussed below. I do not pretend to have stated his views with the precision which he would have given them had he written about them himself. They who care to criticise what I have written will no doubt discover many points of attack in my exposition. There are occasions on which I have expressed a difference between Cobden's opinions and my own, though the occasions are rare and comparatively unimportant. But I am not conscious of having modified the impressions which I received from the long teaching which he gave me when I attempt to show what he believed to be necessary and expedient for his country, and how he has assisted in the growth of Public Opinion.

It was necessary, in order to indicate the changes which have come over this Opinion, to consult the arguments employed by the Press, especially that of the time when Cobden's views were subjected to the ordinary criticism with which public men are assailed. Naturally I have made the fullest reference to the arguments of the *Times*. It is well known that Cobden wished that political and literary criticism were not anonymous. There are many good reasons in favour of such a change. The writer of an anonymous article is strongly tempted to be careless and unfair. He can and often does assail a public reputation —the English press is as a rule scrupulously careful in avoiding all allusion to private character—unjustly, intemperately, and with impunity; for an anonymous writer knows but little of his craft if he does not understand how to make dark insinuations. Even when he is called to account for the misstatement of facts, the editor of the paper can relegate the disclaimer to an obscure corner of his issue. In literary criticism again, anonymous writing too frequently gives evidence that the author of the article has never read the book which he reviews, and occasionally is so fulsome in its laudation as to suggest the worst suspicions of reciprocal praise.

But the advantages of anonymous political and literary criticism far outweigh the disadvantages. So much do they outweigh them that one regrets that, of late years, the world has been informed about many of the persons who write for, and nearly all those who manage, the London press. But if such writing ceases to be anonymous, it will either lose its liveliness, or engender strong personal animosities. Few Englishmen would, I imagine, care to see the system of the French press introduced among us, with its brag, its mendacity, its malignity. It is one thing to be attacked by a system, a company, a joint-stock proprietary, another to be always jostling against a man who gets his living by disparaging your reputation, and distorting your utterances.

Besides, it is a supreme advantage to be informed at any given moment of the precise value or popularity of your opinions, and to be instructed in the line of attack which can be made on them. I have assumed throughout these pages that this is the policy adopted by the most considerable paper in England on all unsettled political topics. Of course it does so only on those which are unsettled. On all matters which bear on public and private morals, it reflects with fidelity the traditional ethics of the English character. The anonymous press may powerfully contribute to the maintenance of such a character. A high standard of commercial and public honour are of comparatively little social significance in an individual; but they have a great force when they are seen to be the habit of a great newspaper. I have alluded below to the memorable case of Bogle *versus* Lawson. The moral effect of such a trial in the case of an individual would have been hardly perceptible; it rose to the dignity of a national act when it was undertaken by the *Times*. In what I say therefore of this paper, I am merely referring to its attitude on controverted political topics, and am treating it as an important register of current opinion. It is plain that it would wholly cease to perform this function if the opinions expressed in its leading articles came to be considered merely as the personal views of their several writers.

There is however another motive before me in publishing this volume. Cobden was during his life reputed to be the founder of a political party, which got the name of the Manchester school of politicians. The leading tenets of this school were very successfully travestied during his life. It was described as being a peace-at-any-price party,—as the party of sordid manufacturers, who were intent on nothing but their own gains, and who were ready to sacrifice labour to capital, as unenglish, and eager to Americanise our institutions, as enemies of the great British Empire, as contemptuous towards culture, and Philistine in its enjoyments, as delighting to set class against class, as animated with the bitterest feelings against landlords and farmers. My readers will find these several charges referred to in the subsequent pages, and I hope refuted.

The school which Cobden—I will not say founded, for all who have assisted the solid progress of good government and national prosperity have belonged to it, but—strengthened, affirmed that freedom was the natural condition of the individual, and that restraint must always be justified in order to be defended. In the presence of an outrageous and ruinous wrong, the old Corn Law, it assailed the principle of protection to agriculture with irresistible force. But it was the accident of a fact which caused the assault to be made on this position. It attacked every kind of protection, on the ground that the assistance given to one interest was an injury, a restraint, an indefensible control on other interests, which were depressed, impoverished, and dwarfed in consequence. The promoters of this doctrine knew very well that the orderliness and control which law imposes are the guarantees of personal liberty; but they understood by the beneficent operation of law that government or order which protects all equally, not that which gives a licence or advantage to a few at the expense of the rest of society. Every man is benefited by the police of justice, a section only is benefited by privilege.

Commercial freedom, *i.e.* the right of each individual to employ his labour innocently to his best advantage, and to spend the produce of his labour in the best market which his discretion and opportunities give him, is only one form of the great struggle for social freedom. If the Legislature of this country, like a grand jury, executed a high trust on the principle that it would award to the best of its judgment fair and equal law, just and impartial taxation to all, it would, as far as the result is concerned, be unimportant whether it were elected by millions or by hundreds. It is sufficiently manifest that it does not do so; and though the British Legislature is perhaps as fair as any which can be found, it is perfectly notorious that it has throughout the greater part of its history assisted or recognised those interests only which have been represented in it. Hence the legitimate demand for an extended franchise, on the ground that the existing mechanism of government is not equitable.

Men are pretty well agreed as to the morals of Christianity, but they differ hopelessly as to its dogmas, as to its best form of government, as to its relation to secular interests. If they could effect a compromise on these topics, they could formulate such a common Christianity as might be taught in national schools. But no reasonable person believes that they can. Hence the protection which the Legislature practically accords to one theory about the relation of religion to secular interests in the maintenance of a State Church, is a restraint on freedom, and the disciples of Cobden's school claim religious equality as a right which it is unsafe and unfair to refuse. It is true that the demand for such an equality may at times appear a sentiment. But when it is seen that a great public duty, the genuine education of the people, becomes impracticable under such circumstances, the demand for a change becomes urgent.

Instances like these could be extended and multiplied. The only real answer which can be made to such claims is the doubt as to whether the demand can safely be granted, and whether the concession of freedom on these and similar topics may not lead to disorder and anarchy. The answer to this doubt is partly derived from the facts of experience, partly from the reason of the case. Disorder and anarchy have generally, in the history of social civilisation, arisen from no other cause than the excesses, the arrogance, the conspiracies of a privileged class. Occasionally they have ensued from the revenge which has been taken by a liberated and insulted people, when it suspects with more or less reason that the yoke will be imposed on it anew. Democracies have crushed oligarchies remorselessly, but only when they have been stimulated to vengeance by intolerable wrong. It is almost superfluous to say that the civilisation of Greece, of Rome, and of Medieval Italy was destroyed or arrested by the ambition and violence of aristocratical parties. I do not say that the distribution of power is a preventive of the excesses of power, but experience has shown that it makes the excess increasingly difficult. Nor can it be asserted that every stage of society is equally able to use political power discreetly. A king was necessary in order to recover and further civilisation in the Middle Ages, and a church like that of Rome was necessary also, during the same epoch, in order to form a check to the despotism of kings. But we all know that both monarch and pope became mischievous when they had done their work, and that England in the sixteenth century was immeasurably worse off than it had been in the fourteenth.

To say that a transfer of power from a limited class or order to a popular vote is merely a transfer of the forces which govern society, and that under such circumstances men are just as certainly controlled as they were before the change was effected, is a truism. Society exists by the control which it exercises over men, and there is no guarantee for liberty except by order and law, which are essentially coercive. But the question is, under what circumstances is the control of society most generous, because it is least oppressive, least unfair? It appears to me that there can be but one answer to this. It is that form of government in which political power is most widely distributed, in which opinion, except of course that which denies the fundamental principles of morality, is least of all coerced, and in which neither disabilities are inflicted, nor privileges conferred by law. Except during a few years of Queen Anne's reign, when a standing quarrel with the Commons led it to reject the Occasional Conformity Bill, I cannot discover any period in which the House of Lords, in its legislative capacity, has effected any reform whatever for the English people. I am now speaking of those reforms which the wiser men of both traditional parties in Great Britain acknowledge to have been expedient, or just, or necessary.

It is not easy for the majority in any country, governed by such a system of popular election as our own, to inflict a wrong by law, because they are themselves the objects of the law which they enact. It is easy to discover numerous examples of wrong inflicted by a government which is administered at the discretion of a narrow section in the community. It is not easy to discover the means by which a popular government can oppress or injure any particular interest in the community, because it is invariably the case that such an interest has a very effective representation in the majority. But the social history of this country swarms with illustrations of the contrary facts, of the manner in which interests which have been fortunate enough to appropriate power to themselves have used such power for the systematic injury of their fellow countrymen.

Take for example the case of an organisation which is at present causing considerable alarm in many persons' minds, and, in the opinion of some writers and speakers, is threatening many important national industries with subversion, or at least with impoverishment. I allude to the combination of workmen for the sake of obtaining higher wages. Whether such combinations have had this result, is, I think, problematical, notwithstanding the very general impression among artisans, that wages have been increased by the action of those associations. Even if they have done so, (unless people fall into the exploded error, that the more money they have the richer they are, whatever the worth of the money may be,) it is manifest that a general rise in wages, unless it were assisted by some economy of labour, would produce an exactly equivalent effect on prices, and that the labourer would be no better off after his efforts had been successful. A trade-union, then, if it achieve its end in the direction or object which it purposes, must affect some favoured classes of labour only, and cannot be generally beneficent, though it must be allowed that the advocates of trade-unions invariably contemplate the extension of the system to every kind of labour. But if the combination produced all the evils which are said to belong to it, or to be hereafter consequent from it, it has two justifications. There is no more reason why men should not enter into a labour partnership, and enact bye-laws adverse to those who do not join it, than that men should not subscribe their capital to form a bank, and decline to transact business with those who are not their partners, or than that professions like the bar and medicine should not be permitted to maintain the stringent regulations, by which they surround professional practice. Still less is there any reason why those who attempt to enforce their bye-laws should be visited by the exceptional terrors of law, unless it be shown that there is something in the position of an artisan which renders it just that he should be made liable to a control from which the professional and trading-classes are free. It is a maxim that where combination is possible, competition does not operate, and the experience which all men have of the facts bears out the maxim.

It may be confidently stated that, considered as matters of abstract right or expediency, the justice and soundness of Cobden's views have seldom been questioned by politicians of respectable character and average abilities. Reasons were alleged against concession to his views during the course of his public career, and reasons are now alleged against the acceptance of some of those reforms which he recommended, but did not live to see in practice. But it may be affirmed, beyond controversy, that no man has ever leavened the public opinion of England more thoroughly and more extensively than he did, that no man has familiarised his countrymen more fully with principles which were once considered paradoxes. It is allowed that on many subjects, the views which were once bitterly assailed or mercilessly ridiculed as they were first promulgated by him, are now adopted and avowed without hesitation or gainsaying.

Cobden acted with the Liberal party. But he was not a partisan. From the beginning of his career to its close, he declared himself willing to accept reforms from all hands. It is easy to see why he acted with the Liberal party, for the nation has obtained every improvement in law and finance, every development of civil and religious freedom, every concession to justice and equity from those administrations which have been brought into power by the Liberal party. It is true that in many cases these reforms have been granted slowly, grudgingly, and imperfectly. But there will not be, and cannot be, any reaction from a genuine Liberalism. It is only when a government which has been brought into power by liberal opinion, plays false with its principles, or declines to develope its policy, or makes ignoble alliances, or affronts the convictions of those who have made it what it is, that the progress of liberal opinion is arrested, and its vigour is paralysed.

Oxford, Oct. 2, 1873.

CONTENTS.

CHAP.		PAGE
I.	THE PARLIAMENT OF 1841	1
II.	THE DEFENCE OF THE CORN LAWS	36
III.	THE LAND QUESTION	73
IV.	INTERNATIONAL RELATIONS—WAR AND PEACE	109
V.	MILITARY AND NAVAL EXPENDITURE	146
VI.	FINANCIAL REFORM	183
VII.	INDIA AND THE COLONIES	222
VIII.	PARLIAMENTARY REFORM	261
IX.	COMMERCIAL DIPLOMACY	302
X.	EDUCATION	313

ESSAYS.

COBDEN AND POLITICAL OPINION.

CHAPTER I.

THE PARLIAMENT OF 1841.

COBDEN's entrance into Parliament occurred at a crisis of political feeling. The great flood of enthusiasm which carried the Reform Bill of 1832, and which had given the Whigs a long tenure of power, had ebbed. The public had gradually come to the conclusion that Lord Melbourne was a politician without convictions, the most serious imputation which can be uttered against the reputation of a statesman. The Administration was branded with the charge of nepotism, and apparently with justice. The finances of the country were in a desperate condition. There had been an annual deficit, and in the summer of 1841 the revenue was two-and-a-half millions less than the expenditure. The principles of taxation were hardly understood by any man. When the public knows nothing of political economy, it is almost certain to ascribe a failing income to the maladministration of Government.

The manufacturing districts were suffering from the direst distress. Some of the most important industries were struggling for existence, others were almost paralysed. Of course contradictory causes were assigned for these serious and menacing facts. Some said that the manufacturers had glutted the market. Others averred that the industry of the country was in course of being annihilated by the competition of cheap foreign labour. Meanwhile the condition of the labouring classes was being rapidly deteriorated, and discontent was general. As is customary, when the community knows nothing of the laws by which the industrial forces of society are governed and directed, the working classes imagined that they would discover a remedy for the miseries under which they laboured, by a fundamental change in the political institutions of the country. It was the least fault in the Charter that its political purposes were crude and premature, or that under good government and a sound system of finance they would be superfluous and inconvenient. The Chartism of 1841 was compromised by economical fallacies which, had they been accepted as a course of policy, would have been simply destructive.

These delusions were the consequence of the unreformed Parliament. The nation had been kept in a state of political infancy, and when it was suddenly emancipated, it fell into the natural error of childhood, that, namely, of believing that a Government can be, and should be, characterised by energetic beneficence. It is only by very slow degrees that nations arrive at the knowledge that the functions of government are limited to administration and defence, and that no Government can, without risk of serious injury, assume the duty of arbitrating between contending interests. Again, it is only by very slow degrees that Governments can resist the flattery which assigns them such powers of action as can make nations virtuous, thriving, and happy. Thirty years ago nearly every class of society believed that the Government was bound to protect it, and it meant by protection, assistance against rivals, domestic and foreign.

The Administration of Lord Melbourne had clung to office with a pertinacity which is utterly unintelligible to our habits of political action, and our familiar ideas of political morality. The Government had been defeated over and over again on questions of vital importance. Before it dissolved Parliament in June, 1841, it had been twice put into a decisive minority on a question of finance. The elections gave the Conservative party an overwhelming majority, but the Government did not resign until it had been forcibly ejected from office by a non-confidence vote. Though it was perfectly well known that Parliament was adverse to the Ministers, a rumour was current, and was credited, that the Ministers would resort to the expedient of a second dissolution. It illustrates the habit of the period, when one finds no evidence which would prove that such a line of action would have been thought unconstitutional.

The enemies of Lord Melbourne's Administration were under some impression that the Whigs intended to govern under the sanction of the Queen's personal preferences. Such kinds of administration had existed

in the days of George the Third, and the experience
of the reformed Parliament was raw and incomplete.
Hence the opposition inculcated a doctrine now familiar
to us, that the monarch in a constitutional kingdom
should be absolutely at the discretion of his or her
advisers, and that Parliament (in this case the
Commons) should define the advisers in question. It
cannot, I think, be doubted, that the attitude of the
Conservative party at this crisis, settled, and settled
permanently, an important principle in the conduct
of the constitution, and that this precedent was of
infinite significance in the progress of constitutional
Government.

It is of course impossible to say whether the Whigs
of 1841 had any purpose of using the Queen's personal
friendship for the chiefs of their party, as a means
for lengthening the tenure of their power. It is well
known that there were grounds why the Queen should
have preferred the services of men who had shown
antagonism to the Orange party. Whatever may have
been the faults of Lord Melbourne's Administration,
it is certain that his loyalty to the Queen was sincere,
generous, and chivalrous. It is equally certain that
there were men who did not scruple to malign her,
and that they were not unsupported.

The fear, whether factious or sincere, that the Queen
would suffer any personal feeling to stand in the way
of such a change in the Administration as was demanded
by the nation, was refuted instantly by facts. Many
of the principal persons who were connected with this
important crisis in the political history of the United
Kingdom are still living, and the circumstances of the

case cannot be brought to light as yet. But, I conceive, that even at that time public men were well aware of the fact, that in this country there never is, or can be, a reversal of any precedent which confessedly assures the progress of constitutional liberty and political justice; that in this particular at least, the English nation has effectually assisted the growth of social civilisation; and that, though the process by which necessary change is effected is very slowly developed, the process is a real and irreversible growth. There is no reason to doubt that the Queen was well acquainted with the situation; there is even less reason to doubt that she was surrounded by advisers from both the great historical parties, who could inform her of the facts, and who would loyally assist the facts of which they informed her, by their own action.

I have touched on this point, because the statement is, I think, necessary in order that the position of parties in 1841 may be understood. But there is another topic which requires some attention, if one would wish to understand fully how the public mind was influenced at the same crisis.

An imperative necessity, so imperative that neglect threatened social ruin, constrained the Government to make a radical change in the administration of relief to the destitute poor. The urgency and the magnitude of the case demanded thorough and speedy remedies. Of course pauperism is no natural product of modern civilisation, but is the outcome of mischievous laws, which have disgraced, and do disgrace, our statute-book. As long as these laws exist, pauperism will always grow, and will always need sharp and energetic remedies. It is only to be regretted, that instead of palliating the consequence, we do not eradicate the cause. In 1841 hardly any one had discovered the cause. It was not to be expected that, even had the cause been known, any politician would have ventured on the surgery needed towards destroying it.

I can well remember, when I was a boy, that my father pointed out to me farms on which the poor-rate absorbed all the rent of the land. I can remember instances of agricultural labourers who saved notable sums out of the allowances made to the fathers of large families under the old Poor Law. Had the system been continued, whole districts would have been impoverished, and the country work-people would have been irremediably degraded.

The new Poor Law was assailed with the greatest bitterness. No words were too hard for the authors and advocates of the measure. The workhouse test was considered to be the most revolting cruelty. The policy which demanded a separation of the sexes, even though the parties were married, as long as such persons occupied the workhouse, was looked on as an assault against the sacredness of the marriage tie. It was asserted with passionate vehemence that the poor had a right to employment, and that the parish was bound to find it for them. Fortunately for the nation these invectives did not induce statesmen to retrace their steps, or accept that dangerous doctrine, from which communism is the inevitable consequent, that the state is bound to find work for its unemployed labourers. The ministry of Sir Robert Peel continued the system which Lord Melbourne had instituted.

Foremost in the attack on the new Poor Law was the *Times* newspaper. Though this paper had the widest circulation of the whole London press, it was by no means as influential as it became a few years afterwards. It was eminent, however, for the pains with which it collected accurate news, and for the prudence with which its literary managers preserved their incognito. The attacks of the *Times* had begun to be formidable, its defence of a statesman and his policy was soon found to be exceedingly valuable. But when Sir Robert Peel expressed his acknowledgments to this paper for the service which it had rendered him, during the period of that political diplomacy which culminated in the repeal of the Corn Laws, the *Times* was able to boast, that its services to the Minister were granted on public grounds only, and that no person, external to the proprietors, had ever yet broken into the privacy of the editor's room.

The *Times* rose to the position of the leading London journal, and thenceforward held an uncontested position, mainly from an act which is without a parallel in the annals of journalism, whether one considers its boldness, its gallantry, or its singular usefulness. One of its foreign correspondents detected or gave notice of the most gigantic fraud which had yet been attempted in the experience of society. The parties to this fraud were persons in great repute, of high social standing, and of abundant resources. They attempted, by means of forged circular notes, to defraud a number of foreign bankers. So skilful were these forgeries, that the clerks of

Messrs. Glyn and Co., whose circular notes had been imitated, were hardly able to detect the imitation of their genuine paper. So matchless was the effrontery of these scoundrels, that, when the *Times* exposed the villainy, one of the confederates, Bogle, commenced an action for defamation against the printer of the newspaper. No pains and expense were spared on the part of the *Times* to collect the evidence necessary in order to justify the libel. For nearly a year the attorney of the newspaper was abroad, collecting all the facts which bore on the case. At last, after Bogle had vainly endeavoured to hurry on the trial before the evidence was matured, and just about the time at which Lord Melbourne's Ministry was ejected from office, the great case of Bogle *v.* Lawson was tried, and resulted in the gift of a farthing damages to the plaintiff.

The *Times* now obtained, as it deserved, the position of the leading journal in the commercial world. It appears at the same time to have stereotyped its peculiar policy, that namely, of waiting on events, of putting itself into constant opposition as long as political changes were merely advocated, of slowly acquiescing in them when they became inevitable, and of ignoring its previous hostility when they became accomplished facts.

The *Times* was by no means the most vituperative of the political newspapers. But the language of its leading articles would not be endurable to any reader at the present time. On July 15, 1841, it compares Lord Howick on the hustings, to 'a dying rattlesnake, darting out its venomous tongue with futile malignity against its destroyers.' In our day, most newspaper writers know more of natural history, and are more courteous to their victims. The style of writing, of which a specimen has been quoted, now lingers only in American newspapers. But the chief figures of speech are reserved for the dissenting ministers who met at Manchester in June in order to remonstrate against the Corn Laws. The mildest epithet employed against them is that of Jacobin.

Before the downfall of the Melbourne Ministry, the *Times* was not bitter against the Whig Administration. It was taken to task in April for having quoted with approbation a story of some Conservative who declined to support an association for the maintenance of his own principles, on the ground 'that when one gets rid of one set of scoundrels, we have another set in their room.' On the same occasion it praises the Nottingham Chartists, and speaks contemptuously of both Lord John Russell and Sir Robert Peel. Just at that time, however, Mr. Walter was seeking the suffrages of the Nottingham electors, and though the editor of the *Times* was impersonal, its proprietor was not. Mr. Walter's seat at Nottingham was not secured at the general election. His relations with this constituency were commented on with characteristic relish by Mr. O'Connell. When, on June 4, the Melbourne Ministry was put into a minority of one, on a no-confidence vote, and the Government recommended a dissolution, the *Times* became powerfully Conservative. At first, indeed, it did not pretend to defend the sliding scale, but charged the system with 'working injuriously, and with occasionally humiliating frauds.' But it will not write them down, because it 'is disgusted at the Corn Laws being mixed up with the trickery of ministers.' But as soon as ever the League, fortified by the return of Mr. Cobden to the House, began to work energetically against the system, the *Times* attacked the League, and its Coryphæus, as it called Cobden, with excessive bitterness. These attacks continued till the gradual conversion of Sir Robert Peel made the repeal of the Corn Laws an accomplished fact.

The feud—if it can be so called—between Mr. Cobden and the *Times*, lasted long after the first occasion of the quarrel. It is singular that this paper nourishes personal animosities against those who have attacked it, or disparaged it. It never forgave O'Connell. The contempt with which Cobden treated its morality was a permanent cause of offence, and the dispute between the Statesman and Mr. Delane left lasting memories in the editor's mind.

In my opinion, Mr. Cobden erred in undervaluing this remarkable political instrument. It is the first business of politicians to form an estimate of the forces which are arrayed against their opinions, and perhaps of the arguments by which these forces are sustained. It was not indeed Cobden's practice to interpret a course of political action by the question whether its completion 'lay within the range of practical politics,' and it is fortunate for the progress of social civilisation that he was undeterred from ventilating a theory, because the public mind was unprepared to accept it. They who had the benefit of his friendship and his experience recognised as his most marked characteristic a conscientiousness on all political questions which was perfectly fearless, and a sagacity and a prescience which are never accorded except to those who shape their public life by an unflinching rule of political integrity. But even to such rare persons it is of supreme use to know what is at any given time the precise value of the opinions they announce in the minds of that influential part of the public which gives its cue to 'the leading journal,' or takes its colour, as the case may be, from the same publication. Errors in judgment are not of course so serious as errors about the forces arrayed against a judgment. But however wise and right the judgment may be, they are still errors, and the misconceptions which such errors induce are vexatious and misleading.

The Free Trade party in the Parliament of 1841 was exceedingly weak. They had succeeded in winning Stockport, Stoke upon Trent, Brighton, and Gloucester at the general election, but their prospect of carrying the reform which they contemplated was by no means cheering. Mr. Charles Villiers could number about 120 supporters to an annual motion which he made on the subject. I was informed by Sir William Clay that this motion was once his own, but that he surrendered it to Mr. Villiers, and adopted as his political client the motion against Church rates.

It is true that the minority which was hostile to the Corn Laws was very intelligent and clear. When Lord Melbourne's ministry was defeated in the Lords on the Corn Law question, a protest of singular ability was inserted in the Lords' Journals, under the signature of the Duke of Sussex and other peers. There was no period since the first enactment of the Corn Laws in which persons of great reputation were not found who gave all the force of their abilities and characters to the cause of free trade. But nothing seemed more hopeless than the struggle. Not only had Sir Robert Peel come into office with a clear majority of 90, but he was reputed to have owed his success with the country to his opposition to the fixed duty of Lord John Russell. His majority was even greater, if the number of votes cast for his Government be considered. Nearly 530,000 electors voted for his supporters, while the Ministry, notwithstanding the advantage of being in office when the contest took place, (a far more important element in a general election at that time than it is now) polled only a little more than 273,000 votes.*

The forces which gave Sir Robert Peel so decided a majority were those of the landowners, the clergy of the establishment, the farmers, and the Chartists. The landowners believed that their rents were imperilled by the action of the Free Trade party. The clergy of the establishment were influenced partly by a similar reason, partly by their dislike of the latitudinarian principles, ascribed truly or falsely to the Whig government. Besides, the Oxford movement was not yet unpopular, for it was as yet professedly loyal to the Anglican establishment, and the *Times* supported this movement by every means in its power. The farmers were intensely hostile to the advocates of free trade in corn, and it was reported at the time that the loss of the counties to the Liberal party was due to the operation of the Chandos clause.

* *Times*, July 31.

The hostility of the Chartists was partly exhibited against the economical reforms of the Whigs, and especially against the new Poor Law, partly against what was supposed likely to ensue from the cheapening of corn. The Chartist organisation included most of the artisans in the large towns, and was formidable by its zeal and activity. Ostensibly its purpose was political reform. But it is a maxim in politics, that no movement can rouse the mass of the people unless it be connected with, and is held to be the means of effecting, a notable amelioration in the material condition of the working classes. The points in the people's Charter were a mere mask, under which great economical changes were threatened and expected. It is almost superfluous to say that they who coquetted with the Chartist on the hustings, or in the canvass, never intended to grant a single point in the Charter, and still less to concede any of those objects for the ultimate acquisition of which the Charter was intended to be an instrument. In the early days of the agitation against the Corn Laws, the Chartists gave more trouble to the advocates of free trade than any other class of the community.

On the other hand, the mercantile classes were generally favourable to an amendment in the revenue laws. The Nonconformists were similarly minded. The manufacturers of the north of England repudiated protection to their own industry, for they knew well enough that a protected industry is certain to be debarred from a foreign market. The Dissenters had not yet forgotten that they had been reluctantly emancipated, and the line between them and the adherents of the Anglican Church was still drawn sharply. They were still marked with the badge of inferiority, were still liable to imposts which were more offensive than onerous, and were still excluded from important civil rights. It is almost superfluous to say that an established church is invariably on the side of privilege, and that the sympathies of those other ecclesiastical organisations whose members buy their liberty by disabilities are always given to the advocates of progress and change. It will be seen in time to come, whenever an absolute equality between sects is effected, whether the enfranchised sects keep alive a traditional loyalty to the agencies by which they have been liberated, or are insensibly led into that conservatism, or at least acquiescence in customary institutions, towards which religious systems generally tend. It is, I think, clear to present experience, that the various dissenting bodies are far less sympathetic with measures of social and political reform at this time than they were thirty years ago, and there is reason to believe that the causes which ordinarily operate upon those who are relieved from disadvantages and disabilities will be furnished with no exception from the Nonconformists of the future.

'To expect,' says Adam Smith, 'that the freedom of trade should ever be entirely restored in Great Britain, is as absurd as to expect that an Oceana or Utopia should ever be established in it.' Forty years after this prediction was penned, the merchants' petition was presented to both Houses of Parliament, and accepted as the authoritative exposition of a policy which should be adopted in practice as soon as ever financial exigencies permitted. Sixty years afterwards the organisation which finally overthrew protection was fully formed, and was steadily pressing onward to victory. This victory necessitated the acceptance of another theory of finance. Previously, industry was made to wait on the necessities of the Exchequer, and the means which might be adopted, with greater or less wisdom, in order to satisfy these necessities. As a consequence, industry and invention were crippled in a thousand ways. Taxes were laid on production which effectually thwarted the energies of industrial agents, as well as curtailed the power of purchase which the consumer might have possessed. But after the principle of free trade was adopted it became necessary to make finance wait on industry, and to extract a revenue—soon proved to be elastic and increasing—from the growing resources of the general community, and from its power of consumption.

In the days of the great economist, the landowners were indifferent, or at least comparatively so, to the assistance of protective laws, while the mercantile and manufacturing classes were passionately attached to these treacherous and delusive props. The condition of Great Britain, as far as regards the principal industrial classes in the community, was very like that of the United States, where the western farmers and southern cotton-growers are advocates of free trade, while the Pennsylvanian coal and iron masters, and the New England manufacturers, are the sturdiest partisans of strictly protective tariffs. It is important to point out the causes of that change of feeling which led to the agitation against the Corn Laws.

The English legislature had long controlled the trade in food. The readers of Adam Smith are acquainted with the sketch which he gives of the various Acts by which the mercantile intercourse of England with foreign nations had been regulated, and with the real or affected motives which governed Parliament in its enactments. But during a considerable part of the eighteenth century this country was visited by a series of abundant harvests. Between the years 1700—1768, the price of wheat reached fifty shillings and upwards only six times. Between 1769—1846, it fell below this price only thirteen times. Hence, in the days during which Adam Smith was gathering his inductions, the landowners strove to keep up the price of corn, by granting a bounty on its exportation. After his work was published a series of deficient harvests commenced, the produce of the soil became insufficient for the wants of the population, and the landowner enhanced, or thought he enhanced, his rents by the sliding scale.

During the epoch in which this country exported corn, it was plainly to the advantage of the landowner that there should be as free a trade as possible in foreign commodities. An exporting nation always deals in the best market when it has the fullest possible list of objects against which to exchange its exports; deals in the worst when it stints the number of articles which it can purchase. Nothing proves more clearly how deficient a nation is in economical science, than the fact that, having the discretion of regulating its own financial system, and carrying on a considerable export trade, it suffers itself to be limited in its choice of a foreign market in order to assist the manufacturer who produces for home consumption. Such a concession to the manufacturer has characterised the financial policy of the United States, of France, and of our own colonies, and in each case the interests of the whole community have been sacrificed to the sophistries of traders and manufacturers.

Again, in the days of Adam Smith the fallacy which governs the fiscal system of the countries referred to above, influenced the mind of the English manufacturer. So inveterate was the delusion, that even in the face of facts Smith defended the Navigation Laws. He saw that they were indefensible in theory, but he conceived that they were assisting a great political necessity. But had he investigated the circumstances, he would have condemned those laws as conclusively as he did the East India Company's trade, and the monopolies of the home trade. He would have found that they neither aided the defence of the nation, nor enlarged its trade, nor strengthened its mercantile marine. Nothing shows how difficult it was in those days to disengage oneself from prejudice, than the fact that so acute a mind as that of Smith was possessed by a delusion which would not now impose on the tyros of Conservatism.

The English manufacturers saw that the monopoly which a protective system gave them was an intelligible advantage. Whatever else it did, it gave them the sole possession of the home market, and precluded the foreigner from underselling them with their own countrymen. They were not far-seeing enough to detect that it hindered them from competing with the foreigner in his own market, and even from making their footing good in a common market. Hence, in so far as they could influence their Government, they attempted, under the machinery of the 'mercantile' and 'colonial' system, to create for themselves a privilege in such countries as they could bring within the reciprocities of mercantile diplomacy, under the so-called Commercial Treaties, of which that negotiated by Methuen with Portugal was the type; or of which they could control the trade, as they did in the case of the Plantations.

Had Adam Smith lived to see the developement of British industry, in the discoveries or inventions of Watt, Arkwright, Cartwright, and others, he would have discovered the reasons why the principles of free trade took hold on the minds of those very manufacturers who had hitherto opposed it. Those inventions rapidly made England the rival, and the successful rival, of all other manufacturing countries. Then came into play precisely the same motives which influenced the landowners of Smith's time to desire a free and wide foreign market. The manufacturers found that they were at a disadvantage in restricting the number of articles against which their goods could be exchanged. But of all restrictions the worst was that on the importation of corn. Countries which habitually produce more food than is requisite for the wants of their inhabitants, are precisely those in which a manufacturing community finds its largest and most willing body of customers. If they could buy food they could sell goods. Nor was this all. The free importation of food would enable the manufacturer to collect a larger number of hands for the industry in which he could engage them, to provide them with greater plenty, and to offer them the prospect of more regular, and therefore remunerative employment. The advocacy of free trade was not mere enthusiasm on the part of philanthropists who wished to see their own countrymen better off; for enthusiasm rarely influences a considerable percentage of society, even under the most favourable circumstances. In matters of finance and the regulation of trade, an intelligent self-interest or an unintelligent self-interest influences, as the case may be, those who maintain this or that kind of policy. It was an accident, and a very important accident, that the advocates of free trade could point to natural justice, could dilate on the outrageous wrong of the system against which they arrayed themselves, and could prove that the change which they wished to bring about would be beneficent as well as just. But it is doubtful whether the justice of their cause would have made it successful, had it not been ultimately seen that the concession must be made. Again, it was an accident, and a very important accident, that the Potato Famine supervened on the agitation for the repeal of the Corn Laws. But such an event would not have overset a just law, any more than a season of qualified prosperity would have long endured an unjust or mischievous one. The real assistance which the incident gave against the law was, that it made that sudden which might have been dilatory, and precipitated a crisis which was impending.

The summer of 1841 was a period of great commercial distress. Even if the character of those who testified to the facts had not been beyond suspicion of exaggeration, the circumstances were sufficiently patent. The population of most manufacturing towns was rapidly thinning, and the inhabitants who remained were in serious straits. Cobden stated that in the borough which he represented (Stockport) one house in every five was empty. Harrowing tales were told of the miserable poverty to which the factory operatives were reduced. It was affirmed that men had died at their looms from the exhaustion of famine. The Queen's Speech recognised the fact, and, inviting the attention of the Legislature to its causes, suggested an examination into the system of Corn Laws. It was known that the Government contemplated the substitution of an eight-shilling duty for the sliding scale.

The Anti-Corn-Law League, which was then in a youthful but vigorous existence under the leadership of Cobden, characterised a fixed duty as a fixed injustice, though, as O'Connell affirmed of himself, when during the debate which led to the resignation of the Melbourne Administration he declared himself an uncompromising enemy of all taxes on food, they would have accepted the fixed duty temporarily as an instalment of justice. But it is not easy to see how the Whigs could have ventured on free trade. Lord Melbourne had stated that, in his opinion, a man who would propose a repeal of the Corn Laws was mad;

and this avowal was conceived to be so positive, that the Duke of Wellington was able to twit him with abandoning his principles when he proposed the eight-shilling duty. They who, being wise after the event, charge the Melbourne Administration with inability to interpret what was necessary for the well-being of the country, forget that there always have been, and always will be, two classes of politicians. One of these classes administers affairs, the other initiates reforms. The two functions are rarely compatible, and have been rarely united. The difference between a wise and an unwise Administration consists in the intelligence with which a Government accepts the demonstration of those who initiate reform, but do not or cannot carry out their demonstration into practice. But for the Melbourne Administration to have proposed free trade in corn would not only, to judge from ordinary probability, have been to invite expulsion from office, but an ostracism which might be as prolonged as that which the Whig party endured from the death of Fox till the passage of the Reform Bill. A party will never forgive those leaders who render its accession to office improbable or remote.

Sir Robert Peel has been charged with violating his pledges to his followers, because he carried the abolition of the Corn Laws in 1846. But he gave no pledge whatsoever. When he appeared in Parliament after the election of 1841, his rivals constantly charged him with having no policy. He was absolutely silent as to his intentions. No trick or taunt would make him show his hand. His tact was consummate. His measures, when he came to grapple with the difficulties before him, social and financial, might be criticised. The coarse and clumsy expedient of an Income Tax, its naked and flagrant injustice, has been and will be condemned, though to do Sir Robert Peel right, he never contemplated its permanent retention, and would not have condescended under any extremity to the sophistries which have been alleged on its behalf. The belief which he honestly entertained, that much of the commercial distress of the time was due to the action of the banks, and the palliative which he devised in the Act of 1844, have been sufficiently discussed by every economist of repute. Fortunately, the ingenuity of the money market has discovered a remedy for the crude and pedantic provisions of the Bank Charter.

But whatever may have been the value of Sir Robert Peel's measures, his administrative abilities were, I believe, the highest which have ever been exhibited. He came into office absolutely unfettered. He insisted on the fact at the very moment when the division which gave the *coup de grâce* to the Melbourne Ministry was about to be given. . 'If,' he said, on September 27, 'I were bound to maintain the existing Corn Law in all its details, as a condition of agricultural support, I would not have it on those conditions.' He said this after O'Connell had uttered an unanswerable invective against his party, the fierceness and eloquence of which must have strongly moved him. It was with a perfectly clear appreciation of the position which Sir Robert Peel had voluntarily chosen, that Lord John Russell, at the conclusion of the same debate, observed, that 'Sir Robert Peel had no right to say that he was shackled and thwarted by party considerations, because it was clear that the party to which he belonged could not resist Liberal measures if he were to propose them.' If this was a sneer it was also a prophecy.

Again, Sir Robert Peel had, and deserved to have, a reputation for perfect political integrity. He was undoubtedly influenced by the natural ambition of conscious power. That he had a profound insight into the causes of the crisis with which he had to deal cannot be maintained, for to maintain it would be to assert that all his earlier avowals on the question of free trade were a dishonest dissimulation of his convictions and his intentions, just as in the case of Catholic Emancipation. He believed that the Corn Laws were defensible, and on public grounds. Had he imagined, as Lord Stanley rashly and candidly avowed, that the object of the Corn Laws was to keep up prices, and so keep up rents, no language would be too strong for the condemnation of the attitude which he took on the subject. But Sir Robert Peel was not an economist. He did not understand the principles which had been demonstrated to exhaustion by a generation of thinkers. An admirable speaker, a consummate tactician, a ready debater, a man of unimpeachable probity and purity, he thought like a Conservative and wrote like a schoolboy. His vision was exceedingly narrow, and he gave the most erroneous interpretations of current facts. He believed in over-production, and that over-production could be effected by the rivalry of bankers. He believed that the distress of 1841 was caused by the reckless advances of money-lenders and in the over-issue of convertible paper, and he imagined that he had discovered a perpetual remedy against commercial panics in his celebrated Act of 1844, though it has been proved to demonstration that the Act in question aggravates their severity, according to the predictions of the ablest thinkers on the currency. He gave the preference to a sliding scale over a fixed duty, on grounds so grotesque and crude that one is amazed that any statesman could believe and utter them. But no person who has given any study to the character of Sir Robert Peel could doubt that, however open he might be to the influence of a fallacy, he was utterly incapable of deliberate sophistry.

'I had adopted,' said Sir Robert Peel in his Memoirs, vol. ii. p. 99, 'at an early period of my public life, without, I fear, much serious reflection, the opinions generally prevalent at the time among men of all parties, as to the justice and necessity of protection to British agriculture. They were the opinions of Sir Henry Parnell, Mr. Ricardo, Lord John Russell, Lord Melbourne, as well as of the Duke of Wellington, Mr. Canning, and Mr. Huskisson. I had, however, been a willing party, both in 1828 and 1842, to the reductions which took place in the amount of protection fixed by the Corn Law of 1815, a law which was based on the assumption that wheat could not be profitably grown at a price less than 80s.' But he adds, 'I had always refused to fetter the discretion of Government by any assurance that an amount of protection should be steadily adhered to.'

In his Tamworth address of July, 1847 (and which is reprinted at length in the 'Apologia pro vita sua,' which goes under the name of his Memoirs, and which was published nearly seven years after his death, by his literary executors, Lord Stanhope and Mr. Cardwell), Sir Robert Peel recounts the reasons which led him to modify his views on free trade in corn. He speaks here of being influenced 'by the conflict of arguments on the principle of a restrictive policy,' 'by the many concurring proofs that the wages of labour do not vary with the prices of corn,'—a position which had been demonstrated by Adam Smith three quarters of a century before, and had been insisted on by nearly every economist and every advocate of free trade,— 'by the contrast presented in two successive periods of dearth and abundance in the health, morals, and tranquillity and general prosperity of the whole community, by serious doubts whether in the present condition of the country cheapness and plenty are not ensured for the future in a higher degree by the free intercourse in corn, than by restrictions on its importation for the purpose of giving protection to domestic agriculture.' 'It has been weakened,' he continues, 'by the following considerations, which were in a great degree new elements in forming a judgement on this vital matter. The general repeal of prohibitory duties, and the recent application of the principles of free trade to almost all articles of import from abroad, made the Corn Laws an object of more searching scrutiny and more invidious comment, and narrowed the ground on which their defence could be maintained.' He then appeals to negative proof from the refutation given to those anticipations of panic which were entertained in consequence of the changes which were made in the duties on salt and fresh meat, cattle and sheep. Under these it was supposed that the price of meat would fall to 3*d*. a pound. Here he gives a reason why he does not anticipate a decline in the prices of corn. 'There has appeared,' he says, 'of late a tendency to increase in the consumption of articles of subsistence much more rapid than the increase of the population.' Then he gives a list of imports the increased consumption of which was noteworthy; and concludes by stating that he 'saw no middle course between keeping the Corn Laws inviolate, and a measure involving their absolute repeal.'

The Memoirs by which Sir Robert Peel purposed to vindicate his public character, (and which in my opinion so completely vindicate it, if we take one ground only, that of his manifest integrity and conscientiousness, and his perfect freedom from any taint of sordid ambition,) give a different, but by no means a contradictory, account of the circumstances which led to his change of mind on the subject of agricultural protection. This account is to be gathered from the correspondence between the Prime Minister and Sir James Graham and Lord Heytesbury on the subject of the Irish Potato Famine.

The earliest letter in this correspondence is from Sir Robert Peel to Sir James Graham, of the date of October 13, 1845. The Home Secretary had informed him of the disquieting rumours about the disease, which, with considerable exactness, was called the Potato Cholera. On this occasion he writes: 'I have no confidence in such remedies as the prohibition of exports, or the stoppage of the distilleries. The removal of impediments to import is the only effectual remedy.' Two days after he says: 'Interference with the due course of the laws respecting the supply of food is so momentous and so lasting in its consequences, that we must not act without the most accurate information.' The sentence is obscure and awkward, but it probably means that there ought to be no relaxation of the existing law unless the necessity for such a step were proved to demonstration. But on the same day he writes to Lord Heytesbury: 'The remedy is the removal of all impediments to the import of all kinds of human food, i.e. the total and absolute repeal for ever of all duties on all articles of subsistence.' Sir James Graham replies on the 18th, that 'It is useful to observe how the Almighty humbles the pride of nations,' (an euphemism, I presume, for his regret that it might be necessary in the face of facts, and in consequence of a great national calamity, to repeal a law which was enacted in the interest of a few, and to the injury of the many); and on the 19th combats the idea that the Irish ports only could be opened, while protection should hold in Great Britain, since he foresees that the Government will offend the agriculturists on one hand, and the free traders on the other, and so run the risk of missing the necessary Act of Indemnity.

Before the Cabinet met, on October 31, Sir Robert Peel sent Dr. Lyon Playfair and Mr. Lindley to Ireland, with a view to procuring accurate information on the facts of the case. These gentlemen confirmed the worst suspicions. Besides, news of a similar kind came from various parts of England. In Lancashire the potato crop was at that time nearly as important as it was in Ireland. It was found out that the disease affected the whole of England, and the same information came from Scotland. It is well known that the Scottish Highlands, particularly the Hebrides, suffered nearly as much as those parts of Ireland did in which the disease was most disastrous.

One cannot but regret to read, in Sir Robert Peel's Cabinet memorandum of November 1, 'That in the event of great Irish distress there will be no hope of contributions from England for a mitigation of this calamity. Monster meetings, the ungrateful return for past kindness, the subscriptions in Ireland to Repeal Rent and O'Connell Tribute will have disinclined the charitable here to make any great exertions for Irish relief.' Sir Robert was biassed by political partisanship. He remembered the Clare election too keenly, and the fierceness with which O'Connell had attacked his Government, and thereupon credited the English nation with a resentment of which it has always been incapable. It is superfluous to say that when the fact of the distress became known, men of all shades of opinion vied with each other in assisting Irish destitution. The English people is thoroughly permeated by one at least among Christian principles. It remembers no grudge, and forgets all enmities at the sight of genuine and helpless distress.

Mistaken as Sir Robert Peel's estimate of English charity and English character was, it was wisdom itself compared with certain sentiments uttered by the late Duke of Portland, in a letter addressed to the Prime Minister under date of November 2. 'Considering,' says his Grace, 'their conduct' (i.e. of the lower orders of the Irish), 'I cannot think the Queen's Government ought to show them any favour or give them assistance in any way. But if,' he adds, 'a subscription be got up—it would add much to its value if it appeared to be promoted by the great beneficed clergy in both countries, and those who have the reputation of bigoted attachment to the Established Church.' It is difficult to conceive more meanness and malignity than is contained in this passage. It is amazing that Sir Robert Peel had so little consideration for his friend's reputation as to print it.

Sir Robert Peel proposed, in the face of the sudden and overwhelming difficulties of the position, to throw open the ports at a shilling duty. But only three members of his Cabinet supported him. These, he informs us, were Lord Aberdeen, Sir James Graham, and Mr. Sidney Herbert. Much precious time was lost, and, as events proved, very many lives were sacrificed to the hesitation of the Cabinet. Sir Robert Peel informs us that he ventured on a very singular transaction. In concert with Sir James Graham, and through the house of Baring, he 'secretly purchased a large quantity of Indian corn.'

The kind of arguments alleged by those who counselled delay was as follows. The Duke of Wellington feared 'that it would be found that this country would cease to be the desirable and sought-after market of the world, if the interests of agriculture should be injured by the premature repeal of the Corn Laws.' If this sentence has any meaning whatsoever, it suggests that the foreign trade of the country would decay as soon as ever its foreign trade was increased. It is not easy to see by what process the Duke arrived at the alarm which he professed.

Mr. Goulbourn was more intelligible. He objects to any change on four principal grounds. His first and most elaborate argument refers to the attitude in which the members of the Government would stand as public men. His second is, that until 'the peculiar burdens on land' were adjusted, the amount of taxation to which it was liable (being as he said 2s. 8d. in the pound), it would be unfair to remove protection, and that there ought to be previously to, or simultaneously with the change, a new law of parochial settlement, a removal of the Land Tax, or the advantageous 'facilitation' of its redemption, a modification or repeal of the Malt Tax, and the lightening of the duties on the conveyance of real estate; that some of these changes would be of serious effect on the public finances, and that the situation was full of difficulty. His third reason is, that the British agriculturist ought to have protection against the competition of the foreigner, who not having the same charges on him, is, or ought to be, able to supply articles at a cheaper rate. His fourth, and apparently his most important, is that the party must needs exist, in order to check the revolutionary effects of the Reform Bill, and the menace of unrestrained democracy. It would not be easy to collect, in the space of a single letter, so much ignorance and presumption.

Lord Stanley, who finally seceded from Sir Robert Peel's Ministry, and would take no part in its reconstruction, after Lord John Russell's abortive attempt to form an Administration in December, took an easier course. He denied the existence of the distress altogether. In a somewhat similar way he was slow to admit the magnitude of the circumstances which characterised the Cotton Famine of 1863, as I heard at the time from Mr. Cobden.

Sir Robert Peel has left it on record that he was prepared at first to propose that a new sliding scale should be adopted on the following principle. An eight-shilling duty should be levied on wheat—and on other kinds of grain porportionately, when the price of the imperial quarter should stand at or below 51s., and should decrease a shilling with every shilling of rise, and that this should be the scale for 1846. That the next year it should be 7s. on 51s., and so forth, the next 6s. on the same value; the plan proposing to extinguish the duty altogether in the course of eight years. He professes to have borrowed the idea from Ricardo.*

How the difficulties which Sir Robert Peel found in his Cabinet were insuperable, how for reasons of patriotism and prudence he refused to advise a dissolution, how he resolved to resign, how Lord John Russell undertook the task of forming an Administration and failed, how Sir Robert Peel was recalled, how

* Something analogous to this plan may be found in Ricardo's works, Macculloch's edition, p. 493.

the distress which had to be met became more and more appalling, how the Corn Laws were cut up root and branch, how a disappointed and indignant party ejected Sir Robert Peel from office on an Irish Coercion Bill two days after the repeal of the Corn Laws, how he foresaw this vengeance impending, how the Conservative party which he had formed was broken up by the rancorous malignity of those who would have wrecked the country rather than accept free trade, how Sir Robert Peel foresaw that revolution was impending unless the restrictive policy were abandoned, how the Duke of Wellington justified the repeal by the apology which he first uttered in 1828, 'that the King's (or Queen's) Government must be carried on', and how Sir Robert Peel was traduced during the rest of his life by the most malignant hearts and the most unscrupulous tongues which ever sold themselves to a faction, are matters of familiar history and need not be commented on.

I have dwelt on these particulars because it is essential to state them in order that my reader may recognise what were the forces against which Cobden had to contend in dealing with one of the great questions to which he dedicated the early part of his political career. It will be seen that at no period of the agitation were the economical reasons which Cobden alleged confronted by any arguments drawn from the science with which he was familiar. Protection was treated as a compensation for peculiar burdens, as a stimulus to the investment of capital in the soil, as a condition without which the British farmer would be unduly weighted in the race of foreign competition, as a means for guaranteeing the independence of the nation, as a state of things which, though it might not be justified on abstract grounds, was so habitual and familiar, that it could not be dealt with except by disturbing colossal and important interests. Some country gentlemen were candid enough to state that they could not pay the settled interests out of their estates if protection was tampered with, some admitted that the object of the Corn Laws was to raise prices and to raise rents, some imagined that protection was a barrier against democracy. Some, despairing of argument against the masters of argument, advised that the agitators should be put down by force. One farmer, a Mr. Chowler, publicly boasted that the farmers had all the horses and would ride them down. Cobden answered the fool according to his folly, and told him that they had all the asses too.

Sir Robert Peel declined to dissolve at the crisis of December, 1845. He could have done so with abstract propriety, for it is a tradition in Administrations, though not I believe a very old tradition, that while a Government may dissolve a Parliament which has been elected under its predecessors, it is debarred from adopting this expedient with one which has been elected under itself. But Peel had three reasons for not adopting this course. He was sincerely anxious to do his duty by the Crown, and he was convinced that he should put the Queen into great difficulties if he advised a dissolution. Next, he tells us himself that he was convinced he could carry the measure of repeal, that he had never failed in what he had determined to undertake, and that he would not, if it were possible, fail in this. It is I think plain that he foresaw the insuperable difficulties which Lord John Russell had in forming a Cabinet, and that he could not, except in very general terms, assure him of his support to whatever free-trade measures the Whigs might propose. And thirdly, he saw how difficult it would be for him to frame a policy with which to go to the country. How could he, he alleges, oppose certain persons (whom he names) at a general election, when the chief policy of those persons was exactly that which must under existing circumstances be his own.

Had Sir Robert Peel gone to the country in the winter of 1845 with a free-trade policy, he must have identified himself with the Whigs. Had he gone with a protective policy, he would have been in a hopeless minority. It would have been discreditable to do the former, suicidal to do the latter. After parties were reformed, it was natural enough for the advocates of commercial liberty to ally themselves with the advocates of civil and religious freedom, even of civil and religious equality; and undoubtedly as time passes on, the alliance between those who were called Peelites — the name is quoted by Peel himself within a few days of his defeat and resignation — and the Radical party is inevitable, and must be close. But such an alliance was impossible in 1845. Nor have I any doubt, had no Potato Cholera or Irish Famine occurred, that an appeal to the country would have resulted in the repudiation of protection, if not in 1845, yet very speedily after. The agitation for free trade, as the election of 1847 showed, had roused the spirit of a crusade. The Whigs, discredited in office, but progressively popular when in opposition, would have been drawn closer to the Radical reformers and to Radical measures. The creation of forty-shilling freeholders, as Peel foresaw, would have lost the Tories the counties, as protection had lost them the towns. The old cries would have been easily raised, and would have been caught up with alacrity. The danger which Mr. Goulbourn saw, and would have stemmed, of revolutionary changes and an unrestrained democracy, would have been precipitated if his advice had been followed, since nothing is more certain to induce violent change than violent efforts to resist change; as Sir Robert Peel foresaw. For, as modern experience has proved, the Liberal party approaches the Radical platform when out of office, and the Conservative does so when in office, and each for very sufficient reasons.

CHAPTER II.

THE DEFENCE OF THE CORN LAWS.

THE principal arguments which were alleged in favour of protection to British industry, and especially to British agriculture, are contained in the first of the two protests which were drawn up after the third reading of the Corn Importation Bill in the House of Lords. The author of this protest was, I presume, the late Lord Derby, then known as Lord Stanley, and sitting in the Lords by summons during his father's lifetime. The protest is subscribed by eighty-nine spiritual and temporal peers, for a few bishops gave their signatures to the document. Some of the bishops, however, voted in favour of the repeal, and were not obscurely rebuked for having intruded upon secular business in the House of Lords. But the remonstrants did not disdain the names of those prelates who agreed in the protest.

The protest consists of twelve counts, and as it presents a summary of the reasonings which influenced the seceders from the party of Sir Robert Peel, and as it contains the essence of the speeches which were delivered in favour of protection, I shall quote it at length. The eighty-nine peers are dissentient—

'1. Because the repeal of the Corn Laws will greatly increase the dependence of this country upon foreign countries for its supply of food, and will thereby expose it to dangers against which former statesmen have thought it essential to take legislative precautions.

'2. Because there is no security nor probability that other nations will take similar steps; and this country will, therefore, not only be exposed to the risks of failure of supply consequent on a state of war, but will also be exclusively subject to an unlimited influx of corn in times of abundance, and to sudden checks whenever short crops shall reduce the ordinary supply from the exporting countries, or their Governments shall deem it necessary to take precautionary measures for their own protection, thus causing rapid and disastrous fluctuations in the markets of this country.

'3. Because under a system of protection the agriculture of this country has more than kept pace with the increasing demand of its increasing population, and because it is to be apprehended that the removal of protection may throw some lands out of cultivation, and check in others the progress of improvement which has led to this satisfactory result.

'4. Because it is unjust to withdraw protection from the landed interest of this country, while that interest remains subject to exclusive burdens imposed for purposes of general and not of special advantage.

'5. Because the loss to be sustained by the repeal of the Corn Laws will fall most heavily on the least wealthy portion of the landed proprietors, will press immediately and severely on the tenant farmers, and through them, with ruinous consequences, on the agricultural labourers

'6. Because indirectly, but not less certainly, injurious consequences will result to the manufacturing interest, and especially to the artisans and mechanics, from competition with the agricultural labourers thrown out of employment, but principally from the loss of the home market, caused by the inability of the producers of grain, and those dependent on them, to consume manufactured goods to the same extent as heretofore.

'7. Because the same cause will produce similar evil results to the tradesmen, retail dealers, and others in county towns, not themselves engaged in agricultural pursuits, but mainly dependent for their subsistence on their dealings with those who are so engaged.

'8. Because the effect of a repeal of the Corn Laws will be especially injurious to Ireland, by lowering the value of her principal exports, and by still further reducing the demand for labour, the want of which is among the principal evils of her social condition.

'9. Because a free trade in corn will cause a large and unnecessary diminution of annual income, thus impairing the revenue of the country, and at the same time that it cripples the resources of those classes on whom the weight of local taxation now mainly falls.

'10. Because a general reduction of prices, consequent on a reduction in the price of corn, will tend unduly to raise the monied interest at the expense of all others, and so aggravate the pressure of the national burdens.

'11. Because the removal of differential duties in favour of Canadian corn is at variance with the legislative encouragement held out to that colony by Parliament, on the faith of which the colonists have laid out large sums on the improvement of their internal navigation; and because the removal of protection will direct the traffic of the interior from the St. Lawrence and the British ports of Montreal and Quebec, to the foreign port of New York, thus throwing out of employment a large amount of British shipping, severing the commercial interests of Canada from those of the parent country, and connecting those interests most intimately with the United States of America.

'12. Because the adoption of a similar system with regard to other articles of commerce will tend to sever the strongest bond of union between this country and her colonies, will deprive the British merchant of that which is now his most certain market, and sap the foundation of that colonial system, to which, commercially and politically, this country owes much of its present greatness.'

Another protest, drawn up apparently by the Duke of Richmond, but much less numerously signed, commented on the burdens of land, and the injury which would ensue to those whose incomes were regulated by the Tithe Commutation Act. It may be added, too, that while the eighty-nine peers who signed Lord Stanley's protest signed all its clauses, the signataries to the second protest selected special clauses as the reasons for their dissent from the action of the Legislature.

The opinions of Lord Stanley in 1846, and indeed in 1852, when Mr. Disraeli brought forward the last

Protectionist Budget, and was defeated, were the opinions of Sir Robert Peel in 1841, and would probably not have been wholly repudiated by Lord Melbourne and Lord John Russell, when their Government gave way to that of Peel. But they were wholly false and fallacious. They have been refuted by experience, and would be admitted at the present day to be utter delusions. The theoretical refutation of these opinions was first supplied by Cobden and his associates in the Free-trade agitation, and this refutation was accepted by an increasing number of those who listened to the speeches which were made at the instance of the League, or read them when printed and published. Now in the progress of political science, the labour which induces the public mind to reject as false and mischievous a system in which it previously acquiesced as necessary and permanent, though originally artificial is exceedingly onerous, while the service is of the greatest possible value. And furthermore, it is to be remembered that the United Kingdom is the only civilised community which has accepted commercial free trade, though the acceptance and maintenance of this policy has incontestably been the cause of its great industrial and commercial developement, just as the establishment of a system of protection, partial or general, has been followed in the countries which have adopted it by an arrest of economical progress, or at least by its retardation. No country affords a more striking proof of this fact than the United States of America do.

It will be seen that the protest of Lord Stanley does not attack free trade in the abstract, does not assert that interference with the principle of free exchange is theoretically defensible, though it goes very near such a view when it dwells on the danger which may ensue from a dependence on foreigners. The question as to how far the political independence of a nation is compromised by those circumstances under which an enemy may hold back anything, the acquisition of which is essential to its defence, may and does arise in practical politics. It would probably be considered unsafe for a country to neglect the manufacture of munitions of war and rely on foreign trade for their supply. It is certain that no country has ever failed to secure itself against such a contingency. Nay, it has been found impossible, or at least highly inexpedient, to trust to the likelihood of sufficient or serviceable domestic supply. There have been occasions, and there are objects, on which a Government does not find it wise to trust contractors, but must needs itself manufacture for its own wants. There are occasions on which it is thought expedient that for some supreme reason of state policy the Government should supply an artificial stimulant to some industry or some product. It is well known that Adam Smith's defence of the Navigation Laws was laid on the basis of public policy. The great economist was in error, and the refutation of his error might have been found in that part of the political history of England which immediately follows on the enactment of those special provisions, when the Dutch burnt the British fleet in the Medway, and the London merchants were reduced to the ignominious expedient of sinking a barrier in the Thames, and guarding the passage by a chain.

It is not difficult to extend the alarm which may be felt at the neglect of those precautions which leave a state defenceless, into advocating the sustentation of those interests which afford a supply the curtailment of which might be attended with inconvenience. It may be granted that the authors of this protest entertained a genuine alarm at the risk which the country ran of being dependent on foreign nations for a supply of grain, though beyond doubt other reasons stronger and more personal urged them to insist on the necessity of agricultural protection. But if they did entertain a sincere dread of this contingency, it was easy to show, even in that day, that the dread was an ignorant fear, and akin to the ridiculous mistake into which Lord Stanley fell when he directed attention to the dangerous fertility of Tamboff. It was argued, with overwhelming force, that a free trade in corn made the risk that the supply would be interrupted wholly problematical, since it inevitably extended the area over which supply would be forthcoming. Later experience has proved that the benefit of such a trade is even wider, since the corn trade of this country is rapidly growing to such an extent, as to further the importations of a perpetual harvest. In short, free trade has demonstrated the truth of the paradox, that the more dependent this country is on foreign supply the less precarious is the supply itself.

The old sliding scale brought the country within the maximum of risk. If it were desirable that the United Kingdom should be independent of foreign

THE SLIDING SCALE. 43

supply, such a policy should have been furthered by absolute prohibition or by a high fixed duty. Experience showed that the former was impracticable, and the slightest acquaintance with public opinion proved that the latter would have been intolerable. The design of the sliding scale was to effect a fixed price, and to relax the restriction on importation when the price of home produce marked its maximum. It caused ruinous fluctuations in price, for the foreign importer poured as much corn as he could into the market when the duty became nominal, and thereupon effected a rapid reduction in price as soon as the market was affected by the sudden influx. The farmer ran great risk of ruin when prices were very high, and similar risk when prices were too low to be remunerative. But the sliding scale was precisely one of those plausible expedients which profess to do the least possible harm to the general public, and the greatest possible good to the parties interested in agriculture. In effect, it did the greatest possible harm to both. No one demonstrated this position more completely than Cobden did, as, for instance, in the seventh of the speeches on Free Trade contained in the volumes which were edited by Mr. Bright and myself.

A very singular delusion occupied the minds of the landowners and farmers, a delusion so gross that in this day we are amazed at the persistency with which it was maintained. The agriculturist was instructed that the principal object on which he should allow his energies to converge was the production of corn, and not of corn only, but wheat. He erred in good company, for this delusion permeates the economical writings of Ricardo, one of the acutest thinkers who ever reasoned from wrong premises. In the settlement of the tithe question the commutation was based on corn averages entirely, though, fortunately for the tithe owners, on the three principal kinds of gramineous corn, for the other elements of farm produce were previously liable to tithe in kind.

Hardly any persons discovered, during the period in which agitation was carried on against the Corn Laws, that a reduction in the price of wheat would be followed by an exaltation in the price of barley and oats, and still more notably in that of other agricultural produce, as meat, butter, cheese, wool, and poultry. The reason for this rise is strictly economical. The more plentiful is the supply of the first necessary of life, that is, a necessary which is in universal demand, and in nearly equal quantities by all, the wider is the field from which the demand for the second necessaries of life are forthcoming. If wheat be cheap, barley and oats, *cæteris paribus*, rise in price, for the public can consume more beer, and use the services of horses more freely. But the case is still stronger in the articles of meat and dairy produce. Cheap bread means dear meat, and the reverse is equally an illustration of one economical law. The horrors which Protectionists predicted about the abandonment of land then cultivated, and the consequent diminution of rent, have been proved to be fallacies as gross as witchcraft and astrology were. The rent of agricultural land has steadily risen, and for the reason that the price of those secondary necessaries to which allusion has been made has grown steadily.

No one, it is true, saw more clearly than Cobden did how deficient was the production of British agriculture. It was so, as the Protectionist party admitted thirty years ago; it is so now, as many eminent personages, who are the heirs of Protectionist opinion, acknowledge now. But Cobden also traced the cause with perfect logical exactness to the absence of security to the tenant, a consequent upon the system under which land is let throughout the greater part of the South of England; to the barbarous absurdity of entails and settlements of land, under which the majority of proprietors are compelled to deal with life interests only, and are therefore deterred from permanent improvement, as well as judicious business arrangements with their tenants; and to the excessive preservation of game, especially ground game. The mischief done by game is vastly increased in these days, for the custom of battue shooting has been encouraged by the high authority of men who, we may hope, were ignorant of the mischief they were doing. The prosperity of labour and capital has made meat and dairy produce dear, but the dearness is greatly enhanced by the wanton waste of resources consequent on excessive game preserving, and the insecurity of the tenant.

It is almost superfluous to say that the theory of dependence on the foreigner being a grave political danger is an exploded fallacy. Unless nations resolve on adopting a policy of absolute political seclusion, they always wish to sell, and wish to do so with greater eagerness the more their industry is devoted to raw produce. Cobden therefore insisted that the general industry of the country would be assisted by a trade with those communities which produced raw material largely, just as he foresaw that the farmer would be compensated for cheap wheat by a rise in the price of all other agricultural products. Nor was he slow to discover that the reciprocity of a beneficial trade was one of the surest preventives to that quarrelsomeness which politicians are apt to foster, and for which nations suffer. Men who know that they have to lose a great deal by going to war, will think once, twice, thrice, before they take an international difference out of the region of diplomacy and carry it into warfare; and politicians are finding that some of the mischief which they cause will react upon them. The punishment which such men endure for wantonly dividing nations, and hounding them on to each other's throats, is not yet severe enough, though it is increasingly deterrent.

A policy of exclusion from importation, facilities being given for exportation, increases the 'dependence' of the country which adopts such a course. In other words, a protective system places the country which accepts it in a position of disadvantageous trade. The proof of this position is not difficult, for it is derived from the elementary principles of commercial intercourse. Since all exchange between country and country is of commodities—the fact is equally true, though not so plain, of the trade between members of the same political society—that country is placed at the greatest disadvantage, which either by the accident of its industry, or by the artificial regulations with which its trade is fettered, has the fewest exports with which to deal in foreign imports, or admits the fewest imports against its exports. This result is quite irrespective of the loss which a protective or prohibitive system puts on the consumer, who might purchase foreign commodities freely, but is either debarred from their use, or curtailed in the free enjoyment of them. For instance, the loss which the protective tariff of the United States puts on the inhabitants of that country is threefold. The most obvious is the fact that the general public does not get the article which it needs as cheaply or conveniently as it might, or in other words, its labour does not go so far as it would go, under a free system of exchange, in obtaining the necessaries and conveniences of life. Next, (a fact which is less obvious, but sufficiently demonstrated by experience, and quite capable of explanation in the light of economical laws,) the producer of the protected article, in his eagerness to grasp the home market, is debarred or debars himself, as the case may be, from entering into competition in the foreign market. At the present moment, to take an example, the United States could take the first place in the coal and iron industry of the world. As it is, they have no place at all in those industries. The same fact may be illustrated by many other instances.

But the most important effect is induced on the producer of those articles which do command a foreign market, as, in the American Union, bread-stuffs and dairy produce. Here the Western farmer, in common with every other inhabitant of the Union, suffers the loss of an exalted price in those articles which are necessary for his own comfortable subsistence, and in those again which he requires in order to carry on his industry to the best advantage. But he also exchanges his own produce to the least advantage. Were the articles which are purchased by his breadstuffs and dairy produce numerous, he could command the best price for his exports. But the choice of exchange being limited, he gets the worst price. Were he to refuse, under the paternal wisdom of the Legislature, and the pressure of the Eastern manufacturers, to sell for anything but gold, the narrowest form under which protection is practised, he would injure his market still more. He would sell what he has to sell for the least possible amount of gold, and he would get the least possible value of articles in exchange for the gold which he buys so dearly. In brief, that country which has adopted the freest possible system of exchange in dealing with that country which has fettered itself with the most restricted system, gets, as a *consumer* of those articles in which it is supplied by the restricted country, the greatest possible quantity of those articles which it imports, at the least possible cost. There is therefore the greatest possible reason in the common allegation of foreign Governments, that free trade suits the circumstances of the British nation. The marvel is, that while they are guided by statesmen whose intelligence on the principles of trade is far lower than that of the noblemen who signed Lord Stanley's protest in June, 1846, the subjects of those Governments do not see that the British policy is equally suitable to themselves.

I have stated above that the protective or prohibitive enactments of other nations are of great benefit to the inhabitants of this country, in so far as they are consumers. Twenty-three centuries ago, the Athenian statesman commented on the fact that his country enjoyed the products of foreign countries as freely and as familiarly as the producers of those articles did themselves, and he doubtlessly knew that this plenty was induced by the free trade policy of the Athenian commonwealth. The fact which was true so long ago, is true now.

But the restrictive policy of foreign countries, though it assists the British consumer, hinders, to some extent, the energy of the British producer. The foreign market is limited by fiscal regulations of a protective character, and the foreign purchaser is put to a disadvantage. But this disadvantage leads him to buy less. He pays more than he needs for the articles which he imports, but he thereupon imports less than he needs. He gives more of his bread-stuffs and dairy produce for British linens, calicoes and hardwares than he would give if the trade between him and the United Kingdom were free, but he takes less of those articles of British industry than he would if his dealings were not restricted. Now it is well known that Cobden, besides identifying himself with a free-trade policy, undertook the functions of a commercial diplomatist, and, as the world knows, with great advantage to both the countries who entered into negotiation, he settled the terms of the Commercial Treaty with France. It is by reason of the œconomical laws which have been referred to above, that a seeming paradox

E

can be explained, i.e. that the French manufacturers gained an advantage in the very articles which were brought into the region of British competition under the Treaty, while similar advantages accrued to the British manufacturers. Both produced more, and both sold on better terms. Had, however, the British Government altered its tariff without any negotiation or reciprocal action on the part of the French Government, all the benefits of the Commercial Treaty would have been secured to the English nation, in so far as they were consumers, though they would have been debarred from some which have accrued to them as producers.

The second of Lord Stanley's reasons for protesting against the repeal of the Corn Laws contains, therefore, the germ of that truth which Cobden, fifteen years after the promulgation of the protest, served to vindicate. But the author of the protest was unconscious of the truth which was latent in his reason. He objected that since reciprocity was not granted, foreign Governments might prohibit exports; forgetting that the prohibition of exports of corn in corn-exporting countries was exceedingly rare, and would be, except under the most utterly abnormal circumstances, an exceedingly unpopular measure, even in the most despotic countries; as was seen by the slowness with which the corn ports of Russia were closed during the Crimean war. He also forgot that the wider the corn market is, the less risk is there of probable failures in the harvest, and by implication, the less reason to fear 'precautionary measures.' Least of all did he see that the parties who had most to fear from the fact that foreign nations would not reciprocate free trade were the manufacturers, whom future danger and present mischief rendered clamorous for the repeal of British protection. But, in fact, nothing can be well more ludicrous than the proposal that the British nation should starve itself regularly, in order to obviate the risk of being reduced to scarcity through the adoption of an expedient which a civilised Government would hardly venture to use, and an uncivilised one would hardly be able to recognise,—a restriction, namely, on the exportation of corn.

It was supposed that the withdrawal of protection would tend to throw land out of cultivation. That the creation of an artificial scarcity by virtue of restricted importation was a stimulus to the cultivation of that quality of land which would otherwise have been left untilled was an opinion entertained, as is well known, by West and Anderson, and was elevated into an economical law by Ricardo. It is more than probable that the supposed cause has never really operated; that the celebrated Law of Rent, which has been elaborated by Ricardo, with all its consequences, is as imaginary as the cosmical theory of Ptolemy; and that had the economical system of Ricardo been an induction from facts instead of a construction from a few positions, this eminently sagacious thinker would never have arrived at such an inference as he promulgated. But political economy has constantly suffered from hypotheses, and has always been developed from inductions.

Even if land had been thrown out of cultivation by the withdrawal of protection, such a consequent was absolutely no argument for the continuance of protection. It was no plea to a starving people and a stunted industry that the rent of the landlord ought not to suffer, or that the beneficence of nature and the reciprocity of food which trade affords should be denied to the public in order that a particular interest should thrive. Under this system of restriction, the farmer and the landowner were taught to consider that the misfortune of the public was their opportunity; a theory as dangerous as it is delusive. It cannot be denied, however, that Lord Stanley's objection had some plausibility. It is a matter of profound interest to the public that the soil of the country should be well cultivated, since every country has, in relation to a portion of its agricultural products, a partial 'protection' by nature, while in certain other products the protection almost amounts to prohibition. Thus, for example, home-grown corn is protected by all the cost of carriage from those regions out of which it is exported, and by the charges levied by intermediaries. Hence the cheaper the corn, the greater the protection. The facilities for importing wheat are greater than those for importing barley and oats, and hence, while free trade has reduced the average price of wheat, that of barley and oats has risen in spite of free trade.

But in the case of meat and dairy produce of a perishable kind, the protection is almost absolute. The Western world sends large quantities of cheese and bacon to the English market, though the cost of these articles is enormously enhanced by freight and trade charges. But meat and butter are hardly obtained except from the United Kingdom, for the art of preserving these articles for a distant market is almost in its infancy. It is therefore not without reason that the public looks with anxiety to the successful cultivation of the soil, and though it is not perhaps yet alive to the causes which hinder that success, it certainly is beginning to see the inconsistency of those who insist on the paramount necessity of improved agriculture, and who demand that they should be able to abuse their ownership for mischievous and selfish gratifications. The hindrance which is put on agriculture by the excessive preservation of game, by the laws regulating the devolution and permitting the settlement of land, and by the system of short tenancies, were perpetually exposed by Cobden. True to his habit of dealing with the effects of such anomalies, he traced the mischief principally to the loss which the farmer's interests suffered; since it is sufficient for economical purposes to demonstrate that a branch of industry is thwarted or depressed, to find a reason for the removal of such impediments. But it may be also necessary, in order to waken the political forces which bring about a reform, to invite the public to take a part in the necessary change, by pointing to the evils which are inflicted on society in general by a mischievous economical condition.

Another plea for protection was 'the exclusive or peculiar burdens laid upon land.' There is no country in the world in which taxation for imperial purposes lies more lightly on land than it does in ours. In common with every other source of income, land is liable to a variable income tax. But its further contribution to the revenue is limited to the ancient land tax, an assessment onerous enough at its first imposition, but long become excessively light when compared with the present value of that on which it was imposed nearly two centuries ago. In most European countries the contribution which rent pays to imperial revenue is very large. The justice of this contribution is to be found in the fact, that alone of all objects in demand its increasing value does not depend on the labour of the possessor. It is true that we are often told of the shrewdness which individuals show in purchasing land for trade purposes, and are asked whether such a perception is not analogous to other business operations. But the price which a judicious speculator in land gets for the intelligence which has guided his purchase, however striking in the particular case, is too trivial to deserve consideration in the general increase of the value of land, and is due moreover to an appreciation of the more rapid rise which will take place in such a particular plot than will occur in other plots.

The rent of land entirely arises from the joint effect of agricultural skill and demand for agricultural produce. I omit designedly (since the omission is only a still stronger illustration of my rule) the rent of building sites. Land which paid a rent of four shillings an acre nearly two centuries ago, and pays a rent of forty shillings now, does not owe this enhancement in the price of soil to the pressure of population, and a recourse being had to inferior soils, and the greater cost of labour in procuring food, as the Ricardian theory of rent alleges, but to a precisely opposite cause. Rent has increased simply because the cost of cultivation has diminished. Undoubtedly if there were a scanty population in the country, rent would fall, and might be wellnigh extinguished. But for just the same reason the price of cotton and woollen stuffs would fall, if the demand for such articles were to diminish. It may be confidently stated that the production of a quarter of corn at the present time is effected at a fourth of the cost at which it was obtained in the beginning of the eighteenth century. Hence rents have risen; and it is certain, that were the hindrances attending the due cultivation of the soil, which have been alluded to above, removed, the rise of agricultural rent would be even more rapid than it has been during modern experience. If, therefore, there be any object of value which is equitably open to growing taxation, it is the rent of land; because its value increases spontaneously, or without effort on the part of its owner.

This produce is divisible into two portions. The owner of the one portion has a very ancient title, one more ancient than that of any private owner whatsoever. It is not easy to say when the title was first acknowledged, but it is certain that it was generally admitted before the Conquest. This portion is tithe. It is absurd to say that a tithe rent-charge is a burden on land. It is really a partition of rent. Its destination may be anomalous; its mode of collection was certainly invidious, though its increase was not intrinsically different from the growth of landlord's rent; and its form of payment obscured the true significance of the charge. Its extinction would no doubt increase the landowner's rent, but so would the extinction of a mortgage. It has been advantageously commuted into a true rent-charge, and not the least part of the benefit arising from this arrangement is the fact that its true nature has been rendered clear.

The chief tax which land pays, or seems to pay, is the rate for the relief of the poor.

The defence which Cobden gave for laying this tax on land, or, to be more correct, primarily on the occupiers of land, is threefold.* First, he alleged that it was 'an ancient tax,' which had followed the ownership of land for three centuries. Next, that ' the poor had the first right to a subsistence from the land.' Third, that ' land is the only property which, in a country growing in population and advancing in prosperity, always increases in value, and without any help from the owners.' One of these principles has been commented on, but something remains to be said for the others.

There is a justification in retaining a tax on permanent property which does not apply to moveable estates. It is that such a tax is capable of numerical interpretation, and is numerically interpreted. A tax on the profits of business is a tax on a variable and uncertain quantity, and cannot in the sale or transfer of such a business be capable of anything like an exact appraisement. Hence, when such a tax is levied, two contingencies arise, one of which defeats its equity, the other its security. Taxes on profits may be

* Speeches, vol. i. p. 419.

transferred from the nominal payer to another person. For instance, a few months ago a deputation waited on Mr. Lowe, and complained of the London co-operative shops. 'We retail tradesmen,' they alleged, 'cannot compete against these shops for cheapness, because they pay no Income Tax, and we do.' This statement either means that a London retail tradesman looks on an Income Tax as part of the outgoings of his business, and charges his customers with it, in the price of the goods he sells, which is obvious; or it means nothing, which is improbable. Hence the customer who pays Income Tax on his own earnings, is forced to pay Income Tax on his consumption also.

Again, it has never been found possible to levy any considerable tax on profits without forcing capital away. It is said that the Income Tax of the United States, perhaps concurrently with other elements in the insane system which is called finance across the Atlantic, has caused a considerable migration of capital from the Union. Taxes, however, may be laid on land and on labour, without materially diminishing the desirableness of the former as a means of investment, and without driving the latter into the habit of emigration. A permanent tax, therefore, on the rent of land is always intelligible, and always fulfils the condition of a tax which is intended to affect a particular description of property, provided it is paid by the landowner and not by the occupier. Moreover, if the tax be an old one and is remitted, the remission does not, as in the case with labour and capital, give energies to both, but is merely a present from the State to an individual who has either purchased an estate at a reduced rate in consideration of the tax, or, possessing an ancient estate by inheritance, has entered upon property the increase in the value of which is wholly due to other causes besides those which give its value to any other kind of property.

The second argument which Cobden alleged contains the gist of the answer to the question,—What is the incidence of local taxation? This question was mooted in 1846, and has been put before the public over and over again since that time as an argument *ad misericordiam* on the part of the landowners. As is well known, a snap division of some significance was given on it in the last (1872) Session of Parliament, on the motion of Sir Massey Lopes.

The statement that the poor have a first right to maintenance from the land, implies that the legal relief of destitution is some compensation or other. But a compensation for what? The answer is twofold. The peasant has been excluded from participation in the soil by enclosures which have annihilated his interest and conferred it on the large proprietor, or by the extension of proprietary rights over limited estates; and he has been constrained by the law which has secured him that legal maintenance when destitute, to work at such wages as would not allow him to anticipate destitution, or even provide against casualty. Now all wages must include as much as is needed to bring up a family to take the labourer's place, must supply what is necessary to insure against sickness, and must find an annuity against old age.

If the ordinary wages of a labourer are insufficient for these purposes (and the most energetic of those people who preach contentment to the agricultural labourer has never averred that his wages can cover these chances), it follows that those who employ him make a better bargain for his labour than they would be able to make if the Poor Law and its rates did not provide him with means against those exigencies and those casualties. Thus, so far from the incidence of the Poor Rate being against the landowner, it really is a means by which he obtains cheap labour, or in other words, is an outlay for which the landowner gets a tantamount return. For as the farmer pays in rent whatever he gets in the price of produce over and above cost and profit, it follows that in his case the diminished cost of labour, due to the Poor Rate, appears on the landlord's side of the ledger in the shape of increased rent. And if part of the cost of the Poor Rate is extracted from those who do not employ labour to get profit, as for example from the tithe-owner and the ordinary occupier in towns, the landowner gets a higher rent by the fact of the Poor Rate than he could if the Poor Rate were not levied at all.

In the speech to which I have already referred, Cobden declared that if the demand on the part of the landowner for a remission of taxation on the plea of peculiar burdens were insisted on, he was fully prepared to enter into the question, and to make the landowner regret that he had ever mooted the matter; since he would not only be beaten in the attempt, but would assuredly be constrained to accept a compromise when the facts were made known, which would be far more disastrous to his personal interests than the very moderate amount of taxation to which he is at present subject, or apparently subject. He would have approached the question from the point of view indicated above, as is clear not only from what he continually stated on the subject, but from what he has left on record as to the risk which would happen to the landed interest as soon as the facts were disclosed.

The only remaining plea of any significance, on which the remonstrant peers based their opposition to the legislation of 1846, was the mischief which free trade in corn would do to the Colonies. The sliding scale was less stringent towards Canada than it was to other countries, and an attempt was made to secure to this colony certain advantages which were denied to the American agriculturist, by demanding certificates of origin from the colonial exporter. It is hardly necessary to say that a certificate of origin is one of the clumsiest of defences against a smuggler, and that the proof of this fact is to be found in many instances of systematic and successful evasion. None of these, perhaps, is better known than that of sworn-off bullion, i. e. bullion the export of which was permitted if the dealer swore that it was not the product of coined British gold. A few pence per ounce was the market price paid to those who took the oath of origin.

This is not the place in which to discuss the colonial system. It is sufficient to say that it entailed a double loss on the colonist and the British consumer, since the basis of the colonial system was reciprocity. If the article could be procured as conveniently from the colony as from any other region, the regulation was superfluous; if it could not, the regulation was mischievous, since it constrained both parties to deal in the least advantageous market. But so enamoured were politicians with the colonial system, that as late as 1846 Lord Stanley could bring himself to say that this country owed much of its greatness to a policy which, sixty years before, had been proved by Adam Smith to be a fallacy and a delusion.

How the material wealth of this country has progressed, despite the sinister predictions of the protectionist party, and how this progress is the admitted product of its system of free exchange, is matter of history. I am aware that attempts have been made to explain this colossal growth by other causes. For example, it is said to have ensued from the gold discoveries of California and Australia, or from the progress of physical science applied to industrial arts. A little reflection, however, will show that those who give such an explanation have mistaken effect for cause. The gold of those countries could not have been obtained except by the exchange of commodities, and the production of these commodities could not have taken place except by the free and abundant importation of food. Similarly, the assistance of mechanical science is the result of a stimulant applied to producers, who see the remuneration for improved processes of production in an extended market for their products.

I have dwelt at length on the allegations which

were made in defence of the protective system, partly because the reasonings with which Cobden met the protectionist were the central principles of his economical theory, partly because it would be an error to suppose that false economical theories are destroyed as soon as ever they are refuted. The theory of protection is always plausible, because it always appeals to the immediate interests of those who are able and anxious to procure it for themselves. Now it takes a very good man to deny himself the prospect of the immediate advantage which protection offers him, and it takes a very wise man to see that the advantage is only immediate, and never permanent.

The service which Cobden did to the cause of free trade was, that he made that which had hitherto been the theory of a few philosophers the practice of a nation. 'I have tried,' says Cobden, in one of his speeches,* 'to popularise Adam Smith,' alluding to one view of that great economist. Mr. Mill has commented on the prodigious advance which is made by a great thinker who has instantly and permanently refuted a fallacy; comparing the change which such a demonstration effects in the mind of a reader, to the sudden enlightenment in the mind of a child when its crude fancies are clearly corrected by the instruction of adult experience. But the service which Cobden rendered in giving instruction to the whole nation, and in triumphantly converting timid and hesitating statesmen, is rarer, and was even more useful. It is true, that in order to effect this result there must be a nation which can be instructed, as well as a mind capable of

* Vol. ii. p. 180.

imparting the teaching, and there probably must be also a set of circumstances which rouse attention and keep up interest. But it is not a little remarkable that though the subject which Cobden took in hand has as great a significance to other nations which boast, perhaps justly, more logical habits of thought than those which characterise our countrymen, and who possess or permit greater facilities for political or economical instruction, the teacher has as yet been wanting, and the conclusions to which we have come in practice are to such persons still buried in the books of thinkers.

It is exceedingly hard for a public man to avoid the seductions of a compromise. We are told, perhaps on high authority, that the course of English political action is invariably a compromise, and that this result is due to the balance of political forms in the British constitution. We are even advised to admire the beneficence of the result, because it is alleged that the balance of these forms is beneficent. The balance is, I believe, a far grosser political fiction than the balance of power was, and the compromise which is so much applauded has nothing, except indirectly, to do with the political institutions from which it is supposed to be derived. It is true that in a social or political constitution, every social element counts for something in the aggregate of forces, either as a check or as an impulse. But it is also true, that where separate interests are endowed with an independent vitality and a power of restriction, one of those interests is certain to rule, and the others have to submit. They may submit after a struggle, and they may check the ruler by the fear that they may recover the ground they have lost and dispute the victory again. Thus it is clear that the Crown governed this country in its interests from the accession of the Tudor dynasty to the expulsion of the Stuarts, some few concessions having been made from time to time to the claim of public rights, and one very serious alarm having been given to this political instrument; that the aristocracy seized the reins at the Revolution, and held it till the passage of the first Reform Bill, using the nomination-boroughs as a means for securing their power; and that the mercantile classes have wielded the political forces of this country up to the passage of the second Reform Bill. It is equally clear that, in time to come, political power will be wielded by a democracy, whose counsels as yet are crude and divided, and which has been hitherto induced to acquiesce in the leadership of the great hereditary Houses of the two historical parties. How long this acquiescence will last cannot be predicted. It may be continued for a generation or more. It may be withheld speedily and suddenly. It is certain that when it is once withheld it will never be regranted.

What is called a compromise is in reality a concession. It is a grant of a little to avoid the surrender of a whole; it is often accepted to avoid that demand for the satisfaction of vested interests or habitual abuses, the compensation for which has been carried to such an alarming height lately, that there is some reason to fear lest legitimate claims may hereafter be ignored. Such compromises or concessions bring about a temporary lull, but never effect a true pacification. Over and over again, persons who have been parties to these arrangements imagine that they have achieved finality, in order to find that the attack on a privilege is certain to be renewed.

In the earliest days of his political career, Cobden was not unwilling to contemplate a compromise. He conceived that a tax on corn amounting to two shillings a quarter might be legitimately levied as a matter of revenue only.* But he soon repudiated even this slight concession. Food, he saw, was the raw material of labour, and all taxes on raw materials are mischievous, this being the most mischievous of all. Thenceforward he argued against a fixed duty with the same energy that he inveighed against the sliding scale. He would have all or none. And with similar perseverance he repudiated the claim to compensation put forward by the protectionist party. Peel indeed made them some grants. He retained a shilling duty, an impost which was reckoned to have put about a million-and-a-half of money annually into the pockets of the British corn-growers. He transferred a small amount of local taxation to the Consolidated Fund. And he sanctioned a very evil precedent, that of allowing landowners to borrow of the Government at rates below the market price of permanent loans.

A politician who repudiates compromises is ostracised from office. It was perhaps no great loss for Cobden, for except during the short time in which Lord Aberdeen held office, he could not have taken part in any Administration. When he was offered a place in Lord Palmerston's second Cabinet he declined it. He could, as he told me at the time, have taken

* Political Writings, i. p. 149.

office under Lord John Russell, but for Lord Palmerston he had an antipathy which, in any man of less genial and conciliatory character, might have passed for prejudice; in one of less purity and singleness of purpose, for an unfair misapprehension of a popular politician.

The rarity of such a man as Cobden was, is not only due to the infrequency with which his peculiar genius is bestowed on mankind, and I may add, perhaps, the scantiness of the occasions on which such a genius may find a subject on which to exercise itself, but in the prodigious sacrifices which such a career exacts. For it, and for his public duty, Cobden sacrificed totally his private interests. It is no secret that when he commenced his labours he was in the fair expectation of an ample fortune, to be obtained by the legitimate process of a lucrative business which he had founded and advanced. His labours, which made the nation rich, made him poor. The man who thinks he can earn business profit without superintending the business in which his capital is invested, expects a law of nature to be suspended in his favour. Had Cobden realised his property when he entered on his public career, he might have had a competence amply sufficient for his modest and frugal habits. But this is not all. Such a public man as he was, unless his fortunes had been abundant, was forced to sacrifice his domestic relations, to neglect his home. Nor was he long in doubt about the surrender which he had to make. The education which a great statesman can give his children is the highest which can be imparted. But it is very rarely the case that he has the opportunity or leisure to grant the boon. Mr. Galton would find it difficult to illustrate his theory of hereditary genius from the families of statesmen.

The effect of the repeal of the Corn Laws reached further than the legislation against which the energies of the League were directed. It is true that, immediately on the repeal, the Council of the League resolved to destroy the organisation which they had so laboriously created. The temptation to continue the machinery by which free trade in food had been obtained was strong. In the first place, men are unwilling to part with any serviceable power, and are very apt to conclude that the purposes which such a power can effect are far from being accomplished by the first victory. They know that when the bond is broken, it is not easy to gather the forces of action together again. They know that there is no gratitude in politics, and that the malignity of beaten and baffled adversaries, particularly of such adversaries as are studiously taught that their ruin has been designed by the reforms of which they have been the objects or the victims, is unsleeping and unsparing. In the next place, the repeal of the Corn Laws was only the reduction of one fort in the great stronghold of protection. The victory, to be sure, enabled the successful combatants to command the other forts, but still they had to be reduced. There were the Navigation Laws, which enhanced freights. There were the differential duties on colonial produce, especially on sugar and timber, which pressed heavily on consumers and producers. There was a fiscal system of Excise, which did its special mischief to various domestic industries. And again, there was another motive for maintaining the organisation of the League, in the threat that when the inevitable reaction of political feeling came, the protectionist party would seek to reverse the legislation of 1846, and certainly to prevent its extension. As a matter of fact, such a purpose held the protectionist party together, till the collapse of Mr. Disraeli's Budget in 1852.

But the leaders of the agitation determined to dissolve the League. They did not indeed intend to be negligent. They declared that they would at once revive it, if any effort were seriously made to carry out the threat of reactionary measures. Had it been necessary, they would have attempted, and perhaps with success, to recall the enthusiasm by which the Corn Laws were swept away in 1846. But there were not a few persons among the less sanguine members of that great Association, who deplored the suicide which the free-trade party advocated and effected. There were some who believed that the League might be advantageously retained as a means for effecting political as well as economical reforms. The wiser and more judicious members of the Association determined on another course. The principal motives which influenced them were two.

In the first place, they were aware that there is no real reaction in the policy of a free country. It is true that there are occasions in the history of every progressive community, when political activity and intelligence are arrested, and some signs induce an alarm that even a reversal is at hand. But since the constitution of this country was formed by the

Act of Settlement, all public questions which have once been fairly debated and decided on, have, with one exception, been never seriously reviewed. The exception to which I refer is the occasional Conformity Act, which the reactionary party in Anne's reign was bent on carrying, which was continually rejected by the House of Lords, and which was finally permitted in 1711, only to last for eight years. But my memory supplies me with no other instance of a deliberate abandonment on the part of the nation of any principle which it has fully discussed and deliberately settled. This is the true finality in politics, and anything short of such a settlement, however loudly partisans may talk of a compromise, is merely temporary. My reader will recall to memory many such achievements in the progress of constitutional liberty, in which victory means that the conquerors will never be dispossessed. After 1846, the revival of a sliding scale or fixed duty on corn was as impossible as an attempt to restore the Stuart prerogative, or a general warrant, or an Act to licence the Press, or a rotten borough, or a restricted franchise would be now.

Again, it was certain that all other forms of the protectionist system would follow the doom of the principal offender against free trade. One by one these minor anomalies were found to be indefensible, and fell almost without a struggle. The differential Sugar Duties and the Navigation Laws gave way first, and the Shilling Duty on corn, which professed to be a mere registration duty, but was virtually a small compensation to the landowners, fell last, almost without comment, certainly without remonstrance. The

small band of able men, who under the name of
Peelites had been originally the most energetic advocates of protection, vied with the Whigs, who were
also converted from fixed duties, in carrying out the
experiment of Peel's first great Budget, and in developing a sound system of finance. Since the repeal of
the Corn Laws, the old Tory remnant, under the
alias of a Conservative party, has rarely been in
power, and then for the most part only on sufferance.
It appears necessary that its traditions should be kept
alive, and this can only, it seems, be effected by an
occasional and brief permission to form an Administration. But it is powerless to reverse the past, and
the farsighted agents of commercial freedom in 1846
could fairly assume as much, when they discussed the
continuance or suspension of their organisation.

It was an indirect service to the science of political
action, but a service of the highest kind, when the
Free Traders dissolved the League. The agitation for
every social reform, and the mechanism by which such
a reform can be achieved, ought to be limited both in
their objects and in their duration. In this country
we have no associations in permanent opposition to
Government, except those which are ridiculous and
powerless. If men propose to themselves some political
reform, they are careful to define the purposes for
which they unite, and to forecast the dissolution of
their organisation when the object which they put
before themselves is achieved. We do not pretend to
reconstruct society, we simply fasten on some mischief,
and strive to mend it. We do not labour for gener-
alities, nor even for general reforms, but seek to deal

with special mischiefs. It is no doubt very difficult to win the results we aim at, but perseverance can generally gain its end, or at least, assuming that its purpose is capable of proof, can make ultimate success inevitable. Unless I am mistaken, no nation has ever succeeded in attempting to remodel itself. The Abbé Sieyès was the very reverse of a statesman in all that was practicable. Cobden was the type of one. The two men are in absolute contrast, in their means, and therefore in their ends.

The result, however, of the Anti-Corn-Law agitation, and the revision of the fiscal system in this country, contained in it the germs of a thorough and a pacific revolution. It was not only a precedent in the assault of untenable positions, but it was a formal notice that every kind of interference with natural liberty, and every grant of a special privilege, however imposing and sacred the privilege or institution might be, was open to challenge and might be challenged. It made no objection to that orderly delay in the acceptance of a reform, which requires the education of public opinion, by agitation and discussion, till that public opinion pronounces in favour of a change. The essential feature in the action of the Free Traders was that they did not attempt to found a clique of doctrinaires, but to correct hostile opinion. Hence it has followed that from the time of this remarkable movement, all parties have agreed that there is an opinion, which is to be developed, interpreted, and adopted. A generation ago men took guarantees from those whom they admitted to political equality or civil rights, and strove by exacting pledges to affirm finalities in politics. In these days such a process would be an anachronism. For example, when the Test Acts were repealed, Dissenters were called upon to declare that they would make no attack on the Anglican Establishment. The promise was of course futile, for it could only in the nature of things affect those who were enfranchised. At present, the most conservative of statesmen, as far as ecclesiastical matters are concerned, allows that, if public opinion demands it, the Establishment must go by the board. Such an admission is not, as foolish people say, destructive, but eminently protective to the institution about which it is allowed, for it must as a consequence be shown, not only that the Establishment is useless, but that it is mischievous.

CHAPTER III.

THE LAND QUESTION.

Perhaps few of Cobden's utterances have been more frequently quoted than one which is contained in the last speech which he made in public.* 'If,' he said at Rochdale, 'I were five-and-twenty or thirty, instead of, unhappily, twice that number of years, I would take Adam Smith in hand, and I would have a League for free trade in Land just as we had a League for free trade in Corn. You will find just the same authority in Adam Smith for the one as for the other; and if it were only taken up as it must be taken up to succeed, not as a political, revolutionary, Radical, Chartist notion, but taken up on politico-economic grounds, the agitation would be certain to succeed; and if you can apply free trade to land and to labour too—that is, by getting rid of those abominable restrictions in your parish settlements, and the like,—then, I say, the men who do that will have done for England probably more than we have been able to do by making free trade in corn.'

Another passage is equally significant:† 'It is no use your talking of your army and navy, your export and your imports; it is no use telling me you have a small portion of your people exceedingly well off. I

---

* Speeches, vol. ii. p. 367. † Speeches, vol. ii. p. 116.

want to make the test in a comparison of the majority of the people against a majority in any other country. I say that with regard to some things in foreign countries we do not compare so favourably. The English peasantry has no parallel on the face of the earth. You have no other peasantry like that of England—you have no other country in which it is entirely divorced from the land. There is no other country of the world where you will not find men turning up the furrow in their own freehold. You will not find that in England. I don't want any revolution or any agrarian outrages by which we should change all this.'

Again:* 'I believe we have no adequate conception of what the amount of production might be from a limited surface of land, provided only the amount of capital were sufficient. There is no reason whatever why I should not live to see the day when a man who lays out £1000 on fifty acres of land will be a more independent, more prosperous, and more useful man, than many farmers who now occupy five or six hundred acres, with not one quarter or one tenth of the capital necessary to carry on the cultivation.'

Again, after having given two arguments in justification of the practice which casts 'local taxation' on real estate, he adds,† 'But I have another reason why this property should bear those local burdens, and it is this,—it is the only property which not only does not diminish in value, but, in a country growing in population and advancing in prosperity, it always increases in value, and without any help from the owners. These gentlemen complain that those rates

* Speeches, vol. i. p. 407.   † Speeches, vol. i. p. 430.

have increased in amount during a recent period. I will admit, if they like, that those local rates have increased. During the last hundred years they have increased, I will say, seven millions of money. That is taking an outside view. Well, but the real property upon which those rates are levied—the land and houses of this country—has increased in value four times as much; and therefore they stand in an infinitely better situation now, paying twelve millions of local rates, than ever they did before in any former period in the history of this country.' These references might be multiplied, for Cobden was never weary of advocating a thorough and searching reform of the Land system in the United Kingdom. I shall take occasion hereafter to comment on the manner in which they were discussed by the public prints, and especially by the *Times*; for there is no doubt that, on the whole, the last-named paper is a very fair exponent of the sentiments entertained at any given time by those classes which have hitherto been dominant in the administration of public affairs, and absolute in the Legislature.

Researches into the social history of this country prove that, four or five centuries ago, land was very generally distributed. In every English parish or manor, portions of land held at a fixed rent, or at a fixed service commutable into a small money payment, were occupied by an agricultural population. The estate of the feudal superior contained a considerable portion, and probably the best portion, of the village. The income of this personage was derived partly from the profits obtainable by the cultivation of his own domain, partly by the rents and other payments due from his tenants in perpetuity; for in those times for which we have the evidence of rentals, the precarious tenancy of the serfs, if indeed it ever existed, had wholly disappeared. As these tillers of the soil held of their manorial lords, so the manorial lords held of the Crown, either immediately or by intermediate stages. In theory, and in early times, perhaps in fact, the tenant of the Crown had only a life interest, or even a narrower tenure. In practice, however, these grants of the king to his tenants soon became estates of inheritance. But the earlier state remained as a legal generality. The English law invests the sovereign with the ultimate ownership of all land, and the nation, partly by having conferred no higher title than a parliamentary status on the House of Brunswick, and thereby repudiating the ancient theory of hereditary right, partly by commuting the estate which it bestowed on the Crown by the Act of Settlement into a fixed annual sum, has succeeded to and enjoys whatever actual or reversionary interest was possessed by the English sovereigns. To speak, as some persons have lately spoken, of the rights of the Crown in the London parks, or even in any portion of that which was the hereditary estate of the monarch, as distinguished from his private acquisitions, is either foolish adulation, or transparent sophistry, or consummate ignorance. It is almost as absurd to speak of any resumption of these estates by the monarch on a future devolution of the Crown. The English monarch does not possess an inch of his public estate by any but a parliamentary title, and the power which gave being legally competent to take away, the authority which enacted the Act of Settlement has an absolute power of repealing the Act. The value which we assign to our institutions will not be heightened by an error about their origin or their sanctions.

Up to the time of the Reformation, the condition of the yeomanry, the descendants of the small freeholders and the inferior tenants of manorial lords, was progressively prosperous. The old English nobility committed suicide during the long civil war of the fifteenth century, and their estates were in many cases divided among their social inferiors. But little more than half a century after the Battle of Bosworth another estate was all but annihilated, and a new aristocracy was founded on its ruins. The dissolution of the monasteries was long foreseen. The lands and the feudal privileges of these institutions were parcelled out among the dependants of the Crown. It is probable that the monasteries were indulgent landlords. It is certain that their successors were rapacious.

Complaints about the extensive and irregular inclosure of common lands precede these events. But the complaint becomes systematic at the latter part of the sixteenth century and onwards. It appears that these usurpations were founded upon some indefinite custom. At last the aid of the Legislature was invoked, in order to give a formal sanction to these proceedings. The first Enclosure Act was passed in the reign of Anne, and for a long time the private appropriation of public lands was attained through the Legislature. At last, the principle, if we can call it so, which gave the principal landowner the power of increasing his estate, on something like the ratio by which prize money is distributed, and which was justified by the plea that such inclosures increased the national supply of food, was formulated in the establishment of a Board of Enclosure Commissioners, whose business it was to facilitate spoliation.

The practice of primogeniture in the form with which we are familiar, is, I believe, peculiar to this country. It appears to have prevailed in Normandy before the French Revolution. Its origin in England may be traced to the policy of a foreign conqueror, whose interest induced him to establish a fortress in every county held by his own creatures, and who commissioned it, to overawe a subject people. Such a person was well aware how important is the concentration of force for the purpose of garrisoning a country. It was equally obvious that the dependence of such nobles on the Crown would be secured by their fewness, and that if the estates which they held were parcelled out among their dependants, an organisation might be effected which would perhaps paralyse the royal power. Primogeniture was not instituted in Kent, and the men of Kent have taken up from time to time a very energetic attitude, from the days of Wat Tyler to the epoch of the Kentish petitions.

The primogeniture of antiquity was a very different affair, however, from its modern representative. This custom only affected land and the incidents of land. Personal estate was divided generally according to the rules of the civil code. But in the middle ages, personal estate was far more valuable than real.

Most of the nobles and wealthy landowners cultivated their own estates, and the stock of a well-tilled farm was, as a rule, worth three times at least the fee simple of the soil. Of this the eldest son took only an equal portion with his brothers and sisters. The growth in the value of land and the adoption of a system of farming occupations have not only greatly modified the relations of an elder to a younger son, but have intensified that concentration of power, under the conditions of modern government, which it was the purpose of the first William to develope for personal, or at least temporary objects. Nothing but a few accidents in administration, and especially that which limits the financial system of the country to the discretion of the Lower House, prevented the United Kingdom from being governed by a very narrow oligarchy, and probably from being split up into a number of principalities like those of Germany at the close of the last century. The Upper House actually did rule this country from the Revolution till the passage of the first Reform Bill.

It is indeed not a little remarkable that the hotly-contested and hardly-won privileges or usurpations of the House of Commons have greatly obviated the power which the constitution of the House of Lords indirectly confers upon it. I have referred to the most significant, the origination of all money bills in the Lower Chamber. Another is the fact that in cases of malversation the Commons have the sole power of impeachment. A third is the peculiarly invidious character of an irresponsible veto, and the hesitation with which it must be exercised. Those ardent politicians who aim at destroying the House of Lords have made a very unintelligent interpretation of political forces. The framers of the Scotch Union were wise in abrogating the rule which had prevailed since the accession of the House of Stuart, that a Scotch peer might be elected to an English constituency. The framers of the Irish Union committed a grave error in permitting Irish peers to be eligible. To destroy the House of Peers, as long as the custom of primogeniture and the power of settlement exists, and for two or three generations afterwards (unless indeed, what every sensible man would deprecate, the great estates were violently broken up and distributed), would be to hand over the constituencies to men of great wealth, and of considerable means for conciliating popularity. As it is, a seat in the House of Lords is a form of dignified ostracism, and like ostracism, is a means for curtailing the inordinate influence which arises from the accumulation of great wealth and of admitted social position in a few hands.

The practice of entail had a beginning which is widely distinct from its developement and extension. Its object was to create a body of male tenants who might be dependent on the grantors of the estate in fee, and whose estate should revert to the grantor on the failure of male issue. The framers of the Statute of Entails did not contemplate the application of the law to their own patrimonies, but only wished to develope a new form of subinfeudation, to create a body of retainers, who might aid the lord against the sovereign, the law, or the public. It was only during the civil wars that the tenancy in tail was made a means of securing his estate to the principal lord, under the machinery of a use or ancient trust. Hence after the middle of Edward IVth's reign, when the crown seemed to be firmly fixed in the line of York, the judges decided that there was a way for breaking the continuity of an estate tail under the process of a common recovery. By degrees the other securities which maintained the estate tail were broken down, and before the end of Henry VIIIth's reign the estate was nearly as liable to voluntary or involuntary alienation as a tenancy in fee simple. At present it only differs from such an estate in two facts, that it cannot be devised by will, and that it must be alienated under one form of conveyance only. Those persons therefore who meet objections to entails in England by stating that there is no material difference between an estate in tail and one in fee simple are technically in the right. It is true that an estate tail, even under present circumstances, is a barbarous and absurd form of ownership, and is indefensible. But it is not, as many people are apt to think, an inalienable perpetuity.

Another form of conveyance, which has superseded, or rather included, the old estate tail, does amount to a practical perpetuity. I refer to the conveyance under what is called a strict settlement. Here the first taker of the estate has a life interest only conveyed to him, with a series of limitations in tail over the issue of his marriage, or failing these to other persons under the same conditions. It is true that the first taker may, with the consent of his son, or other person occupying such a position, and being of full age, alienate the estate, or charge it. But in practice, when the son comes of age, and when he wishes to form a fresh settlement on his marriage, the estate is tied up anew with similar limitations. This ingenious evasion of the English Common Law, which we are told with some irony professes to abhor a perpetuity, was the invention of two conveyancers of the Revolution, Palmer and Bridgman. The validity of the process was disputed for a time, but we are informed that when these two persons administered the law which they created,—Bridgman became successively Chief Baron, Chief Justice of the Pleas, and Lord Keeper; and Palmer Attorney General,—they gave effect to their own proceedings, and that the conveyance was thereby established. With some modifications, the scheme of these two lawyers is the basis of the modern settlement. I have dwelt on these particulars mainly because in ordinary conversation people speak very loosely of the 'Law of Entail,' as if it were the mechanism by which estates are tied up. The real process by which the result is effected is by the form of a strict settlement.

It is clear from the language which Cobden used, that he contemplated two things. He wished to remove all hindrances to the easy and economical transfer of land; and he wished to develope a process by which, under the natural operation of a free exchange, the labourer might be resettled on the soil from which, in his energetic and suggestive phrase, the labourer had been divorced. He wished to do this also for two reasons. In the first place, it is the interest of the farmer that he should be able to use his capital in such a way as would produce the largest possible quantity of return with the least possible labour, a

result which cannot possibly be obtained by any
prudent man who has a precarious or even terminable
tenure of land, and who is debarred by the terms of
his tenure or by the custom of farm-letting from compensation for unexhausted improvements. The other
reason is the general good of the public; for the
public is interested in an abundant return from cultivation. It is true that since free trade in corn has
been established, the interest of the public in an
abundant crop of corn is lessened. It is not rendered
superfluous, for a deficient harvest involves a rise in
prices. But the public is greatly interested in an
abundant supply of other agricultural products, as for
example, dairy produce, meat, poultry, and eggs, articles
of which modern British husbandry affords a very limited
supply. Another fact which did not escape Cobden's
sagacity in dealing with the land question, was the
exceedingly slight contribution which land affords in
this country, when contrasted with the same property in
foreign countries, to the national revenue. But this fact
may be reserved for future notice. It will be convenient
to treat the four points which are stated above in order.

The English law is very lenient on the landowner
who holds his land. Most of the local taxation, about
which so great a complaint is made, is beneficial
outlay, and most of that beneficial outlay is extracted,
by a process familiar to political economists, from the
occupier; for it is an axiom in taxation that taxes
tend to remain upon the person who immediately pays
them, or in other words, that it requires an effort, which
is made with very varying degrees of ease or difficulty,
to shift a tax which is paid by the first payer to the

shoulders of another. The direct taxation on land is the ancient land tax, an assessment of 20 per cent. imposed in the reign of William and Mary, and never reassessed since, and the quota which land pays unquestionably to a variable Income Tax; unquestionably, for the law interposes, perhaps from some obscure consciousness of the rule which I have given above, to adjust the tax, for it authorises the tenant to deduct the Income Tax from his rent. On the other hand, the law claims no Probate Duty from the landowner, and enacts a Succession Duty which is not calculated, as in personal estate, on the actual value of the property, but on the probable duration of the legatee's life. The law therefore, while it gives the landowner every facility for accumulation (and more illustrations could be afforded of the fact), takes care that, as long as he holds his land, he shall be lightly assessed to public burdens.

But the law is prodigiously deterrent to those who wish or need to sell. It puts upon the vendor the practical obligation of proving his title, for it visits an innocent purchaser with confiscation if he buys inadvertently from a fraudulent seller, or even from a *bona fide* but illegal possessor. In all other objects of value, the man who buys openly and fairly acquires an indefeasible title to his property, and the penalties of fraud are visited on the dishonest seller. In land, the reverse rule holds. So preposterous a condition, so ludicrous, if it were not so unjust, a rule, probably arose from an anxiety on the part of Crown lawyers to substantiate the claim of the Crown to the reversion or resumption of legal grants. Hence the ancient rule was, that an action of ejectment against a defective title might be based on any evidence of adverse possession gathered at any time previous to the date of legal memory, the first year that is of Richard I. Even under the less absurd arrangement of modern times, the period of prescription is lengthened far beyond the time allowed in any other civilised country. As a consequence, the cost of conveyance is enormously increased, though it is probable that few titles are without a flaw. What can be said for the law of titles in a country where such a case as that of Tichborne is rendered possible? This law-suit has, to be sure, made an obscure family notorious, but at what a cost of public money, and of public time.

That the complications of title have been developed in order to gratify a morbid anxiety for preserving estates against contingencies more or less remote, and have been perpetuated in the interests of a professional class of conveyancers and attorneys, cannot, I think, be doubted. But it is possible that the latter may have overshot their mark. Cobden used often to tell a story with great glee, as to how he held a conversation with a country attorney on the effect of the accumulation of land in few hands, and how his companion ruefully allowed that, as half a county passed under a single conveyance, the gains of lawyers were curtailed by the very ingenuity which they had displayed. When Washington was urged not to lay hands on the custom of primogeniture in his native State, on the ground that it would put an end to all carriages and four, he is said to have answered, 'But think how many carriages and two we shall see!'

It will be plain that the expense attending proof

of title operates as a progressive tax on small holdings. Most economists reprobate a tax the percentage of which increases with the value or profit of the object which has been made liable to the tax. Thus, for instance, a progressive Income Tax has been generally considered a violent act of spoliation, though it is capable of a scientific defence under Adam Smith's first rule, 'that taxation should be proportioned to the ability of the tax payer.' But a tax the percentage of which increases with the smallness of the object on which it is levied is utterly indefensible. It is said to be often the case that the costs attending the transfer of small portions of land are equal to two or three years' rent of the land itself. But there is no reason, except morbid vanity or professional interest, why the transfer of land should not be as easy as that of railway stock, or even consols. Land can be surveyed, registered, identified. A new Doomsday might be made, in which all ownerships and all charges on ownerships might be and should be inscribed, and such a Doomsday should be open to public inspection. Pledges of personal property are published, there is no reason why pledges of landed property should not be equally matters of publication. A *bonâ fide* and public purchase of goods relieves the purchaser from any liability of confiscation through defective or fraudulent possession on the part of the vendor. There is no reason why a similar rule should not hold good in the case of land. It is monstrous that an innocent buyer should be liable to the effect of forgeries like those of Roupell, when he has not been privy to his crimes. Under an effective system of registration, the possibility of fraud would be so remote that exceptional provision need not be made against its occurrence.

With that clear good sense which distinguished his insight into all economical questions of a practical character, Cobden saw the sufficient means for removing the anomalies which characterise the present tenure of landed estates in the United Kingdom in the assimilation of landed to personal property. He would not have interfered with the right of making a will of lands, but he would not have exempted the succession to real estate from the taxes which are levied on the devolution of personal property. He would not have agreed to that rule which, under the name of Hypothec in Scotland and the Landlord and Tenant Law in England, makes rent a secured debt, and so puts the creditor of personal estate to a disadvantage in trading with his debtor. There is nothing, he argued, but superstition or selfishness in the distinction which is made between investments of capital in a part of the earth's surface, or in a portion of the earth's products, or in a loan of money to a trader. They are all forms of the same fact, viz. property, however different the origin of the first may be from that of the other kinds, and however peculiar may be its place in the economical elements of social life. He would have made the process of transferring land as easy as that of any other bargain and sale.

No man believed more thoroughly than Cobden did in the principle that a civilised society, if its action be not hampered by absurd restrictions, will work out the problems of its own being by natural and orderly processes. Given freedom of exchange in all directions

and over all kinds of property alike, and there is and
can be no need of any reconstruction, of any violent
interruption with the natural distribution of wealth.
And conversely, if wealth is unnaturally accumulated,
such a result is unquestionably due to some abnormal
or irregular interference with a natural process; for
the rectification of which evil, the removal of the cause
and patient waiting for the consequences of reform
are the only remedy which is consistent with the well-
being of society I do not know whether he ever had
heard of the expressive lament of Pliny—*latifundia
perdidere Italiam*—but he had thoroughly caught the
spirit of that publicist, for his condemnation of the
system by which the labourer was divorced from the
soil, and his wish that he had the youth and vigour
necessary for a campaign against the English land
system, are expressions of the same sentiment which
the Roman stated in different terms. But he would
not have dreamed of nationalizing the soil, or of
making the State a vast bureaucratic land office, or
of extending instead of limiting the function of civil
administration. He thoroughly endorsed the doctrine
of Adam Smith, that the interference of Government
in the details of private life, or in the energies of
industry, or in the distribution of property, or in the
factitious creation of social orders, was not merely an
impertinence, but a mischievous error. The occasions
on which a Government can help or intervene are, a certain very well defined province of action excepted, exceedingly rare, and ought to be looked on with the gravest
suspicion, and permitted with the greatest hesitation.

From his point of view, free trade in land, by which,

I repeat, he meant the extension of the principle of free exchange in all its fulness to landed estates, and the removal of all restrictions on its transfer, either voluntarily, should the owner desire to sell it, or involuntarily, if its owner became hopelessly embarrassed, would bring about the second of the objects which Cobden contemplated in a reform of the English land laws. It might be slowly effected, but it would be surely effected. The small purchaser in a wealthy or progressive country can always, and always will, outbid the large buyer, if facilities are given for easy transfer. If, as people allege, and as I believe with overwhelming evidence in favour of their view, a small or peasant proprietary is the most thriving, the most industrious, the most thrifty of cultivators, and if under small freeholdings the capacities of the soil are developed to the fullest possible extent, and the rate of production raised to the very largest amount, this small proprietor, if no legal hindrance is put in the way of his existence, will be, and ought to be, naturally developed. It is as great an error to develope him by artificial means, as Feargus O'Connor tried to develope him at Minster Lovell, and as some amiable theorists would wish to develope him now, as it has been to permit the law to assist in forming the process by which he has been unnaturally extinguished.

A true statesman differs widely from a mere politician, and from an advocate of reconstruction; from the former in the fact that he never accepts a compromise on a true principle, from the latter in that he is satisfied with particular reforms, and has confidence in the power with which society uses legitimate opportunities for bringing about the best state of things possible under the habits and institutions with which it is familiarised. That the English people has no attachment for its land laws is manifested by the fact that it never retains them in a British colony. But that it would remodel its social state at home, or acquiesce in a theory which would suspend all existing facts, in order to rearrange them through the instrumentality of Government, is a fancy which nothing but the impatience to see everything instantaneously reconstructed on a new plan would ever suggest or deem feasible. From the days of Plato down to our own time, there have been good and well-meaning men who have framed schemes, more or less optimist, of a beneficent despotism, which should annihilate first, and create afterwards. Most of these schemes have never been intended to imply anything more than a protest against existing usages; none of them have ever reached the earliest stage of practical acceptance. Once or twice in the history of the world impatient attempts have, it is true, been made to force social changes on a hostile or apathetic people. These attempts have as invariably ended in ruin and reaction. The rapacity of the Roman nobility wrecked ancient civilisation. But the student of social facts cannot fail of seeing that the Roman nobility was exasperated and demoralised by the abortive but well-meant agrarian projects of the Gracchi. Men must be ripe for a truth, before it is a truth to them.

Even upon the difficult question of the relations of landlord and tenant Cobden seems to have entertained the view that perfect freedom of contract was the best for both parties. He advocated leases, and rational leases. He ridiculed, during the time when he was vindicating free trade in corn, the preposterous clauses in ordinary farmers' leases. But on the other hand, he stated,[*] on March 8, 1849, that while 'free trade owes it to the farmer to carry out its principles, by removing every impediment to the free employment of capital and labour upon the soil,' and that if the farmer makes out his 'complaint of the interference of the Malt Tax with his business, that therefore it is not inconsistent with my principles to remove that impediment out of the farmer's way,' he adds, 'I do this without pretending to any particular affection for the farmer above other classes. If I did so I would follow your error, by attempting to legislate for a particular class.' It is not easy to anticipate what would have been Cobden's line of action in relation to the Irish Land Bill, and whether he would have acquiesced heartily in a law which protects one of the parties to a contract. He might have done so, for according to his principles there was a justification for such a departure from the strict rule of mercantile bargaining. Freedom of contract is a fiction, when one of the parties to the contract is wholly in the power of another. Now this is the case when the latter deals in an article which is wholly limited in quantity; still more so when the article has by the direct act, or by the permission of the Legislature, been accumulated in few hands; yet more when the social and religious feelings of the two parties are unnaturally at variance; and most of all, when the

[*] Speeches, vol. i. p. 397.

community is in such a condition that the mass of the people have no industry but the occupation of land, and the purchase of this occupation is forced to an unnatural height by the competition of tenants. But all these circumstances converged in Ireland, to say nothing of the fact that the proprietors were bankrupt by their extravagance, and had been settled on lands which had over and over again, by successive acts of an alien Legislature, been confiscated from the ancestors of the people who are now tilling them.

There is no reason to interfere between the parties to the contract for a lease of lands in Broadway or in the neighbourhood of Boston, although the causes which operate to create rent are as dominant in these parts of the American Union as they are in London or Manchester, and are quite as much illustrations of the unearned increase of land as any which could be quoted from our immediate experience. The fact is, the American Union is so wide, that if individuals are unwilling or unable to purchase or rent land in the immediate neighbourhood of great commercial activity, they can, without abandoning the political and social habits of their country, and the numberless associations which such habits bring with them, seek a spot where they can bargain to greater advantage, or obtain virgin soil at a nominal price. Nor, again, is the American Union, or indeed any other civilised country, hampered and restrained by a system which gives an opportunity to the worst faults of a monopoly by fostering every means for accumulating and retaining land. Men do not grumble at the injustice of nature, but they are irritated irreconcileably by the injuries of law. Nay, it is one of the misfortunes which are sure to ensue from erroneous legislation, that it always begets a disposition to remedy one wrong by another, to repudiate as obsolete the adoption of those natural processes by which the effects of an error are slowly but surely righted, to cry out that it is too late to reform a process, and that immediate necessity requires fundamental change.

It is I think clear that capital cannot be freely used upon the land of another, unless provision is made that the occupier shall be in some way or other compensated for what are called unexhausted improvements. The lessee of land for building purposes can distribute the loss of a terminable annuity, such as the reversion of his outlay to the landlord at the end of his term, and thus recover the loss over the term in question. It is certain indeed that nothing but necessity will reconcile men to this process. In this country it is all but impossible, even when the Government grants favourable terms, to float terminable annuities in the market, though such a form of security may be no loss, but even a gain to certain parties who purchase them. But to the mass of the public, a property which is annually diminishing in value is exceedingly distasteful. There are districts where, it being the custom to lease lands on chief or permanent rent, lessees will not look at short terms of years. I have been told by a person exceedingly competent to give information on the subject, as he is a very large landed proprietor in the district, that terminable leases would have been an insuperable obstacle to the growth of Manchester and its neighbourhood, where the system of permanent leases is customary.

But whatever may be said of buildings, the case of farm holdings is still stronger. A landlord cannot, in England at least, for it appears he did so in Ireland, exact the fullest rights which the law gives him over the occupancy of his tenant. Hence persons are apt to dwell on and to vaunt the generosity with which the landowner does not avail himself of all the powers which he might employ. In my opinion this generosity is really the necessity of the situation. Englishmen would not tamely acquiesce in a practice which continually revalued their occupancies, and made their own outlay the basis for an enhanced rent. The rent of agricultural land is therefore seldom the maximum annual value of the occupancy, in many cases is considerably below such an amount, though when such easy terms are given, they are generally considered as the condition of political allegiance. But whatever may be the motive of the landowner and the understanding of the tenant, the concession is precarious, is occasionally withdrawn, and always may be. Now there is nothing which operates so greatly as a discouragement as insecurity does. It used to be an argument against tithe that it discouraged improvements in agriculture, because it taxed unequal outlay at equal rates. But the case is far more strong when a system of rackrents is attempted to be induced on improving tenants. It is admitted, I think, that British agriculture is far below what it might be, and that British stock is generally improved to the highest efficiency which skill can improve it. The reason is not far to seek. Till stock is generally improved, no operation of the landowner can make it contribute to rent. But a crop may be visited by an enhanced rent, because in this particular the tenant is within the will of his landlord. Hence towards the conclusion of a lease, it becomes the interest of the tenant to reduce within the lowest amount which is consistent with average production and the terms of his contract, all outlay on the soil. It is to this fact, and to the frequent embarrassment of landowners, and their consequent incapacity to make landlords' improvements, that much of the unproductiveness, which has been made the subject of complaint by men of all parties, and the defects of British agriculture are due.

I think it is impossible to doubt that some form of tenant-right will be ultimately obtained, as it is eagerly demanded by British farmers. Few statesmen will now be bold enough to utter the specious apothegm of Lord Palmerston, that tenant right is landlord's wrong. It is now believed that if some loss accrues to the landlord by limiting his power of exacting the maximum which his opportunity of ownership gives him from the outlay or spirit of his tenant, a far greater and less justifiable wrong is inflicted on the tenant by such a procedure; and that in fact the answer to Lord Palmerston's generalisation is another, that, in a still more marked and indefensible manner, 'Landlord's right is tenant's wrong.' Nor can it be said that the recognition of rights which traverse the terms of a strict and a voluntary bargain is unknown in English law. Technically the tenant in mortgage is held to have forfeited his estate if he fails to repay the advances of the mortgagee within the specified time for which he borrows the money and pledges his estate. But the law has long since protected the mortgagor from an injurious but not strictly unjust foreclosure, by according him an equity of redemption. Tenant-right therefore, understood as the repayment of unexhausted improvements and compensation for capricious ejectment, has a precedent in the English law of mortgage. It is even still more defensible, because the wrong or loss is positive in the case of the tenant, and is only contingent, or at best comparative, in the case of the mortgagor.

Now it is not difficult to show how profoundly the public is interested in the adequate cultivation of the soil. The cost of carriage is always a natural protection to the home producer. If it could be reduced to a minimum, the price of wheat in Chicago would not vary from the price of wheat in London. In point of fact, the money value of the article at the latter place is as a rule double that of the same article in the former. Still more is this the case with cheaper kinds of corn, which are also exported from foreign countries, for of course the lower the value of the article is, minus the cost of carriage, the greater the element of such a cost when it is added to the original value. The efficient cultivation of the soil is therefore, as far as these articles are concerned, a double advantage to the inhabitants of any given country. The increased quantity is a positive gain. The diminution of the aggregate cost of transit is a comparative or indirect gain.

There are, however, some articles of which the protection is absolute. Such are those which are perishable, or which cannot be conveyed without risk and loss. A very short sea voyage is sufficient to greatly diminish the value of fat stock. A slightly longer sea voyage is prohibitive of its transit at all. Extend the distance, and even lean stock cannot be imported. Similarly, the distance over which meat may be seaborne is very limited. It is possible that science may hereafter discover a means for preserving this article, so that it may be conveyed over long sea voyages. Attempts are already made in this direction, but with indifferent success. When, therefore, the *Times* answered my complaint that there are more than six times the number of cows per heads of population in Denmark than there are in Great Britain, by saying that such a statement meant no more than that the English people, for wise reasons or sufficient ones, kept some of their cows in Denmark, this clever newspaper must have relied on the ignorance or prejudice of its readers. To those English people who consume or wish to consume milk, butter, and beef, the Danish cows are as remote, and therefore to all practical purposes as unserviceable, as though they were in the American prairies. In a densely-peopled country like our own, where the caprice of the climate and the hardness of labour render it in the highest degree desirable that the nation should be well nourished, a deficient supply of these secondary necessaries of life is a public calamity, and the wholesale dedication of land to other than food-producing purposes is an indefensible waste. Such is the loss induced by excessive game-preserving, and by the maintenance of a huge number of horses for a frivolous and demoralising amusement.

When Cobden spoke of campaigning against the English Land Laws, had he possessed the youth and vigour which he carried into the Anti-Corn-Law League, of taking Adam Smith in his hand, and discovering in his favourite author the same arguments for a free trade in land that could be alleged for a free trade in corn and in other commodities, he was probably thinking of the general principles on which Adam Smith vindicated free exchange. But Adam Smith did not rest his assault on entails—by which he intended to designate all devices which have for their object the inalienability of landed estates—on the general laws which render free exchange the condition under which the economic good of man can be most fully effected. He advocates the breaking up of those estates and the annulling of those entails for special as well as for general reasons. Admitting that they might once have had a political defence, he asserts that this defence has long since been rendered untenable by the growth of civilisation, and that 'nothing can be more completely absurd' than an entail. He discovers their modern justification in the necessity for strengthening an hereditary nobility, and observes that 'that order having usurped one unjust advantage over the rest of their fellow-citizens, lest their poverty should render it ridiculous, it was thought reasonable that they should have another.' He observes that 'a great proprietor is seldom a great improver,' and having sketched what are and must be the leading motives in his action, observes,—'There still remain in both parts of the United Kingdom some great estates which have continued without interruption in the hands of the same family since the times of feudal anarchy. Compare the present condition of these estates with the possessions of the small proprietors in the neighbourhood, and you will require no other argument to convince you how unfavourable such extensive property is to improvement.'* I have never yet heard of any economist, except the late Mr. Macculloch in England, and M. Le Play in France, who defended the institution which Adam Smith so roughly assailed. But both these writers advocate the maintenance or re-establishment of entails and their analogues, for reasons which I dare venture on asserting would never have suggested themselves to any one who gathered his inferences from the actual working of that which he has defended. Economists have, fortunately, seldom been misled into fallacies of sympathy, those *idola theatri* which are so little creditable to the capacity of their victim.

The speech which Mr. Cobden made at Rochdale about a year and a half before his death, in which he spoke of 'the peasantry being divorced from the soil,' in a manner to which no other country afforded a parallel; and in which he went on to say that the consideration which is shown to any class in the community at the hands of the legislature depends very much on the admission of such a class to political power, was the occasion, as many of my readers will remember, of a sharp quarrel between the speaker and Mr. Delane, the reputed Editor of the *Times*.

* Adam Smith's 'Wealth of Nations,' Book III. chap. ii.

Mr. Cobden, in alluding to the condition of the English peasantry, and to a fact in practical politics— now unhappily too notorious to be denied—did not show how the grant of the franchise could possibly better the condition of the peasantry. But he did disclaim any revolutionary proceeding or agrarian outrage, and therefore, irrespectively of his known antecedents, should in common fairness have been presumed to point to remedies which were strictly economical. The only explanation which I can give for the criticism with which the harmless speech of Cobden was treated, is the fact that Vicksburg had fallen and Gettysburg had been fought in the previous summer, that Cobden and his friend were powerful advocates of the Northern side during the American war, and that the classes for whom the *Times* is written were very much dissatisfied with the posture of affairs in the United States, and the prospects of those States with which they sympathised. I infer so much from parts of the article in which the speech is attacked.

Two days after the speech was delivered, a leading article appeared in the *Times*, in which the writer, after calling the two speakers 'the Timons of the political stage,' quotes the passage which I have given at the head of this chapter, and continues, ' What Messrs. Cobden and Bright should show is, not that it is difficult for the poor man to obtain land, but that the law places any obstacle in the way of his obtaining wealth.' Afterwards he states, 'If England were a land of peasant proprietors, the increase of capital employed in agriculture would, from the ruder husbandry that would be employed, and the smaller quantity of stock that would be kept, be less rapid than at present, and consequently the fund to which the poor look for subsistence would be smaller, and the share of the working man less.' 'This language, so often repeated and so calculated to create discontent among the poor and ill-informed, has really one intelligible meaning. "Reduce the electoral franchise, and when you have done so, you will obtain an Assembly which will seize on the estates of the proprietors of land, and divide them gratuitously among the poor." If this be not the true interpretation of these appeals to legislation, Messrs. Cobden and Bright should lose no time in disavowing it, and in pointing out some means of dividing land among the poor by law, other than by the confiscation of the property of its proprietors. If they do mean this, they have not done much towards forwarding the success of the cause of which they are the advocates. It may be right to reduce the franchise, but certainly not as a step to spoliation.'

On the next day another article contained the following: 'What can be the object of this "ugly" allusion to the absorption of small freeholds in connexion with the political weakness of the working classes, and their alleged misgovernment? Is it not in effect to tell the labourer and working man to look over the fences of the neighbouring proprietor, and learn to think that they have a natural right to a share of the soil? Is it not to tell them that they have no voice in the government of this country, which is monopolised for selfish uses by a select landed aristocracy? This is the topic of an incendiary.' The writer then argues as to what would be the effect of 'giving' ten acres, or twenty or even fifty, to a man of this class, comments on the indebtedness of the French peasantry, and says that the interest which they pay on their mortgages is known to exceed that of our national debt. The writer also observes, in a further article: 'He can have only one object, and that is to throw one more bone of contention between the working classes and the landed aristocracy. If that be his game, there is an end of his pretensions as a legislative reformer.—Let him try his hand at a measure which shall aim to multiply genuine agricultural freeholders, and so create a substantial peasant class, without assailing the very basis of property, and placing the conveyance and transmission of land out of the pale of Free Trade.'

It is superfluous to say that insinuations such as those which are contained in the passages extracted from the newspaper were not only misleading and unfair, but were a charge of sentiments which were utterly alien to the man to whom they were assigned. Men who have accepted a single principle of commercial intercourse, and have carried it out, as some may allege, to the verge of pedantry, do not in a hasty moment abandon, or hint at an abandonment of that which is the cardinal fact in their political creed. The criticism of the paper, in so far as it commented on the absence of any scheme in the speech by which the desired object was to be realised, was within the bounds of legitimate comment; not so, however, when it ascribed to the speaker the most odious, violent, unjust, and revolutionary motives. It is of course a common trick with newspaper critics to assert that a speaker's words have a tendency which was never before him or his audience. I suppose there is no person who has come before the public in the character of an advocate of such a change as is distasteful to certain parties, who is not accused of purposes which he never contemplated, and of intentions which nothing but a malignant ingenuity can infer from his statements. At the very least, it is obvious to charge the speaker with setting class against class, as though it were possible to advocate a reform without provoking irritation. Revolutions are not made in rose-water, we are told; and what applies to the greater is true of the less. No one ever witnessed any person being made the object of a reform, however necessary the reform was to the public, and even salutary to its immediate object, without hearing strong expressions of dissatisfaction and dislike from the patient.

Cobden quarrelled with Mr. Delane, as representing the *Times*, and high words passed between them. It is perhaps a mistake in management, that the Editor of this paper has been allowed to abandon his impersonality. But Cobden, I think, was unwise in his indignation, as he was unwise in not keeping himself informed of what his critics in that paper said of him. Not every public man can attain to Mr. Disraeli's perfect cynicism, and avow 'that he thinks no time is lost so much as that which is lost in making explanations;' but he must not be so sensitive that he will not read what is said about him, or if he does read it, be too indignant at newspaper misrepresentation. No rational man believes that the London Press guides or developes public opinion. Its business is to express in convenient words a public opinion which has already been formed. Most Englishmen, particularly in the South of England, have already collected their sentiments on such public questions as interest them, and select the paper which gives the best exegesis of those sentiments, with the best reasonings by which they may be supported. The London newspaper acts very much the same part in political matters, which was performed by those rhetoricians of Athens who composed speeches for those who could not make the speeches themselves, and the newspapers do the work very cleverly. That paper is the best managed for this end which catches and exhibits, with the greatest possible appearance of originality and clearness, what happens to be the prevailing sentiment of the widest circle of men. It is therefore bound to attack all innovators, and the innovators ought to be very glad that they are attacked, particularly whenever common prudence induces the critic of the leader to admit any disclaimer of a misrepresented fact.

The partisan Press performs a very useful function. I know no other process by which it is possible to measure the forces which are opposed to any recommended change; still less can I understand how to anticipate the arguments by which the change itself is deprecated. The vastness of modern society renders it not only impossible to reach the minds of many, but even to find out whether they have any mind at all on the subject. The Press does this work for the public man, and does it very effectually. It not only informs him of sentiments, but of tastes, or it may be of

sensations. It is the largest shop-window conceivable.
It does not make the fashion, but it meets the fashion.
It does not guide the stream, it simply receives and
exhibits it. To ignore it, is to cut oneself out of a
very important element in practical wisdom—the knowledge
of facts, and their prevalence. Unluckily, the
chief organs of the London Press, under the present
distribution of political power, represent a very narrow
class of society. But there is a growing temptation
with public men of a certain type to use the sprightly
libels which the current Press utters against the mass of
the people, as a means towards raising popular hatred
against those for whose pleasure the Aristophanic
cavils of these 'gentlemanly papers' are composed.
It is an evil omen, when one side mocks and the
other gets angry. But perhaps before the crisis comes,
the managers who now put pepper on the future
masters of the English commonwealth, will slowly
but irreversibly begin to butter them. It will not
diminish the circulation of their paper if they change
their tactics. There is no gratitude in politics, and very
little malice, where men are free, and government sits
loosely on the public life.

At the present time, no paper, except one of the
meanest reputation, which writes for the coarsest and
most stupid natures, would venture on an article like
that which appeared in the *Times* less than ten years
ago, on the Rochdale speeches of Cobden and Bright.
It is not the fashion now for the public prints to
charge men of established reputation and high principle
with advocating socialistic principles, with aiming
at a violent revolution of existing usages, and with

sinister purposes against the proprietors of landed estates. The reformer of the Land Laws in the present year is as unlikely to be treated to the criticism which I have quoted above, as he would be to be visited by the invective of Swift, or that of the *Times* of 1841, when, as I have already stated, the present Lord Grey was compared to a 'dying rattlesnake,' with the accompaniments of a 'venomous tongue' and a 'futile malignity.' Nor, I may add, would a rival newspaper comment on the interpretation which the *Times* put on Cobden's speech, as the *Globe* of December 9, 1863 did, as 'a trifling misstatement.' The principles of competition are better understood in our time.

The advocate then of that free trade in land, which is likely to supply the public with increased produce from the soil, and who, accepting present facts and present rights, is agitating or advocating a change in the English Land Laws, need not, I suppose, fear that he will be challenged with purposes of confiscation, and with being an incendiary. He has to deal with different dangers. The true demagogue is not the man who, being ill-informed himself, strives to stimulate a worse informed audience to violent and total change, but the foolish partisan of existing customs, who furiously defends an untenable position. I have never heard or read any avowal more unstatesmanlike and more destructive, than that which declares that a political change is never urgently required before it is demanded by a numerical majority. The condition of modern representative institutions is, that the majority must rule, and the minority must persuade. But unless a statesman is to become a mere clerk who registers with more or less precision the votes of the public on some exciting topic, the business of a Government is to anticipate what is wise and just, before a concession is extorted from irritated and helpless partisans.

The real difficulty in the way of a revision of the English Land Laws lies in the projects of those who desire to make the State the owner of the whole soil. There is no economical problem in which abstract reasoning and practical wisdom are so completely at variance. There cannot be a doubt that no community will ever grant any possessor of the soil an inalienable right to the possession of his land, and an absolute discretion as to the uses which he can put it to. The public good respects property in land, but never permits itself to be the servant of the landowner. The State enforces involuntary alienation every day, and does so with increasing stringency as population increases and a public want is felt. The dearest private sentiment must yield to considerations of public defence, and even of public utility. The proudest peer would be compelled to give up the tombs of his ancestors, or anything else he cares for more, to military exigencies. It appears that even the lion on Northumberland House must yield to the claims of Westminster traffic. Bishop Hatto would in our days, were famine or even scarcity oppressing the people, be forced to open his granaries. Much more the cultivable area of the British islands, the game preserves, the deer forests, the battue shooting, are limited or extended, *durante bene placito*, the judge of this discretion being the public opinion of the future.

Fortunately, we are not now able to say, as the *Times* said in 1863, that large farming tends to produce more stock. We have learnt, that as far as the food of the people is concerned, we are the worst off among European countries. We have reason to believe that the more land is distributed the more produce is obtained, and that if the peasant were not 'divorced from the soil,' we should have a greater abundance of the conveniences and necessaries of life. To bring about the change which shall give plenty instead of scarceness, no reasonable man, least of all no intelligent economist, would advocate anything more than that Free Trade in Land which Cobden wished he had strength and youth to carry out, and which consists in removing all obstructions to the sale of land, and all aids to its accumulation, in order to give a fair trial to the respective powers of large farming under a precarious tenure or a lease, and small farming on a freehold or on a perpetual occupancy.

CHAPTER IV.

INTERNATIONAL RELATIONS. WAR AND PEACE.

COBDEN was a member of the Peace Society. He held the labours of his friend Mr. Richard, now Member of Parliament for Merthyr Tydvil, in the highest estimation. In public and private he denounced war as a barbarous and irrational expedient for removing a difficulty. He saw that it demoralised those who adopted it. He endorsed Bentham's definition of it, that it was 'mischief on the largest scale.' He saw that when the war fit is on a nation, there is no place left for reason and argument; that it was simple waste, unmixed evil. He believed that no war in the world's history was necessary, and therefore that none was capable of defence. At the commencement of the great American war he was disposed to think that the North would have done better if it had let the remonstrant South go. It was only when he rightly understood that the war on the side of the North was virtually defensive, that he embraced the Northern side warmly. The object of the Southern politicians was to extend and perpetuate slavery, and such an object must always involve violent and ceaseless aggression.

Of modern European wars he entertained one uniform opinion, that they were absolutely indefensible. He believed, and urged with great force, that the motive which urged the Government of Pitt into declaring war against France in 1793, was not because the safety of this country was imperilled, or because the nation was morally bound to interfere in the quarrel, but because Pitt was alarmed at the expressions of sympathy with the progress of republican liberty in France. His pamphlet, '1793 and 1853,' demonstrates in the most exact manner how spontaneous was the action of the British Government of the day, and how little war was forced on the nation from without. He held a similar opinion about the Russian war. It is difficult to account for that remarkable piece of Quixotry on the part of this nation, as that 'just but unnecessary war' was, to use Mr. Disraeli's description of it. This war undertook the defence of the most detestable and immoral Government on the face of the earth, a Government of eunuchs and extortioners. It sought to perpetuate the rule of a dynasty and a race which has inflicted beggary and barrenness on what were once the most populous and prosperous regions of the earth; for the Turk has never lost the vices of the savage, while he has faithfully copied all the vices of civilised nations. It attacked a nation which had always stood on friendly terms with us, whose rulers had never, except for a very short interval during a crazy czar's reign, entertained any but the kindliest feelings to the English nation and Government. It inflicted a needless insult on another race, which is certainly, at some time or the other, destined to drive its tyrants

out of Europe, and regain its own liberty. The Greek
has suffered ages of oppression, is fettered by an in-
elastic and superstitious religion, is demoralised by the
foolish attempt to plant a European monarchy in the
midst of a people which ought to have been encouraged
in the construction of a federal republic. It may be
true that the Greek of to-day is in no practical sense
the descendant of the Greek whose genius was so mar-
vellously keen twenty-three centuries ago. But the
modern Greek believes that he is the descendant of
that ancient culture, just as we Englishmen, the col-
luvies of a thousand races, believe that we are descended
from the Saxons of Hengist and the Normans of William
the Bastard.

The war with Russia, ostensibly undertaken to save
Turkey, the Balance of Power, and the like, was
carried on by an attack on two sets of fortifications,
those of Cronstadt and Sebastopol. The former defied
assault, the latter, after a prodigious waste of life
and money, was taken. The death of Nicholas, the
collapse of the Russian finances, and the fall of the
Black Sea fortresses, led at last to peace. Fortunately,
the issue of this war did not add an inch of soil to
the British dominions. Nay, it led indirectly to the
cession of the Ionian Islands. It did not even permanently preserve the conditions on which peace was
declared between England and Russia, for the Russian
Government three years ago repudiated the terms of
the treaty. But it gave fanaticism to Russia, it made
Lord Palmerston Prime Minister of England, and
rivetted the vulgar despotism of Louis Napoleon on
the French nation. The French Empire was the

El-Dorado of scoundrelism, and has been the ruin and disgrace of the French people. Even now, the passionate eagerness of the Monarchical factions at Versailles is nothing but the howl of hungry adventurers, who are longing for the greasy offal with which French monarchs have rewarded their supporters, and Napoleon the Third most of all.

But if Cobden held heroic war in righteous horror, he was even more indignant at the mean aggressions which have too often dishonoured the policy of this country, especially in the East. His pamphlet on the way in which wars are got up in India, his denunciation of the attack on China after the affair of the Lorcha, in 1857, and his comments on the manner in which the Japanese were instructed in the courtesies of European civilisation, and the justice of the British Executive at the bombardment of Kagosima, were cases in point. Under the auspices of Lord Palmerston, this country was presented alternately as the compliant and deferential ally of strong States, the hasty and unscrupulous bully of small or weak ones. It was infinitely more creditable to Cobden that he lost his seat at the General Election in 1857, than to Lord Palmerston that he was able to secure public support for the affair of the Lorcha.

Nor, again, did Cobden fail in the expression of strong sympathy with struggling and oppressed nationalities. He spoke of the intervention of Russia in Hungary, when the liberties of the nation were crushed by brute force and treason, in terms of the warmest indignation; commenting also on the perfect shamelessness with which the leaders of the Stock Exchange supply funds for the most nefarious and shameful objects. But he would not, had it been possible or easy, have counselled the British public to adopt a counter intervention. He would not have done so, partly because he was well aware that very shortly after such a struggle commences, the real interests of the parties on behalf of whom intervention and counter-intervention are entered on, are totally lost sight of; partly because he was convinced that those nations alone can achieve political liberty who are competent to attain it by their own exertions. The independence of Switzerland, a country less populous than Hungary or Poland, has never been seriously threatened but once, during a period of history which has been very protracted. The independence of Poland, whatever may have been the merits of individual Poles, was a standing nuisance to Europe, an anarchy of turbulent nobles and oppressed serfs. Events have shown that Cobden was right. Hungary has achieved independence for herself, by her own exertions and patience, by that statesmanship which watches for and uses opportunities.

The theory of the balance of power was originated by the struggles which accompanied the Reformation, and was finally developed by the Thirty Years' War. Every student of history knows how France seized the opportunity of interfering in the great German War, and how she obtained, as the price of her alliance with Sweden, certain territories which she retained up to 1871. The peace of Westphalia was intended to settle the boundaries of kingdoms and creeds, and if possible to save Europe from a repetition of those sufferings which great part of it endured up to 1648.

Thenceforward the diplomacy of all European statesmen was directed towards maintaining the existing state of things. Hence Innocent XI and Alexander VIII were the secret allies of William III and the English Revolution. It is only lately that the Papacy has declared itself the fanatical enemy of all generous principles of government.

The kingdoms of modern Europe have been created by royal marriages or by foreign conquests, and sometimes by both. Louis XIV of France attempted to extend his dominions by both processes. The House of Austria has been most fortunate by adopting the former method, that of Brandenburg by the latter. The nations of Europe have been made the playthings and the victims of monarchical ambition, till one is amazed that they did not turn on their tormentors, and make short work with them. They did at last in France, and humanity would have made enormous progress had not the insolence of the Duke of Brunswick and the alarm of Pitt driven the French people into a frenzy of terror and slaughter, and ultimately turned them from defence to aggression, till it made them the scourge of Europe. Thenceforward they have been slaves at home and makebates abroad, till at last, it is to be hoped, humiliation has made them free, and taught them to respect the independence of others.

I have observed elsewhere that revolution involves reaction, and that no more striking examples can be given of this maxim than the English reaction of 1660, and that of France after the establishment of the Empire. But it would be an error to imagine that all the fruits of a revolution are lost in the reaction which follows on it. The Restoration of 1660 did not put the Church in the same position which it held before the meeting of the Long Parliament, and the Government of Charles II did not venture on rescinding all the reforms which had been extorted before the Civil War. Similarly solid results were obtained by the French Revolution. The Government of Napoleon was as tyrannical and insolent as that of Louis XIV and his grandson, but Napoleon could not or would not restore the Church, and he dared not restore the aristocracy. He shed the blood of his subjects, but they held the lands which they had wrested from their masters at the great upheaval. The nation was wasted by a military despotism; but though for a time all France was enslaved to its ruler, the slaves were equal to each other before the law. The Revolution totally swept away privilege, and the nation has never endured its restoration. The French aristocracy is a tradition, powerful perhaps in social life, but incapable of any true political force, for its growth or renovation was arrested eighty years ago. An aristocracy which is not perpetually recruited soon withers.

The French Revolution, however, developed another political fact, destined hereafter to induce greater effects than ever it has hitherto done—the principle of nationalities. At the Treaty of Vienna Europe was carved out into a number of monarchies, composed of the most heterogeneous materials, and distributed among the reigning families of the old blood. The ancient claims of the House of Austria, dating from the times of Charles V, were recognised in the cession of the North-east of Italy. The plenipotentiaries at that Treaty settled, without a moment's consideration for popular feeling, or the traditions of an unexplored antiquity, the Republic of Venice on the same power. They confirmed France in the possession of Alsace and Lorraine. They restored the Spanish Bourbons to their throne, the worst race of monarchs which has ever ruled, by means of the worst kind of priests. They restored another branch of this effete family to the throne of Naples, and in it a stock which nearly equalled, for baseness, treachery, and superstition, the Spanish branch. They strengthened Prussia, Austria, and Bavaria, by granting them the dominions of the mediatized princes. They united, sorely against the will of the people, Norway to Sweden. And, finally, they turned a deaf ear to the remonstrances of the Poles. It is true that this arbitrary partition awakened strong feelings of dissatisfaction, against the expression of which the energies of the Holy Alliance were directed. But for fifteen years Europe was in a state of profound repose, the result partly of exhaustion, partly of the vigilance of those monarchs who used their victory over Napoleon to keep their own subjects in bondage.

The first interruption of this calm was the successful revolt of the Belgian provinces, for the achievement of Greek independence caused little or no disturbance in Europe, was indeed encouraged by the great powers. The separation of Belgium from Holland was the severance of two races, which were not only aliens in blood, but in religion. The advocates of the Belgian liberties were greatly assisted by the latter fact. The principle of religious toleration was advocated before

the French Revolution, and affirmed by it. France
assisted Belgium, and England sympathised with her.
Meanwhile the German people, and notably the
Prussian contingent of it, was developing the principle of nationality. German patriotism was encouraged after the disaster of Jena, and during the
dreary period which was brought to an end by the
Russian campaign and the battle of Leipsic; but it was
not encouraged further than as an assistant to the
restoration of the monarchy. Thirty years ago the
advocacy of the principle involved serious risks to the
enthusiast. 'When I was a young man,' said a distinguished German once to me, just after the first victories
of the Franco-German war, 'I was put into prison for
having written a pamphlet in defence of German unity.'
'You only suffered,' said an English friend who was
standing by, 'what every honest German suffered thirty
years ago, or ran the risk of suffering.' As the principle
of German unity took its beginnings in the campaign of
1806, so that of Russia commenced in 1812. But after
the completion of the great Continental war, Russia
seemed likely to be not only nationalist, but aggressive.

The outbreak of 1848 was a unique phenomenon in
politics. It took Governments completely by surprise,
as nearly all great movements among the mass of the
people do, was followed by abject submission on the
part of the Governments at first, and by complete reaction very speedily afterwards. Only one European
dynasty was the victim of it, that of the Orleans
family. But except in England and Russia every
throne was convulsed by the shock. The English
people felt only the quivering of the earthquake,

though the Government was excessively alarmed at the Chartist demonstration of April 10. It is not a little remarkable,—I have the story on Cobden's authority,—that when the news reached London of the downfall of Louis Philippe, and was brought to the House of Commons, Sir Robert Peel crossed over the floor of the House to the late Mr. Joseph Hume, and said, 'This is what would have happened in England if I had not repealed the Corn Laws, but had followed the advice of those people,' pointing with his hand to the back benches of the Conservative party. England was therefore saved from political disturbances by an economical reform, according to Sir Robert Peel. There were however, I think, other causes which shielded her from the storm. These were, the Parliamentary Reform of 1832, the principle that destitution is a legal claim to relief, and the innocuousness of the British monarchy. A proletariat ceases to be dangerous when it is secured by law against starvation. It may become degraded, and its degradation may be the apology for wrong-doing, and for false theories of economical science. English republicanism, too, is only a theory combating with another theory. It cannot become a passion.

The movement of 1848 was partly political, partly socialist. The Governments of Europe were despotic, the condition of labour was grievous. The working classes then demanded a Government in their own interests, and the form which their interests took was that an administration should find them capital, i.e. work and a market. To us, whom experience has freed from the dream of constructing a social republic, who have insisted that Government should sit lightly on us, and who thereupon trust to the harmony of individual interests, nothing is more grotesque than the demand which the leaders of the foreign labour movement make for the active exercise of those powers which a Government is supposed to possess, and which have become familiar to them by their experience of over-government. When the English deputies went to the International Conference at Geneva, they were under the impression that the object of the International Society was the diminution of the hours of labour, and the increase of its wages. They were surprised, and it appears disappointed, to find that such objects were only secondary with the Society, and that the purpose of the association was to employ the powers of Government in the interests of labour.

In Italy the movement of 1848 took more definite aims. In the first place, it was led by men of greater energy and credit than those who were associated with it in other European countries, and it was secretly assisted by the Government of Sardinia. Again, it strove to extinguish the ecclesiastical government of Central Italy. Next it sought to vindicate Italian unity. Lastly, it purposed to take guarantees against the abuse of monarchical authority. But the effort was baffled. The battle of Novara crushed Piedmont, and the French intervention restored the Pope. The time was not ripe for the secularisation of the Roman See. This was partly effected when, against his will, Napoleon was obliged to acquiesce in the campaigns of Garibaldi, partly when an alliance having been secretly but firmly concluded between the Roman See and France in 1870, the loss of Alsace and Lorraine was accompanied by the occupation of Rome. The only other serious outbreak of the epoch of 1848 was the revolt of Hungary. This was crushed by the armed intervention of Nicholas, and there is no doubt that the English nation was inclined to the war of 1854 from the memory of that intervention in 1848. Most of these events were commented on by Cobden in a series of remarkable speeches delivered by him in 1849.

Abortive as this movement was, it gave cohesion to the principle of nationalities, for Governments began to see that they could make use of the sentiment to their advantage. But they did so not without misgivings. The first leader in this new theory of administrative policy was Cavour. In 1847 Cavour was an economist and a Liberal. So timid or so jealous was the Sardinian Government at that time, that when, after the repeal of the Corn Laws, Cavour and certain other free-traders wished to give a banquet to Cobden at Turin, and asked permission of the Government, pledging themselves that the banquet should have no political complexion, and offering to submit the speeches which should be read at the meeting to the censorship of the Ministry, the permission was peremptorily refused. In 1859 Cavour was the Minister of Victor Emanuel, and had contrived to lead Napoleon into quarrelling with Austria. It is true that Napoleon contemplated a very different result from his Austrian campaign. But he had committed himself by the fact of the war to the Italian nation, and events were speedily beyond his power. I have stated above that there is little or no gratitude in politics. Few honest men can have any respect for the memory of Napoleon. But the gratitude of the Italian people followed him to his grave on account of the most, perhaps the only generous action of his public career.

During the time that Cobden was negotiating the Treaty of Commerce with France, considerable suspicions were entertained, or industriously fomented, against the ulterior motives of the Emperor Napoleon. He was charged with meditating the invasion of this kingdom, and the country experienced one of those discreditable political panics which were powerfully assisted by a part of the London Press. It was against these misconceptions and cowardly fears, stimulated, it is impossible to doubt, for professional purposes, that Cobden wrote his last pamphlet, under the title of 'The Three Panics.' But the language of the London Press, and even of persons in the House of Commons, was so irritating, that, as I was informed by Cobden, he had serious thoughts of throwing up the negotiations in which he was engaged, and of returning to England. Even those who had been associated with him by the Emperor were disconcerted at what was said and written at the time, and asked him whether he could seriously carry on the business. On this occasion he told me that he had an interview with the Emperor's cousin, the Prince Napoleon, who said that he could not imagine why European Governments permitted their newspapers to make such continual attacks on the Emperor, especially as he would certainly, if he were in danger, make use of an instrument which would seriously disturb them, and that this was the nationalities. 'The Emperor,' added the Prince, 'can never forget the party which he was associated with in his youth and in Italy.'

To his ultimate ruin, the French Emperor allowed himself to sacrifice his sympathies with nationalities in favour of dynastic conquest or of dynastic considerations. He wished to keep Italy weak by saving the principalities and by maintaining the temporal power of the Pope, but the claims of Italian unity were too strong for him. He was anxious to induce the Government of this country to intervene in the American Civil War, and to secure the severance of the slave-holding States from the Union. He committed himself to the folly of attempting to establish a Mexican monarchy, and persuaded this country to take a part in an expedition from which it retreated with more prudence than honour. He sacrificed the unhappy Maximilian to a vain attempt at forming a counterpoise to the American Republic. He interfered in the Danish war, and is believed in Denmark to be the principal cause why the Danish part of the Duchies has not been restored to Denmark, in accordance with Article V of the Treaty of Prague. He saw with the liveliest alarms the victories of Prussia in 1866, and the consolidation of Northern Germany. He precipitated a war with United Germany in 1870, on a frivolous pretext, and he suffered a defeat which has had no parallel in the history of the world. He did not understand the force of that to which he appealed in the Italian war, and which he attempted to cope with in Germany.

Two influences alone cause war. These are, the

ambition of princes, and the interests of a privileged
class. The greater part of Europe has been, and is,
afflicted by the former of these motives, England and
the American people have been affected by the latter.
The French nation is credited with a passion for
military glory. In point of fact, there is nothing
which the French nation detests more than the sacrifice
which war entails on it. War has been the passion
of French monarchs and French statesmen from the
days of Francis I to those of Napoleon III. Mr.
Cobden has proved in the clearest manner* that the
French people were eagerly anxious not to incur the
hostility of the English people at the beginning of
the Revolution. It is certain that the last vote of
confidence which a plebiscite gave the late Emperor
was accorded from a belief that the policy of the
French Government would be peace. The same may
be said of other nations. The rigour of military
service is unacceptable to the Germans. Russia finds
it by no means easy to collect her conscripts. There is
not a single European country of which it could not be
confidently said that the people look on war with horror.
The feeling of the speaker in Herodotus is as vivid in
our day as it was in his, when, contrasting the blessings
of peace with the horrors of war, he says that in the
former the children bury their parents, but that in
the latter the parents bury their children.

The dynastic ambition of monarchs is however, as
time goes on, less and less capable of gratification. If
these personages wish to wield the forces which they
can obtain from their subjects for their own interests

* Political Writings, I. 396 sqq.

only, they are constrained to become their own ministers. Now a despotism in our days has the advantage of undivided counsels, and of the prompt obedience of its instrument. But it is under the fatal disadvantage of not being able to discover what is the value of the instrument with which it acts. There was no man who filled the imagination of Western nations more than the Emperor Nicholas did. His attention to business was excessive. He spared no cost to make the army which he drilled incessantly as effective as possible. His soldiers were taught to look on him as more than human, as the incarnate object of their highest religious and secular duties. But his instrument was shattered when it came to the trial. He could not with all his vigilance secure the good faith of those in whom he was obliged to trust. He was the victim of gigantic frauds, practised by persons who professed, and probably felt, the profoundest reverence for their master.

Still more striking was the case of Napoleon. No person anticipated that the great army of this personage would collapse so utterly as it did, that it would be found so ill-supplied, that so many of its regiments would exist only on paper, or that the dependants and employés of the Government would, with rare exceptions, be found to be a mere gang of swindlers. Napoleon no doubt felt and found out that he was betrayed, only when it was too late; but he might have anticipated, had he understood the facts, that such a Government as his was, existed to be betrayed, that his agents and subordinates were adventurers who professed allegiance to him simply because it was the most convenient way of promoting their own interests. Nothing proves the character of the Napoleonic Government more completely than the total collapse of the party in France itself. Misfortune does not destroy genuine loyalty to a monarch, as has been proved a hundred times. Misgovernment does not, as the Jacobite party demonstrated in England a century and a half ago. But the attachment of sycophants ceases instantly with the power of that to which they attach themselves.

Hereafter it will be found, I am persuaded, that no great European army will be a trustworthy instrument of war, unless the Government which employs it takes pains to make itself popular. It is therefore with no little insight into the real causes of political and military strength, that the German Government, immediately on the victories which it won, has set itself to work upon political and social reforms, is dealing with the internal enemies of its unity, as it has crushed external opposition to that consummation. It will not, to be sure, abandon its military system, for this is the price which it pays for monarchical institutions. A European disarmament cannot occur till Europe becomes republican; for it is, I believe, a rule to which no exception occurs, that when perfect political equality is established in any community, and the whole machinery of Government is brought under the control of the popular will and public opinion, war becomes an anachronism and an impossibility. And the reason is that military forces are simply defensive under such institutions, and that when all nations cease to be aggressive the contingency of war is at an end. That a free nation should attempt to bring another nation into subjection, or attack it in order to vindicate its honour, is an absurdity. It is only because those who stimulate wars escape all the consequence of the evil which is inflicted, and reap all the advantages of success, that war can be carried on at all.

But it may be said that we have lately seen a war of the most formidable dimensions carried on in a country which boasts of having established and maintained a republic in which the equality of its citizens was the foundation of the Constitution. The answer is, that the war occurred because the facts did not correspond with the language of the American Constitution. The founders of American independence committed the fatal error of permitting the worst form of a privileged class, one which was allowed to hold mankind in bondage. It was on behalf of this class that the war with Mexico was undertaken. It was to support this class that the secession of 1861 was consummated. It was to destroy this class that the Union accepted war, declared the freedom of the slaves, and brought the war to a successful issue.

Since the Revolution of 1688, the power of the English monarch has almost ceased to be political. For nearly a century and a half the forces of the country were wielded by the aristocracy and the chartered merchants, and it was in the interests of these parties that most of the wars were carried on. This was notoriously the case with the wars of 1739 and 1755, which were entered on for the sake of the chartered merchants. Similarly the motives which induced the governing forces of this country to resist the claims and deny the liberties of the American plantations was the dread which the mercantile classes had of losing the imaginary benefits of the Colonial trade. Alison is a ready witness to the fact that the great Continental war was undertaken in the interests of the privileged classes, and to check the growth of democratic sentiment. *Delirant reges, plectuntur Achivi*, is the summary which Horace gives of ancient warfare. The distinction was sharper still in the wars to which I have referred. The people paid the taxes, and the privileged classes reaped the benefit of honours, pensions, and high prices. We owe the Corn Laws which Cobden succeeded in repealing to the attempt on the part of the great landowners to stereotype the high prices which they had obtained as one of the indirect benefits of the great Continental war.

The privileged classes in England were eager to intervene in the American Civil War. They gave the slaveholders all the benefits and, I may add, all the mischief of their sympathy. If the Administration of the time had been honestly neutral, the Alabama and her companions would never have escaped. Had they been indifferent spectators of the contest, the Colonial ports would never have permitted the shelter of their waters, and the supply of necessaries to those vessels, whom it is a scandalous euphemism to call privateers. But by this time the opinion even of the unenfranchised classes was too unmistakeably expressed in favour of the North and the Union to allow those sympathies to be more than verbal and barren. But the most distinct abandonment of the old policy was found in all abstention from interference in the Danish war. The great powers had guaranteed the Schleswig and Holstein succession, and this country was one of the partners in the guarantee. There was a feeling that a small and gallant state was being pressed by overwhelming odds, and that it was resisting on the faith of those guarantees. The inconceivable folly of the Danish Government in attempting to control the German population of the Duchies, was forgotten in the inequality of the struggle which that Government provoked. Fortunately for a sound principle of international action, the British Government declined to interfere, though they based their abstention on the very questionable position, that as they were only one of the parties to the guarantee and as the other parties declined to interfere, the liability was not merely limited, but that the engagement was annulled. The magnitude of the risk, and the sense of relief experienced when the decision of the Government on this question was made known, are described with characteristic clearness and vigour by Cobden in his last public speech.*

I am far from saying that there are no occasions on which a Government should intervene in the affairs of a foreign State. I do not hold that outrageous violence and wrong-doing should be permitted to one people against another people, any more than I think that within the bounds of any country, private individuals should be allowed to gratify their passions upon others. I can anticipate a time in which there may be an international police. In such a case, and with such an understanding among civilised com-

* Speeches, vol. ii. pp. 341 sqq.

munities, I can conceive a force which should compel a Frederic to think twice before he attempted to occupy a Silesia; or, to go further back, before a Louis should seize an Alsace and a Lorraine; and, I may add, a British Parliament endorse the capture and retention of a Gibraltar. But nothing in the present machinery of government justifies one in anticipating that such a police can be expected of it; and certainly no war which has yet been undertaken is of the beneficent and justifiable character which I have indicated.

In the second pamphlet which Cobden published, that entitled 'Russia,' which he put out in 1836, the following 'maxim,' to use the author's words, occurs: 'As little intercourse as possible betwixt the *Governments*, as much connexion as possible between the *nations* of the world.'* The italics are Cobden's. The rule which is laid down in these words was the guiding principle of the writer's political life, in so far as he occupied his mind with international questions; and the rule is as sagacious as it is universal. I do not indeed forget that events have assisted the public opinion of this country into the acceptance of the rule as a guide of conduct, and have brought about the complete reversal of the policy which governed this country from the days of William III to the conclusion of the great Continental war. Thus, the English Government has constantly carried on its wars with mercenaries. We hired Dutch troops in the days of William, subsidised all kinds of foreigners during the war of the Spanish Succession, crimped Hessians in 1730, hired Red Indians during the Seven Years' War, fought against

* Political Writings, vol. i. p. 283.

our own Colonies with Hessians in the American War of Independence, and employed Spanish and Portuguese troops under Wellington in the Peninsula. Now that the progress of civilisation forbids the hiring of foreign mercenaries — the attempted enlistment of troops in the United States during the Russian war, which almost led to serious consequences, and the collection of a Polish legion during the same epoch, were the last instances of the old practice — and since the development of military science has armed nearly whole populations, though at vast cost to their respective countries, we could not, if we would, intervene to any effect in European quarrels. We have an army, which may be effectual for defence, but which is prodigiously costly, and would be wholly incompetent for aggression.

But it is one thing to find that the course of events has reversed a practice which was formerly believed to be of the highest wisdom, and which is viewed by many with the fondest regrets, another thing to have persistently maintained, and convincingly proved, that what seemed to be wisdom was consummate folly. We and other nations are burdened by enormous debts, for which we have to make sacrifices which habit only renders bearable, for objects which never have been and never could be realised. The burden of the Continental war, as Mr. Porter proved exhaustively, fell upon those who were not represented, and were not consulted. The profit and glory of it were the share of the governing classes. The nations were unable to control their Governments, and were therefore made the puppets of a policy which every intelligent person condemns. It may hereafter be the case that diplomacy will do something to justify its operations, but hitherto, with very rare exceptions, it has been the curse and the bane of mankind. It was a just epigram of Bishop Wilberforce, when he spoke of Cobden as an international man. It will be a happy thing for mankind when that race of pseudo-statesmen is extinguished which considers that the security of a country or government consists in the intensity with which an administration can stimulate international feuds.

It was a common practice to charge Cobden with being a 'peace at any price man.' If this phrase has any meaning, it applies particularly to those who are willing to make any expenditure of life and money in order to bring about a temporary peace, but who are also convinced that war is the normal state of civilised man, and that the maxim of an enlightened Government should be *ex bellis bella serere*. The phrase which most nearly represents Cobden's mind is that he was a 'peace at the least possible price man.' He never grudged expenditure for defence. He constantly asserted that this country ought to maintain an army sufficient to deter an enemy from landing on these shores, and a navy so strong that such a landing would be rendered impossible. Acknowledging that the only probable rival to the United Kingdom in this arm of the service was France, he always said* that the British navy ought to be superior to that of France. But he also went so far as to quote the words of Sir Robert Peel: 'In time of peace, we must by our retrenchment incur some risk.' †

* Speeches, ii. 249. † Political Writings, ii. 425.

The impression to which Cobden directed his attention, and on which he bestowed his most effective criticism, was the exaggerated alarm which was excited about the possible designs of France and her ruler. It is possible that Sir Charles Napier and Lord Lyndhurst expressed their genuine sentiments when they did their very best to intensify the panic which was felt in 1860. But if these eminent persons really felt the fears they expressed, the speeches they made did little credit to their knowledge and their intelligence, for not only have they been refuted by facts, but they were wholly baseless at the time. There were doubtlessly Frenchmen in 1860 who were eager to take part in an English invasion, for, to do them justice, military men are generally willing to do some work for the pay and rank which they receive, and on behalf of the service to which they belong; but it is conclusively proved, that whatever may have been the errors which characterised the last ten years of the Second Empire, and perhaps no ruler of whom so much was expected ever made graver errors—the mistake of quarrelling with this country never entered into his thoughts. He is credited with having sincerely and unremittingly adopted the view of the first Emperor, who avowed that the cardinal error in his political career consisted in his not having done his best to disarm the hostility and win the friendship of England.

It is almost superfluous to say that Cobden strongly objected to that erroneous theory of trade—denounced long since by Adam Smith—that it was worth while to conquer dependencies in order that they might be feeders of a restricted or protected trade, and that he looked with peculiar detestation on the policy which, instigated and supported by Lord Palmerston, adopted the practice of conquest, annexation, and humiliation among weak nations in the East. His pamphlet written in 1853, under the title, 'How Wars are got up in India,'* was a searching and powerful exposure of the true causes and motives which led to the Burmese war of 1851. The speech† which he made in February 1857, on the China war of Sir John Bowring and Lord Palmerston, led to a dissolution, unfortunate in its effects on himself, and immediately discreditable to the country, for Lord Palmerston was adroit enough to throw dust in the eyes of the electors. But I suppose that at the present day the true nature of the transaction is known, and that, at any rate, there is little risk that a similar course of policy would be adopted by a British minister in our time. He spoke in fitting terms of the bombardment of Kagosima,‡ in 1863, when the defenceless inhabitants of a Japanese town were bombarded, in order to humiliate the pride of a potentate who suffered, if he did suffer, only vicariously.

I remember an answer of the late Mr. Senior to a Frenchman who said, that if the English ceased to possess India, their reputation or prestige would vanish, and that they would sink into a second-rate state. On the contrary, answered the economist, the real English difficulty is how to well get rid of India. To some vulgar imaginations, and to those cooler judgments which see how vulgar imaginations can be utilised, the possession of a vast and scattered

* Political Writings, ii. 25.   † Speeches, ii. 121.   ‡ Ibid. 111.

empire is a glory and a strength. To more intelligent and honest minds, the strength of a community lies in two facts, the concentration of its resources and the distribution of its wealth. No country is strong which scatters its power, none prosperous which accumulates its wealth in few hands. They who take cognisance of real facts are not misled by imposing phrases, any more than sensible purchasers are by puffing advertisements and glaring shop-windows. The illustrations which history supplies of a refutation to the illusion of a great geographical empire are numerous and overwhelming. The imagination of antiquity was filled by the picture of the great King of Persia. The power of this personage was justly exploded, first by the defeat of one invasion at the hands of two cities, one not so populous as Birmingham, the other half the size of Bedford; next by the ruin of an invasion as large as that of Attila or Tamerlane, which was met by the inhabitants of a district not much bigger than Yorkshire, and not a third as populous; and lastly, by the unopposed march of ten thousand infantry through the heart of the great king's dominions. No state seemed to be in so precarious a position as that of Venice, which had to hold its own against the feudal nobility of Germany and Italy, and which was in its best days nothing but a seaport, with a few miles of suburb in its hands. But there is nothing more surprising, to those who do not estimate the real meaning of power, than the struggle of the Dutch republic in the latter part of the sixteenth century against the overwhelming resources of Spain, at that time the greatest military power in Europe, and the possessor of a transatlantic empire which far exceeded in magnitude and apparent energy anything which has ever seemed to threaten universal empire.

The empire of the English in India can never quit itself of the faults of its origin. Much may be said—taking into account the delusions of the age in which that empire was founded—of the necessity which brought it about; much more of the manner in which the British Parliament checked the rapacity and unscrupulousness of the trading company which gained that empire. It should be added too, that one of the most marked illustrations of the process by which rules of policy have been traditional with a party is to be found in the conscientiousness and generosity with which the Conservative party have approached and handled Indian affairs, and have striven to use the best forces of the British constitution in favour of the native races. In this particular they have been markedly contrasted with their Whig rivals, whose relations to Indian affairs have been far less satisfactory. But the cause of this difference will be obvious to the student of the history of political forces. It is sufficient to say here that British rule in India has necessitated enormous sacrifices from the English nation, that it cannot for physiological reasons be permanent, that its best policy lies in gradually bringing the people of the country face to face with the duty of self-government, that its imperative duty lies in limiting the sphere of its operations, and that its only justification lies in the present exigencies of the situation. In these particulars the policy which Mr. Bright has sketched out, as fundamental to the future government of India, is necessary and inevitable, and is thoroughly in accordance with Cobden's ideas.

The question which Cobden raised in 1857, though he failed for a time, has borne fruit. I grant that the miserable insurrection of the native army, stimulated it may be by fanatical alarms, fomented as it certainly was by the dispossessed and disappointed native princes, has left lasting mischief, and renders a just and true estimate of public duty towards inferior races difficult. It was due to the generous and fearless mind of Lord Canning that the evil resulting from that event was not more serious and more lasting. But I cannot doubt that the public conscience of England in relation to inferior races is keener than it was when Lord Palmerston assumed the exposition of the public mind. I believe that no English statesman in this day would endorse the policy of a Dalhousie, or condone a Sir John Bowring, or commend the gallantry of an Admiral Kuper, or acquit a Governor Eyre. The policy of annexation has passed away, and Englishmen are found who can argue, without fear that they will be charged with a design of dismembering the empire, that we probably possess much which is useless to us, and that if we parted with much which we now hold, that we should be safer and even better off. We have ceased in great measure to be the victims of those recurrent military panics which were the scandal of a past political generation. It is probably the case that we owe this liberation from unmanly fears to the fact that the basis of the constitution has been broadened by the extension of the franchise. We are gradually weaning ourselves from the impression that the retention of a number of trophies, the symbols of past victories, and the cause of inveterate irritation, can ever be wise, unless it be proved to be necessary. We trample on the weakness of Spain by the retention of Gibraltar, knowing that a strong and spirited nation would no more endure such a standing affront than we should the occupation of Dover or Portsmouth by a foreign power. Do we wonder that after enormous sacrifices for the independence of Spain we win no regard from a country whose self-respect we have mortified for more than a century and a half? 'If,' Cobden used to say, 'the Government would let me go to Spain with an offer to cede Gibraltar, on condition that its fortifications were razed or dismantled, I could get from the Spanish Government such a commercial treaty as would be of enormous advantage to the English manufacturers and labourers, and would be an infinite boon to Spain. It would not be much to give away, for Gibraltar is of no value whatever as a check to the entrance into the Mediterranean.'

To Cobden's mind war was a barbarism, a stupid means of doing that which would be much better effected by a rational diplomacy and arbitration. There was a time when societies of men were managed on the principle that the strong should rule, and the weak should submit. It is true that even this practice, wherever society had emerged from sheer savagery, was accompanied by certain rules. If the strong preyed on the weak, they did so under set forms, and they did not permit the process to be carried on, except at their discretion, and by the instruments which they selected. It is not two centuries ago, since a very large number of Englishmen imagined that the essence of government

lay in setting the king above the law, and in inculcating
passive obedience on the subject. Their motto was
a rege lex. The Revolution reversed this position, and
taught for the future *a lege rex* with infinite advantage
to the English people, and with no little security to the
Crown. It is not fifty years ago when it was imagined
that single combat was the only security of the individual's honour, and that if the duel were at some
unlucky moment to be abandoned the world would lose
its best guarantee for good manners. At the present
day a challenge would be an absurdity. But I have to
learn that our generation is any way inferior in good
breeding and true courtesy to the bullies and fire-eaters
of the Georgian epoch.

The same rule will be found to hold good in war.
The time is not far distant when it will become as
ludicrous an anachronism as the divine right of kings,
the passive obedience of the subject, and the practice of
single combat are now. I do not say that we shall
never witness again a war of aggression or revenge. The
issue of the last great Continental war has made the
latter a probable motive, and the former a possible one.
We are informed that the re-occupation of the Rhenish
provinces of France was demanded on military grounds,
and military grounds are appreciated by one side as
much as by another. The exaltation of Prussia by the
war of 1866 was the result of a war of usurpation, and
evil precedents beget mischievous imitations. This only
however is clear. Much of the power which can stimulate or bring about these wars is passing away with the
curtailment of those royal prerogatives and dynastic
forces which have hitherto broken the peace of Europe.

Nothing indicates the progress of political opinion during the last ten years, more clearly than the acceptance of the principle of arbitration in connexion with the privateers of the late American war, and the settlement of the San Juan Boundary question. Arbitrations on minor grievances have not been unknown. Such an award was made in 1863, in a dispute between the British Government and Brazil. But the case of the Alabama and her comrades was one of considerable magnitude, and may fairly be taken as a precedent for the future of the most important kind. I do not venture on asserting that a similar arbitration could have obviated the war of 1870, for the French Emperor, the origin of whose reign was an act of outrageous violence, and the continuance of whose power was simply due to a systematic repression of public opinion, might have felt it unsafe to trust his cause to an international court of judicature, not because he could have alleged partiality in the court, but because a reaction against personal government is sure to follow any ill success which may attend its exercise.

If it be asked, as it confidently is asked, what is to make the decisions of such a court respected in the first place, and binding in the next, and, subsequently, what is to make an application to such a court compulsory in all cases of international difference, the answer is, the growth and the control of public opinion. Fifty years ago it was a common thing for states to repudiate their debts, to ignore the claims of the foreign as well as the rights of the home creditor. It is not too much to say that, in these days, no Government which can pay its obligations ever hesitates about the propriety of doing so, and none which does not, ever gives any other apology than its inability. There is no compulsion whatever upon the defaulting parties, nothing in short but the wrath of the Stock Exchange. We should never dream at present of attempting to collect Jecker Bonds and Spanish Passives by force of arms, partly because we hold that lenders act on their own responsibility, partly because the dread of a Stock Exchange excommunication is a powerful check to the most arbitrary monarch or the most shameless State Parliament. But is it reasonable to doubt that a process which is effective with debts will not be equally operative to preserve the lives and fortunes of the people against the waste and the ruin of war? or when the real effect of the ambition or resentments of princes and ministers is discovered and understood by nations, that they will not find a sufficiently powerful process for preventing the licence and wantonness of which they are the victims?

When the advantage of any particular mode of procedure is thoroughly appreciated, when it is found to confer enormous good and to obviate enormous evil, there is no fear that lack of familiarity with the mode in question will very long hinder its adoption. Professional instincts may be against it, but the habits of a profession may soon be changed by a reform. Hereditary power may suspect and dislike it, but hereditary power is now seldom able to withstand a change which is confessedly good. In order to make their subjects good soldiers, princes have been obliged to educate them. But education implies reflection, and reflection discovers the merits of two courses of action when they are fairly put before a people, and it is found possible to contrast the merits of both. Now that men should habitually acquiesce in that means of settling a quarrel which involves the enforced submission of one party to the dispute by slaying, burning, and robbing him, when it is found possible to determine an arbitration on the subject by reference to an impartial and competent tribunal, is to argue that men are not and never will be able to know what is good for themselves or what is bad, and knowing, will not choose the former and reject the latter. And furthermore, there is no doubt of the constraint which the general voice of civilised nations will put on those who are recalcitrant and restive under this easy discipline, or of the judgment they will form, and hereafter the chastisement they will inflict on those who obstinately persist in the old barbarism. The wanton attack on Germany in 1870 deprived France of the sympathy of all Europe, and compelled her to bear the fullest degradation which a victorious army could put on her. Now it is improbable that for a long time nations will forego military pursuits and abandon the study of military science; but it is also quite possible that under altered international relations they will use these powers and this science in order to keep the peace, and to constrain obstinate and dogged disputants to submit their differences to a tribunal rather than to the arbitrament of the sword.

There is however one part of these international relations on which I may confidently assert that Cobden's unwearied exertions have already borne fruit. I allude to the progress which has been made in the recognition of the rule that private property should be exempt from capture by armed Government ships in time of war. The United States, France and Russia concurred in recommending that this should be a rule in international law. The British Government declined to accede to the proposal, for certain ludicrous reasons, which Cobden in a letter to Mr. Henry Ashworth* attacks and demolishes. A still more important suggestion was made at the Paris Congress, that the American Government would acquiesce in the abolition of privateering by that Congress if private property was exempted from capture. The American statesmen went further. They were willing to abandon all blockades of commercial ports, and confine them to naval arsenals, and towns invested by land. Lord Russell declined to accede to this, for the mysterious reason that a system of commercial blockades was essential to our naval supremacy. Lord Russell did not seem to see that while his theory of commercial blockades being essential to our naval supremacy was a generality which has no apparent meaning whatever, the practice of commercial blockades might be fatal to our national existence. Lord Russell's ill-judged answer closed the cotton ports of the Southern States to us during the American war. The blockade of the corn ports of Southern Russia was suspended during the early part of the Crimean war, and thus afforded a refutation of the most practical kind to Lord Russell's statement. But the fact is, the causes which led our statesmen to decline the overtures of Mr. Cass in 1859, and which were avowed in 1861, were ignorance and prejudice. The mercantile classes knew

* Political Writings, vol. ii. p. 5.

better than the Government, and have constantly overridden such theories as the above-named.

Cobden, in his letter to Mr. Ashworth, proposed three great reforms in international maritime law.

'1. The exemption of private property from capture at sea during war by armed vessels of every kind.

'2. Blockades to be restricted to naval arsenals, and to towns besieged at the same time by land, with the exception of articles contraband of war.

'3. The merchant ships of neutrals on the high seas to be inviolable to the visitation of alien Government vessels in time of war as in time of peace.'

He goes on to say *, 'I will only add that I regard these changes as the necessary corollary of the repeal of the Navigation Laws, the repeal of the Corn Laws, and the abandonment of our Colonial monopoly. We have thrown away the sceptre of force, to confide in the principle of freedom—uncovenanted, unconditional freedom.' This was written on April 10, 1862, at the commencement of that disastrous cotton famine, of which the advocates of the old system embodied in Lord Russell's dictum were the indirect authors.

As the British Government declined to accept the beneficent suggestions of the American Government, America on its side declined to give up, as the parties to the Congress of Paris did, the practice of privateering, with what effects they and we know too well; they in the enormous losses inflicted on their shipping by the Southern privateers, we in the escape of the Alabama and her companions, in the irritation

* Political Writings, vol. ii. p. 30.

caused by these events, and by the disgrace and loss which have come upon us and our administration. We are however, I presume, wiser now, and should acquiesce in the establishment of the rules given above, which were, I understand, formally adopted by the belligerents in the Franco-German war.

It is, I believe, pretty generally known that after the proposals made by Mr. Cass in 1859, Lord Palmerston was not indisposed to renew negotiations on the subject, and that there was actually some progress made towards fulfilling the suggestions of Cobden and the original propositions of the American Government. It is not said, indeed, that Lord Palmerston was particularly keen on carrying the matter forward. But, in the meantime, the situation in America changed. Long before the election of November 1860, it became apparent that the Union was drifting into civil war, or at least that the South would seek to vindicate their meditated secession by force of arms. Mr. Buchanan's administration was composed of the most energetic Southern partisans, and, as is well known, the President was not slow to assist the party whom he served, by doing his best to leave the North defenceless at the time of his quitting office. To the South, blockade-running and privateering were the most important means of defence and aggression. It was believed that foreign nations, depending on them for a cotton supply, would effect the former, and that the South could inflict the greatest possible harm on the North by resorting to the latter expedient. Hence it is currently reported that Mr. Dallas was instructed to let the matter drop, with what effects we know too well. It is to be hoped, however, that much time will not elapse before our Government, in concert with all other civilised communities, will be at the pains to effect a formal settlement of the rules which have been suggested by Cobden, and thus render the position of neutrals, which has lately been stated to be dangerous and difficult, as safe as can be under an international and universal guarantee.

CHAPTER V.

MILITARY AND NAVAL EXPENDITURE.

From the year 1815 to the Crimean war, this country had been engaged in no military operations of importance. Except in chastising the Algerine pirates, and in assisting the independence of Greece, England abstained from foreign intervention. She guaranteed the independence of Belgium, the Luxembourg succession, and that of the Danish duchies. She gave some aid to Greek independence, but interposed to check the further progress of Mohemet Ali's attack on the Sultan. To all appearance it seemed likely that the place which this country had taken in foreign politics had been tacitly abandoned.

From very early times the armies of English monarchs have been well-drilled bodies of mercenaries—the most effective part of the service having been the infantry. The origin of the system, by which the English army has been always distinguished from the militias of the Continent, is as remote as the reign of the first Plantagenet sovereign. Hence the military monarchs of this country were the greatest captains of their age; and enterprising men, either natives of the country, or foreigners attracted by the reputation of the English king, readily supplied recruits for the small but, comparatively speaking, highly efficient armies which these monarchs trained. Edward I was a person of remarkable ability, both as a general and as a statesman. It was under his eye that Robert Bruce, the rival and conqueror of Edward's son, was trained; and it was by tactics like those of his instructor in the art of war, that Bruce defeated the English militia at Bannockburn. Edward the Third and his son were even more eminent captains, winning victory after victory over great hosts of Frenchmen by a small but well-appointed army. The great-grandsons of Edward, Henry V and John Duke of Bedford, were equally conspicuous generals, and like the two Edwards, ceased to be victorious only when their resources were exhausted. After a time these disciplined armies were used for those feuds which led to the great civil wars of the fifteenth century. Henry VII took care, on his accession, to make excesses like those of the dynastic wars of York and Lancaster impossible, by carrying and executing the Statute of Liveries. Thenceforward the active interference of this country in continental affairs ceased. The reputation of past exploits accorded some prestige to Henry VII. The assistance which Elizabeth gave to the Dutch republic was scanty, capricious, and dilatory. The Stuarts scarcely undertook any foreign war. Had Cromwell's life been prolonged, it is possible that he would have taken part in European politics, and there is little doubt, had he done so, that he would have revived the exploits of the Edwards and the great Henry of Monmouth.

The commencement of the modern military history of England dates from the Revolution of 1688. It cannot be said to have been very successful at first. William of Orange was a most unlucky general, whatever may have been his other merits and his general usefulness. It was under Marlborough, probably the greatest military genius that the world has ever produced, and incontestably one of the meanest, most sordid, and treacherous of men, that the English army recovered its ancient military reputation. It has never forfeited that reputation since. Fortunately, its exploits have given very conclusive proof of its adequacy as a means of defence. Unfortunately, its prestige has loaded the country with debt.

The founders of the Revolution, and those who, succeeding to them, maintained its principles, entertained the keenest jealousy towards a standing army. They were determined that, as far as legislation could avail (and a century of arbitrary government had made them exceedingly intelligent in inventing and maintaining constitutional checks), no monarch or minister should make the two forces a means for infringing, or even threatening, public liberty. Since the epoch referred to, the Mutiny Act has been passed annually. It is true that the service is permanent, and that this singular constitutional solemnity may seem no more than a barren protest. But the practice is a continual reminder of the fact, that in this country the sword is the subject of the law, and that the basis of the British Constitution is civil, not military. It also brings under review the whole of the services annually, and though no doubt at the cost of much labour, asserts that the nation, through its representatives, considers the forces as its servants, and not its lords; as an organisation which can have no rights whatever except what have been granted, and no interests which may not be withheld or repudiated.

The jealousy which our forefathers of the Revolution entertained towards a standing army was emphatically and continually expressed. William was forced to dismiss his Dutch guards in answer to this feeling. Nor were these alarms confined to the Lower House of the Legislature. Numerous protests of the House of Lords are on record, in which the annual passage of the Mutiny Act was made the opportunity for expressions of dislike to a standing army, and of remonstrance against even the limited military force which was maintained. For a long time similar protests are to be found, attacking the practice of permitting officers to hold seats in the House of Commons. Towards the conclusion of Walpole's administration constant efforts were made to revive the self-denying ordinance of the Long Parliament. Similarly strong objection was taken to the employment of Hessian and Hanoverian troops.

Meanwhile a singular custom had grown up in the country, amounting to an indirect repeal of the Statute of Liveries, though, to be sure, the old mischiefs of the system of feudal retainers were obviated. Men of fortune were permitted or encouraged to form regiments by voluntary enlistment in the king's name, and in consideration of the trouble and expense which the person incurred who undertook the duty of collecting and clothing the recruits, he was put in command of the

regiment, and allowed to nominate some or all of the
officers under him. This was the origin of purchase in
the army, and explains the local names given to most
regiments of the line. It is said that the uniform of
many, if not all, of those regiments was in fact the
livery of the person who originally collected the
recruits.

It was with armies composed of such regiments,
aided by subsidised foreign troops, that the part which
England took on land in the Continental war was
enacted. Of course the area over which Wellington
carried on his campaigns was for the most part very
local. After the close of the Russian campaign of
Napoleon, when Wellington had driven the French out
of Spain with the assistance of the Portuguese and the
Spaniards, the English general marched into France
and effected a junction with the armies of Prussia and
Russia. Similarly the English army bore the brunt
of Waterloo. But it is easy to see why it was impossible for an English general at the commencement of
the present century to play the part of a Marlborough.
It was impracticable, under any system of voluntary
enlistment, to collect an army which should be numerically strong enough to vie with the continental militias.
What was true in the first fifteen years of the present
century is overwhelmingly manifest at the present time.
If this country adopted the Swiss system of obliging
the whole civil population to practise with arms of
precision, and go through a military drill from time to
time; or the French system, of selecting by lot a certain
per-centage of the population for a prolonged barrack
life; or the German system, by which the whole popula-

tion is made to undergo a short military career, it is obvious that it could not, without a complete subversion of the constitution, constrain such persons to embark for foreign warfare. The physical boundary of the sea would make that impossible which in the case of foreign armies is easy. In other words, the logic of events has reduced the British army to a machine of defence, and has rendered it almost powerless for aggression.

During the conduct of the Civil War in America, among the motives which urged the Northern States to determine on dealing with the Southern Confederacy on no other principle than defeat and submission, and to resolve that they would contest the matter to the last dollar and the last man, none operated more powerfully than the conviction that, if they consented to a separation, they would be obliged to acquiesce in the European system of large armaments. I have already stated that this system is entirely owing to the monarchical forms of government which European communities maintain or endure as the case may be. No republic, in the true sense of the word, ever dreams of a war of conquest, or a policy of aggression and aggrandisement. If France becomes a genuine republic, it will in a short time be absolutely impossible that her people can be stirred to war in order to recover the frontier which was lost in 1871. The peasantry and artisans of that country can have no motive whatever to induce an attempt at regaining the provinces. It cannot possibly be to their advantage to increase the geographical area of the political association known as France. It would be as reasonable as that the British public should voluntarily give their lives and their money in order that certain persons in a certain region may have the satisfaction of calling themselves part of the British people. Monarchs and ministers, particularly as they undergo no personal suffering and loss in the process, may strive, and strive successfully, to rouse that particular form of patriotism which consists in fighting for an idea; but nations which wholly control their own destinies, and which have rendered it impossible that a vigorous foreign policy should be an object of ambition or reputation to their statesmen, or rather to those who constitute their administration, cannot and will not undertake wars of aggression or revenge.

The American people, in dealing with the problem before them, saw that as there was naturally no geographical boundary between the states which had adopted slavery as the basis of their social system, and themselves who had finally resolved on social equality, it would be necessary, if they acquiesced in the severance of the Union, to keep up a large armed force in perpetuity, along an extensive and arbitrary frontier. Such a state of things would have been intolerable. The drain upon the most valuable element of wealth in the Union, labour, would have been prodigious and exhausting. On the other hand, the degradation of free labour, which is the invariable accompaniment of slavery, left a large number of poor whites, even in the thinly-peopled States of the South, for voluntary enlistment. Again, even if a frontier is defined, as European frontiers have been, after the lapse of ages, by geographical peculiarities, by difference of language, of laws, and of political institutions, and thus if one principle or practice markedly antagonistic to the principle or practice of another State is suddenly developed in one of two bordering communities, aggression becomes inevitable.* We can see in Europe how jealous Governments, and indeed peoples, are of a change in the constitution of any among the several states which make up the European family, how steadily politicians, even of a liberal type, dislike and discourage the establishment of any one republic, with what alarm they watch any international association of a political character. Similarly the Americans dislike all monarchical systems in the new world, and will ultimately render them impossible. Much less then would they endure a conterminous Slave State.

I have adverted to the case of the American Civil War at length, because there were persons who taunted Cobden and his political associates with inconsistency in advocating the cause of the North during the Civil War. It was said that they who had maintained peace at any price had suddenly become belligerent, and it was inferred that such a change of sentiment could only arise with sympathy for a particular form of government, which of course, as is done in the fashion of ordinary newspaper criticism, they were supposed to suggest should be transplanted to England. Of course the calumny, though convenient, was ridiculous to all sensible people. No reasonable man strives to get rid by any extraordinary means of the institutions under which he lives, unless they be mischievous, immoral, and intolerable. Even then, as the founders of the English Revolution

* See Speeches, vol. ii, p. 361.

of 1688 did, he strives to neutralise the force of the institution, while he preserves its form. To disturb society by extinguishing political forms is folly and waste; to render such forms powerless for mischief, and if possible powerful for good, is the business of the statesman. It may be the case that some English institutions may simply drop off in the course of time; it is certain that no sensible person will strive to tear them up.

It was, as I well know, with infinite reluctance that Cobden came to the conclusion that it was his duty to lend all his help towards advocating the cause of the North. He hated war with all the hatred which a wise and affectionate nature feels towards a practice which cannot be defended, which is outrageously injurious, and which may be obviated. In those speeches which he made just after the war broke out, he simply deplored the calamity. In private conversation he half wished that the North would let the South go. He foresaw only too clearly the magnitude of the mischief which would fall on the district which he had made his home in his youth, and which was the cradle of his great economical triumphs. When the cotton famine came, he averred that thousands were needed where ill-informed nobles fancied that hundreds would be amply sufficient to meet the crisis. As he forecast all this, the prodigious waste of life, the destruction of wealth, i.e. the means of life, the inevitable and enduring bitternesses which must needs come from so vast, so sanguinary, and so vindictive a war, he shuddered at giving his voice in favour of Lincoln and the policy of the North.

He did however give it. Apart from his detestution of slavery as a social institution, he foresaw that the whole cost of war was a trifle to the cost of an armed peace, the inevitable consequent on the political independence of the South. There were no doubt men who sympathised, as they said, with the Slave-holding States, only because they wished the republic of the West to be ruined by an internecine rivalry. The exclamation that 'the republican bubble had burst' did not imply, as Cobden clearly saw,* that certain parties in England wished well to the South, but that they wished ill to American institutions. To have induced the armies of the Old World on the industry of the New would not perhaps have changed the government of the American people, but it would have discredited their institutions; would not have destroyed the hopes of the nation, but would have retarded and stinted its growth. In the face of facts, then, it was better to endure a temporary evil, however gigantic it might be, than to acquiesce in a permanent, an ineradicable mischief.

There is nothing more remarkable, and, I may add, nothing more instructive in the political history of civilised nations, than the fact that immediately on the submission of the South, the American Government began to disarm on the largest scale. It is well known that the present President of the Union conceived this disarmament to be his first and his most imperative duty, and that his policy has been almost, if not quite carried out, of reducing the regular army of the Union to the numbers which it had before the great war broke out. Next in its significance is

* Speeches, vol. ii. p. 357.

the extraordinary rapidity with which the Union has been clearing itself of its debts, though it has effected this process under the worst system of finance conceivable. The people of America may point with pride to the intelligence with which they have returned to peace, and to the self-devotion with which they have striven to liquidate as rapidly as possible the costs of war.

Cobden repudiated all attempts to obtain the reputation of a sympathy with oppressed nationalities by demonstrations in their favour, or by advocating intervention on their behalf.* History does not, I think, supply us with any instance, with perhaps the exceptions of modern Greece and Italy, in which the armed intervention of foreigners has been any aid to public liberty, though it gives us many examples of the heavy price at which such an intervention is purchased. With rare exceptions, it may be granted, the English people has not attempted to appropriate to itself, through its Governments, any of the conquests which it has made in Europe. It intervened in the time of Elizabeth to assist the Dutch, but it may be doubted whether the Dutch gained much by the assistance of the Queen. It intervened in the time of Charles I to assist the Protestants at Rochelle, but to the condign injury of its clients. It assisted Spain against the ambition of France, and retained Gibraltar as the price of its futile services. And in later days, it freed Spain from Joseph Bonaparte, only to hand it over to the most bigoted and mischievous member

* Speeches, vol. ii. p. 352.

of the Spanish royal house, whose little finger was thicker than the loins of the Corsican.

Intervention in favour of oppressed nationalities and oppressed religions! The assistance of Richelieu to the Protestants of Germany during the Thirty Years' War was the origin of all the calamitous wars which have desolated Europe from that great misery to the calamities of 1870. Napoleon III intervened to save Mexico from itself, to enforce the payment of the Jecker Bonds, and to set up an empire as a rival to the Western republics, and he induced a modern Quixote to enter on an undertaking which sent him to a violent death. Amiable enthusiasts in England have urged us over and over again to redress the wrongs of Poland, and we have fortunately been unable to listen with effect to their harangues. There is no monarchy and no aristocracy which has been a more inveterate nuisance to Europe than Poland has been, none which really deserved less sympathy, except perhaps the Slave-holding States of the American Union. Still more mischievous has been that intervention which consists in putting down internal movements. The declaration of the Duke of Brunswick and his march on France, the violence which Russia put on the liberties of Hungary, the hindrance which the Crimean war imposed on the liberties of the Christian population in Turkey, are cases in point, if instances are needed. What benefit did Denmark obtain from our guarantees?

Against this passion for making war in order to find an army employment there is but one remedy, the relinquishment of the means which stimulate the

passion and supply the temptation. This consists in
the abandonment or the limitation of a professional
army. There is little risk in a militia, aided by a
scientific corps. Switzerland drills all her people, but
her people have no wish to quit the profitable employments in which they are engaged for the trade of
fighting. I do not forget that Switzerland has had a
war of its own since the Peace of 1815, when it had
to deal with the Sonderbund and the Jesuits. In
these days it is able to quiet these disturbers of the
public peace with less difficulty. The great armies
of most continental states, ruinous as they are to the
resources of the countries which feed them, are not,
with the exception of that of France, disposed to be
aggressive. As I have several times indicated, it is
only under certain circumstances that they could
have any such inclination.

The English army is the most costly in the world,
simply because it is a professional army. For the
population of the country, it is the smallest. To
judge from its past history, it is for its numbers the
most effective. The temper which makes the individual enterprising, diligent, and quick to associate
necessary means with desired ends, is equally effectual
for the courage and discipline of the soldier. The
two extremes of English society, that which prides
itself on its culture, and that which is unremitting
in its manual toil, are equally energetic, and equally
courageous. The disgraceful tendency to panic on
military matters which has from time to time characterised public opinion in England has never, I believe,
affected what may be called the educated and the

labouring classes, to use words which very inadequately express the two greatest and healthiest sections of English society. The extension of political enfranchisement to the working classes has, I infer, obviated those periodical fits of poltroonery on which Cobden commented with so much clearness and severity.

But it is impossible to believe that the system of voluntary enlistment will be found adequate, in the existing state of English society, to the army which has hitherto been employed. The Highland clearings and the Irish emigration have greatly limited the number of recruits from those regions which, thirty years ago, supplied the greater part of our military raw material. There remained, till within the last two or three years, the underpaid and unenlightened agricultural districts of England. But a very remarkable movement has taken place in those regions, a movement as significant as it was unexpected. The action of the agricultural labourers in the Midland Counties can result in one of two things only, a considerable rise in the wages of farm labour, or an emigration on a scale which will not be less extensive than that of Ireland, and which will probably be even larger, because under the English land system the tendency is constantly towards bigger farms, and therefore to a progressive loosening of the labouring agricultural population from the soil. Whatever may be the direction which the movement takes, the same effect will ensue, that namely of a notable rise in the price of agricultural labour, and thereupon a diminution of the temptation to enlistment. Evidence bearing on this result is, I am informed, already forthcoming.

The last project of the Government, while it purposes as far as possible to perpetuate the system of voluntary enlistment, seems to have been devised because the old process of recruiting was felt to rest on a precarious foundation. In establishing a set of military centres, the Government seem to have selected such spots for their depôts as gave the fairest prospect, from the fact that the wages of labour have hitherto been low in the neighbourhood of such centres, that recruiting could be carried on under the most favourable conditions. The routine of an office seldom allows the projectors of any change to forecast the future, or to take account of any altered circumstances in the present. But it seems to me that Mr. Cardwell's plan has already been refuted by events, and that its success is as doubtful as the value of the Martello towers and of the Palmerstonian fortifications has been found to be. It appears that there is an end of cheap labour in recruiting, and that either the Army Office must enter into competition with employers, and so raise the cost of the army to a ruinous amount, or they must adopt some other means than that with which they have been hitherto familiar, in order to keep an effective army together.

It is very often said that the conscription of France and the compulsory military service in Germany constitute a real tax on labour and capital from which our method of voluntary enlistment is free. Undoubtedly, if the amount of labour abstracted from directly productive employment is very large, the statement is true. But it is only true because the amount is large. If labour is not superabundant, exactly the same inconveniences ensue, whether the diversion of labour from productive employment is under the compulsion of law, or by the competition of the Government with employers. Under the latter system, which is our plan, the loss would be equal, and the cost will be greater. This, if proof were needed, is plain from the fact that we never can raise a large army by voluntary enlistment, and that we never have done so from our own people. As I have said before, the force of their own countrymen which has been put under the command of our greatest captains has always been small. We have over and over again fought out our wars with mercenaries. Can any one doubt, if it were, or rather seemed, necessary for the English people to have an army as large as that which M. Thiers has decided on as necessary for France, that the cost of enlarging the force would increase geometrically. Exactly the contrary phenomenon characterises such armies as those of France and Germany. They are increased, man for man, at a decreasing cost to the public exchequer, whatever may be their effects as a check on productive industry.

It is possible that the extension of a system of military drill to a whole population may be made exceedingly inexpensive. It is obvious that it may be made the means for inducing a considerable physical and even moral improvement on the health and the habits of a people. It has long since been demonstrated that there is a limit to the time during which effective labour can be carried on within a given space, or, in other words, that long hours are not always cheap labour. It is only too manifest that the habits of the working-classes in this country are susceptible of great improvement. It is certain that, while the discipline and drill of an army like our own tells with remarkable success on certain persons, the traditions of the army, the inevitable character of many among its recruits, and the enforced celibacy of the greater part of a purely professional force, render certain vices peculiarly prevalent, entail certain very intelligible social evils, and tend to justify certain energetic police regulations which are excessively repugnant to a very large section of the community, and in particular to a class which demands and deserves very careful consideration. Nothing can be worse for an institution than an impression that it is essentially immoral, that it produces grave social mischiefs which extend beyond its own immorality, but which are fostered and defended by such a character, or habitual practice, and that it is at war with the best instincts and experiences of human life. When there is added to this, that a proposal is made to create a number of centres in which such a system may permanently infect the life and habits of a country, a nation must be very enamoured of traditions if it calmly acquiesces in so dangerous an experiment. It need hardly be said that, in such a case, belief in the presence of a danger operates as powerfully as the danger itself.

Besides the economical and social difficulties which beset the new scheme of voluntary enlistment, it should not be forgotten that a system of short time enlistments contains a further danger. To take a number of young men from the agricultural districts and train them to arms, is to make them good soldiers perhaps, but to damage their prospects as hired labourers on their return to civil life. When such men quit the army and seek anew their former occupation, it is not likely that they will command such good wages as those do who have continued unremittingly in the same employment. A man does not become a better carter, ploughman, shepherd, or even ordinary farm hand, because he has devoted five or six years of his life to the acquisition of military drill; and therefore when he seeks employment on his discharge he will probably be compelled to acquiesce in low wages. Such a result would make the discharged soldier a centre of disaffection in every village. And if it be said that the State should under such circumstances find civil employment for its discharged soldiers, the answer is obvious. It will be a grievous loss and wrong to the community if its offices are to be the appropriated prospect of such persons as would voluntarily enlist. It would also be a great error, for the absorption of the military element in the civil population could be effected with far greater ease, and with no risk whatever.

I have never met with any military men, who profess to see, and who are able to see a little beyond the immediate facts of the case, from whom I have not had the same answer as regards the future of the British army. They assume that this country must always have a sufficient and well-selected scientific force. They allow that the officers of the rank and file of the army must hereafter be really professional soldiers, who can command the respect of their men by their smartness, intelligence, and character, and that the race of vulgar men who have hitherto entered the army as a passport to social rank must be excluded or discouraged. An officer can command the unhesitating obedience of his social equals, if he has such a character as will justify his authority. It is the greatest of mistakes to imagine that the rank and file of an army must be taken from a rank of life which is as rigidly separated from the order which commands it as a Brahmin is from a Pariah, or that the British army to be perfect should have for its original elements the scum and dregs of society, that its soldiers should be crimped from the waifs and strays, and its officers gathered from empty-headed and wealthy idlers. The effect of relying on the former contributory is to be found in the wholesale desertions from the ranks, and of the latter from the disclosures which have been made about more than one military academy.

In a country like our own, which every disinterested person admits in his calmer moments to be all but powerless, and progressively powerless for the work of aggression, but which ought to be, and might easily be made to be, invulnerable for attack, such military men as I have talked to say that something like the Swiss system is ultimately the only means for obtaining a large, cheap, and efficient force. Of course, when official persons are consulted on the subject, they invariably answer with the familiar *non possumus*. They tell you that the country would never endure a compulsory drill, just as it would never endure a compulsory education. That is, I believe, an error or a sophistry. Even though the Volunteers are discouraged by the authorities of the army, and are confessedly looked on with great suspicion, the number of these civilian soldiers is considerable, and, as far as can be made out, are not inferior in discipline and orderliness to the average soldier of the line. Playing at soldiers is not an unattractive amusement, and under good management, they who play well are insensibly trained to very considerable effectiveness. Under the new arms of precision and long range, the value of mechanical motion is less than it was, and is far inferior to that which is assigned to the skill of the marksmen, and the excellent physical training which the exercise in the use of arms involves. There is no reason why the Saturday half-holiday, now becoming very general, should not be utilised for purposes of military drill; why, if necessary, any employment of artisans in such exercises should not be compensated by a pay which should correspond with the loss of time that the drill involves; and even why the submission to such a regulation should not be made the basis of some political or social privilege, immediate or prospective. It is unnecessary to comment on the effect which such a drill would have on the physique of the nation, and how it might be made to assist order and sobriety. The best feature, Cobden used to say, in the Volunteer movement, is the help which it gives to the physical training of those who fall in with it. But he added always, it will not in itself diminish the professional force, and its expense. The reason is that the latter differs radically from the former in its origin and in its constitution.

A national militia may be guided very effectively by officers who are by no means absorbed in their profession. Grant and Sherman were two of the ablest captains in the history of modern warfare. Both had a military education, but neither of them had been uninterruptedly engaged in military occupations, before they were called on to take their part in the great enterprises with which their names are permanently connected. History supplies us with abundant instances of men who have achieved the highest military reputation, though they had passed great part of their life in civil functions. The army of ancient Rome was a militia, led by statesmen, and this army conquered the world, entirely because the whole nation was put through military drill. Cromwell was a civilian; but he defeated generals who had learnt their craft in that most consummate of schools, the Thirty Years' War. The natural genius of Marlborough was opposed to the skill of men who had spent a life in training themselves. Nay, it has often been found that an army is by no means strengthened by excessive training. There is no European army on which so much pains has been taken as on that of Austria, and there is certainly none which has suffered so many reverses.

It used to be, perhaps still is, a boast, that the dominions of the English Crown never lose the sunlight. It was certainly true that, wherever those dominions were, there one would assuredly find the British red coat, trained and maintained at the expense of the British tax-payer. Twenty years ago the British army was scattered over the habitable globe. No small part of the force was employed in the defence of the colonies, or rather in assisting the gains of the colonial tradesmen by the expenditure of the British Exchequer. English people were told that this policy enhanced the reputation and vindicated the prestige of the British arms. It was strange that these assurances perfectly satisfied the public, except of course when it was stimulated to panic by disclosures as to the defencelessness of our own shores, and by the sensation speeches of a Napier or a Lyndhurst. But even then no one seemed to reflect on the fact that to disperse an army was to weaken it, and that to scatter it over the world was to render the object for which it was collected impracticable. It was strange that even the minds of traders did not perceive that an army is, so to speak, a reserve against sudden calls, and that a man of business invites bankruptcy who is aware that there are pressing claims on him, but who invests all his ready cash in foreign and colonial bills, which he cannot make instantly use of in order to avert a crisis in his affairs.

In 1849, Mr. Cobden, speaking[*] at Leeds, made the following statement:—'Sir Robert Peel has, again and again, in his budget speeches pointed out clearly the vast expenditure in our colonies. He has, again and again, said that two-thirds of our army are either necessary for garrisons in our colonies, or else to supply depôts at home to furnish relief for those retiring; or else that thousands of men may be always on the wide ocean, visiting one place or another. He has pointed that out, time after time: and he has repeated these things so often, that I have long been of opinion that Sir Robert Peel is anxious to diminish public taxation, by preventing this waste of national resources. He saw the mischief;

[*] Speeches, vol. L p. 425.

he would like public opinion to be directed to it; and if public opinion enabled him to effect a change, I am sure that Sir Robert Peel is the man who would like to accomplish it.'

'You send drilled Englishmen to serve as policemen to Englishmen in Australia, New Zealand, and the Cape of Good Hope. Do not you think that Englishmen there are quite capable of taking care of themselves, without putting you to the expense of doing it? What have they been doing lately? You have spent two millions of money, in the last four years, to defend the settlers of the Cape of Good Hope against the inroads of the barbarous tribes of Caffres. What is taking place at this very moment? Why, these very men, whom you have treated as children, incapable of defending themselves against a few untaught savages—they have proclaimed your own governor in a state of siege, invested your own troops, refused to allow them even provisions, and sent away a ship under the colours of the Queen; and in their speeches and letters, the leaders of the anti-convict movement do not hesitate to declare that they are ready to defend their country, if necessary against the whole force of the English empire. Do you not think there is sufficient pluck about them to defend themselves against a few untutored savages? The same thing is going on in Australia. They quote the example of America; and some of the people are holding their great meetings on the 4th of July, the anniversary of the American independence. I do not respect them the less—I respect them the more. I think they would be unworthy the name of

Englishmen, if they did not stand up against their country being made the cesspool for our convict population. But what I want to show is this; that there is not a shadow of pretence for requiring our armies to defend them.'

Again, the same speech contains the following passage:—'I think it is a great mistake to suppose that, in order that you may display a great power to the world, all the power should be put into the shape of cannons, muskets, and ships of war. Do you not think that, in these times of industry, when wealth and commerce are the real tests of a nation's power, coupled with worth and intelligence—do you not see that, if you beat your iron into ploughshares and pruning-hooks, instead of putting it into swords and spears, it will be equally productive of power, and of far more force, if brought into collision with another country, than if you put all your iron into spears and swords? It is not always necessary to hold up a scarecrow to frighten your neighbours. I believe a civilised nation will estimate the power of a country, not by the amount laid out in armaments, which may be the means of weakening that power, but it will measure your strength by your latent resources—what margin of taxation you have that you can impose in case of necessity, greater than another country, to which you may be opposed—what is the spirit of your people, as having confidence in the institutions or government under which they live—what is the general intelligence of the people—what is, in every respect, their situation and capacity to make an effort, in case an effort were required? These will be the tests which intelligent people will apply to countries; not what amount of horse, foot, and artillery, or how many ships you have afloat.'

In a speech delivered in the House of Commons on June 12, 1849, Cobden pleaded for the principle of non-intervention, and for the practice of arbitration. His motion was rejected by more than two to one, as might have been and was expected from the House of Commons of the time. But a different temper has been induced on the habits of English politicians in the present day, and it is not too much to say that no person contributed more to such a change than Cobden did by his persistent advocacy of a policy of generosity and common sense. In the course of this speech, commenting on the waste of wealth which is the consequent of huge warlike equipments, he pointed out the increase in the number of the national army and navy, and of the prodigious stock of destructive implements at that time in the possession of Government. Cobden was remarkably accurate in his facts, and he informed the House, and through it the country, that the stock of barrelled gunpowder stored up in the Government arsenals was equal to nearly three years' consumption during the height of the French war, and equal to fifteen years' consumption at the present rate, while the number of ball cartridges in stock was 65,000,000. The inferences which he drew from this practice were obvious.*

Ten years ago, Mr. Goldwin Smith, for whose abilities, clearness of vision, and integrity of principle

* See Speeches, ii. 169.

Cobden entertained the highest opinion, drew down on himself the customary criticism of the *Times* for advocating a rational policy towards the colonies, particularly in relation to their military defence. Mr. Goldwin Smith argued that to squander British troops over British colonies was to weaken the resources of the country, and to degrade and demoralise the colony. The time was not ripe for the acceptance of so judicious a policy, and consequently the exposition of current public opinion was given in a philippic on the Oxford Professor. It is superfluous to say that the *Times* took nothing by its action, and that Mr. Goldwin Smith continued to vindicate a policy, which the *Times* of our day is perfectly willing to endorse. The defence of the colonies is now left to themselves. If they provoke war with native races they must bear the brunt of their own acts. The home country is supposed to be quit of any liability towards the defence of the colonies, unless they were attacked as part of the British empire by a power with which we might happen to be at war. But the facts that they are entrusted with their own defence, that they are self-governed institutions, and that the bond between them and the mother country is nothing better than one of sentiment, and in some particulars of convenience to the colony, have freed them from the danger of aggression. If England were at war with France or Russia, there is no reason to believe that those countries would discover any strategic reason for attacking the British colonies.

The reform of the British army has been commenced from above, in the abolition of purchase. I have already indicated the origin of the singular custom which was put an end to only lately. The purchase and sale of an office of trust is one which is wholly alien to the institutions of a free country, though it was only in comparatively recent times that it was abolished in civil offices, and then after long and unwearied efforts. It speaks much for the character of the army that a practice radically so vicious should have done so little harm to the service when it was wanted as an arm of defence or warfare. The most unfriendly critic of the British army, whatever he might have said about the effect of the custom in time of peace, could not have averred that it produced any notable mischief in time of war. But, as I have already observed, the traditions of victory and success, as they give force to national courage, may have acted as a check on the entrance of those into the army who might be deficient in this instinct or quality, and would certainly confirm those who might be wavering or half-hearted.

Large as the price was which the country paid for the abolition of saleable commissions, and dubious as the morality and the policy were of allowing the over-regulation price to those who thought proper to retire, the principle involved in the change was worth the outlay. There is no reason to believe that the spirit of the army will be diminished or enfeebled by the change, or that the traditions of the service will cease to be operative to those who belong to it in future. But it is undesirable that any class of public servants should have a permanently vested right against the nation, and should be able to govern the details of the service to which they belong. It is inexpedient that the power of doing a work on which public safety is supposed to depend should be conditioned by an outlay of money. It is true that the higher departments of the military service were not brought under the purchase system. But practically the avenue to the higher service was closed by the necessity, which was imposed on all, of purchasing step by step up to that grade from which the most trusted servants of the public had to be selected.

The army and navy, said Cobden, with more plainness of speech than was agreeable, were a great preserve for the younger sons of the landlord class. As war is the profession of a monarchy and an aristocracy, so a costly public service is apt to be, and hitherto has been, the necessary consequent of primogeniture. If the whole paternal estate is bestowed on the eldest son, certain professions or callings must be, and will be, set apart for the disinherited cadets of the family, and of these the army, the Church, and the civil service, since the ordinary functions of the person who enters on these callings are a very simple routine, and two of them at least have to do, or seem to have to do, with the government of men, are, under favourable circumstances, peculiarly attractive to younger sons. In both the system of purchase was developed and extended. A century ago, a commission in the army was frequently held *durante bene placito*, and men were dismissed the service who were not compliant enough to the Court. Similarly the genius of the Anglican Church, as it was constructed by the intelligence of Thomas Cromwell, made the parochial clergy the dependents on the bishops, the bishops being themselves dependent on the Crown. In the army, custom, in the Church the ingenuity of lawyers, made the commission and the benefice a property and a freehold. Such is the course of human nature. If society allows a wrong to be done by law, (and whatever be the political merits of the custom of primogeniture, it cannot be disputed that it inflicts an injury on the younger children,) it is generally the case that society is burdened with the maintenance of its own victims. Pauperism in the poorer classes, and a costly system of public services for the benefit of the higher, are the necessary result of a system which divorces the peasant from the soil, and allows a younger son only a barren social rank.

Cobden, with his customary prescience, foresaw[*] that the modification of the army, and a curtailment of the expenditure upon it, would ensue from an extension of the franchise, and therefore advocated change in the system of parliamentary representation, for this among other reasons, because he hoped that by it the country would be led back to economy in its military and naval expenditure. It is clear that though this result has not been achieved, the nation is on the road to it. The English people has been invited to give the first impulse to the progress of public affairs. At first indeed it will be wholly unconscious of its real power. It will know but little of the business with which it has to deal. It will temporarily attach itself to those ancient traditional parties which have guided the business of the nation since the Revolution, will be

[*] Speeches, i. 429.

Conservative or Liberal as an uninstructed sympathy influences individuals or groups of individuals. It will gradually however, but irresistibly, develope a policy of its own. At first it will incline to be sectional, to consider itself as a party with interests antagonistic to those of such classes as heretofore have managed the affairs of the people. It will advocate the direct representation of its own interests, induced to such a course by the impression that the depositaries of political power have hitherto used the forces of legislation in order to sustain particular interests— land for example—commerce—the home trade. It may tend towards accepting theories about the reconstruction of society, and think of processes by which it is feasible to reverse that assistance to the artificial distribution of wealth which has characterised our legal system, not only by doing away with the laws which have aided such a result, but by an interference as unreasonable as that which is resented, in order to hasten the remedial process which its instincts teach it to be necessary, but for the natural development of which it has not the requisite patience. It may even please itself with those socialistic schemes which have been sketched by angry partisans in France and Germany.

These, however, will be only temporary and occasional fancies. It is one of the peculiarities of a thoroughly popular Government that it does not lend itself in its vindication of principles to the ends of a section of society, however large that section may be. There is no fear that the working-classes in England will make use of the forces of Government in order to develope trades-unions. It is the essence of a trades-union that it is partial in the protection which it affords to the labour which is associated under it. If all labour were contained in such unions, the mechanism of a union could not possibly do any good whatever to labour in the gross. But the English working-men who have enjoyed the advantage, real or supposed, of these labour combinations, are the teachers of their own industrial creed to all labour without distinction. They have given warm sympathy and material support to the movement among the agricultural labourers; though the enrolment of such persons in labour combinations would do much towards neutralising the advantages which the protected trades acquire. It is stated that the American artisan looks with great jealousy and disfavour upon the Irish and Chinese immigration. But there has never been any step taken to check the flow of such labourers to the Union, for the Know-nothing party, who were reported to have had such aims before the Civil War, were not supposed to belong to the working-classes.

When the English nation becomes alive to its strength, and reasons upon the process by which it is governed, and when it is informed about the sacrifices which it has to make in order to keep up the present scale of Government expenditure, it cannot I think be doubted that it will insist on economy. Under our system of taxation, under indeed any system of taxation with which modern finance is familiar, the pressure of large expenditure falls far more heavily on narrow than it does upon large incomes. And the reason is obvious. No tax which is levied on articles the use of which is wholly voluntary, is half so productive as a tax levied on articles the use of which is necessary or habitual. The doctrine which would put all taxation on the rich is odious and unfair; but the sacrifice which the poor have to make in their payments to public purposes is really very heavy, and the only way in which any tendency towards the doctrine to which I have referred may be obviated is to reduce public expenditure within the narrowest limits consistent with good faith, security, and good government. It is no apology for excessive expenditure to say that the burden of taxation has become relatively lighter, because the nation has grown more numerous and more wealthy. The extortion of the past, the prodigious burden borne by the people for the fifteen years after the great Continental war, will not make the public acquiesce in present waste. And as soon as ever the 'future rulers' of England are convinced that much of the cost of administration is a levy on the resources of the many for the benefit of the few, it is certain that the Services will be thoroughly and radically reformed.

The last speech which Cobden made in Parliament * was an attack on Government manufacturing establishments. It is possible that a Government may not feel itself able always to trust private manufacturers. Frauds have been practised on governments, contracts have been obtained by bribing government clerks, as we are told, and goods, supplied by dishonest dealers, have not come up to sample. But such occurrences are the result of a want of diligence or a want of good faith on the part of those whose business it is to see that contracts are honestly fulfilled. The difficulty in

* Speeches, vol. i. p. 577.

the way of dealing with such contingencies is not insuperable, and even if it were, it is amplified instead of being diminished by the creation of Government manufacturing establishments, for it is plain that the superintendence of a great manufactory is far more open to mismanagement and loss than the examination of contracts is.

A Government office, and by parity of reasoning a Government manufactory, conducts business in a manner which would be utterly ruinous to a private trader, whether one considers his reputation for punctuality and despatch, or his capacity for interpreting the relations of expenditure to profit. A Government office takes a fortnight to answer a letter on the purest question of routine. A banker or lawyer or other professional person would soon lose customers or clients, if he wearied their patience or imperilled their interests by such negligence. But no one can say that the public offices are undermanned. A distinguished statesman and minister told me some time since, that when he entered on the office which he accepted on a ministerial change, his predecessor had thrust so many officials into the department, that if the public interest were consulted, no fresh appointment ought to be made for a dozen years to come. But the fact is, the nation must use the office, and cannot therefore bring it under the conditions of competition; and, still worse, the regular officials have what is virtually a freehold office. A merchant who suffered his clerks to acquire a claim to permanent places in his counting-house, and who was therefore debarred from ejecting the idle and incompetent from his business, would soon find his affairs in a very critical state. There is, I think, no more curious fact in the history of the English Government than this, that the necessary precautions which were taken in order to secure the independence of the Judges in the Act of Settlement, have been made to extend to all Government officials whatever, when an exactly reverse policy was indicated by the circumstances of the case.

The managers of the Government manufactories never seem to have made an estimate of the capital and plant invested in their buildings and workshops, when they gave an account of the costs and charges of what they turn out. As a consequence the establishment grew with amazing rapidity. Estimates were granted for new buildings and implements, and the article produced was valued only at the raw material and the labour consumed in making it. Hence a perfectly delusive balance-sheet was published, and Parliament was thoroughly mystified. Besides, the establishment was not stimulated to invention and improvement, but was utterly conservative and unchanging in what it manufactured. I have heard it stated by gentlemen who are engaged in the manufacture of textile fabrics, that the possibility of getting good business profit depends on the readiness with which the owner of the factory adopts improvements as they occur in the process of manufacture. But the Government workshops had no motive to improve, since they were supported by none of those stimulants which induce prudence in an ordinary producer, who might wish to keep clear of the *Gazette*, and to realise a modest fortune. They built wooden ships long after wooden ships were exploded, and manufactured munitions of war after patterns which the progress of science had antiquated long before.

There was of course no master's eye. The waste was therefore enormous, in some cases ludicrous. If it were worth while to recall them, plenty of stories could be told of the recklessness with which expenditure was entered on, and the obstinacy with which routine traditions were maintained. Valuable materials were condemned and sold as old stores, the Government not infrequently purchasing, and at a greatly enhanced price, the very articles which they had previously disposed of. A sudden and mischievous activity was made to alternate with a capricious and motiveless sloth. The whim of some irresponsible official was easily gratified, when he insisted on the supply of something which was proved to be useless long before it was ordered, and which was found to be useless as soon as ever it was manufactured. The Government manufactory was influenced by the pressure exercised on behalf of one projector, and resolutely declined to consider the merits of other inventors. Perhaps no cases can be found in the history of that unlucky race which busies itself with inventions more painful in their disappointments than those which are supplied from the records of the Government building-yards, foundries, and workshops. The discoverer is stimulated by those ordinary motives which lead men to anticipate rapid fortune by the successful adoption of his project. He flatters himself that in imparting his scheme to the Government, he is serving his own interest, and is a patriot to boot. But if I can trust what I have heard and read, the lottery of the patentee is more than ordinarily uncertain when the Government is invited to make an estimate about the value of his patent.

It is no small matter that the system of Government manufacture tends to develope in the minds of such working-men as are engaged in these establishments the two pernicious doctrines, that Government may properly find employment for labour, and that it is expedient that labourers should have a vested interest in their employment, when that employment is accorded by the State. The rule of the Civil Service, that all officials have a quasi-freehold office, has some defence in the case of offices where trust is required, where the power of supervision is not very great, and where the labour given is not to be tested by tangible results, but is merely an exact routine. But in the case of that industry which can be very well done by piece, and which can be tested by competent persons, provided the inspector does his duty honestly, the workman who is hired by a Government should conform to the ordinary conditions under which similar labour is hired by private employers. In ordinary business nothing would be more fatal than such relations between employers and workmen as would put the former at the mercy of the latter, and what is true of private manufacture ought to be acknowledged as a rule by the State.

Public opinion on this subject has made no little progress in the direction which Cobden indicated. The change has not come too soon. Nothing demonstrates the necessity of a reform more completely than the

fact, that though it was urgently demanded, it was
highly unpopular. It is notorious that the closing of
the public workshops on the Thames was viewed with
great disfavour. The demagogues of both traditional
parties have tried to make capital out of the reform.
Fortunately for the people, the chiefs of both traditional
parties were equally compromised by the alteration,
or, as I should prefer to say, showed equal wisdom in
grappling with the mischief. The Government of Lord
Derby and Mr. Disraeli began the policy which that
of Mr. Gladstone has carried out in some degree. For
it must be remembered that the responsibility of expenditure rests with administrations. No private
member of Parliament, however acute, diligent, and
persevering he may be, ever makes any notable impression on the estimates. It is possible to criticise
these estimates in the gross, it is hardly practicable to
handle them in detail. There is abundant room for
criticism. The expenditure of this country is growing,
and ought to be reduced. Its amount has no defence,
whether one considers our own necessities, or the
practice of other nations. But as yet the public is too
ill informed as to the process by which this expenditure
grows, and administrations seldom have the courage
to institute reforms.

CHAPTER VI.

FINANCIAL REFORM.

When Cobden first entered into public life, the fiscal system of this country was as bad as could be conceived. The exigencies of a protracted and costly war had led Pitt and his successors to levy taxes on every article which could be made to yield a revenue. There was no time to reflect on the question as to whether the tax imposed on the public was mischievous, or vexatious, or capricious, or merely oppressive. Money was urgently wanted, and money was relentlessly obtained. Even if it had been discovered that the fiscal measures of Pitt were ruinous and exhausting, it was doubtful whether the discovery would have availed. A financier has always one answer to a demonstration that his schemes are unfair, partial, mischievous. This is, the tyrant's plea of necessity, the concession that taxation is not, and never will be equitable, and that all which can be expected is an approximation to fairness.

During the great Continental war, English financiers had a storehouse of precedents from which they could extract expedients for taxing the people, in the methods which the Dutch had adopted in order to maintain themselves during their long war of independence. In

Holland, to be sure, the struggle was desperate, and at that epoch fiscal science was in its infancy. It is also true that the Dutch were, according to their lights, perfectly equitable in distributing the taxation which they imposed. No kind of property escaped their exactions. They never dreamed of letting one class off, still less of affording that class considerable exemptions. There is little doubt that Pitt was very unwilling, when he imposed the legacy duties, to relieve the landowners from all contribution to this tax, especially as they were reaping the prodigious benefits obtained from the corn monopoly, and this under the pressure of many inadequate harvests. The statesmen of the age could not have been ignorant of that law of prices which was well known to Davenant and Gregory King, that when a scarcity occurs in a necessary of life, the diminished quantity sells for very much more than the average quantity does. The landowners, too, had the advantage of another law in prices, which, as far as I can discover, I was the first to demonstrate, that when a scarcity takes place in a necessary, the rise is always greatest in the cheapest kind or quality of the article demanded and consumed. Under these circumstances, then, the landowners gained the maximum of advantage, the poor suffered the maximum of loss. It was in the face of these facts that Pitt was constrained, by the resolute bearing of the country party, to omit all succession duties on land, and on *money to be laid out in the purchase of land*, while the duty was exacted to the fullest amount which seemed prudent and productive on personalty.

Statesmen like Pitt, who knew generally what was

right, and would have done right had the times permitted, were followed by persons like Vansittart, who did not know what was right, and would not know it when they could. It was under the administration of the financier, whom the peerage knew as Lord Bexley, that the most grotesque feats in taxation were performed. It must be allowed that when Vansittart quitted the Exchequer, a new epoch commenced. Twenty-one years before Cobden's entrance into public life, the Merchants' Petition, drawn up by the late Thomas Tooke, was presented in both Houses; and not long afterwards Mr. Huskisson and others attempted certain reforms in the tariff of customs and excise. Remissions of taxation in one direction, impositions in another, and, in general, adaptations of fiscal charges on grounds intelligible, and frequently approximating to sound economical principles, were made between the date of the Merchants' Petition and the accession of Sir Robert Peel to office in September 1841.

Two circumstances contributed greatly to the policy which Peel adopted in 1842. One of these was the Budget of Lord Melbourne's Government in 1841. This Budget proposed to apply, in some degree at least, the principles of free trade to the important articles of corn, sugar, and timber. It is true that the proposals of the Whig Government were rejected. But it is the fashion for the leaders of parties not to look at the measures which their opponents bring forward, but to the power which these opponents have for carrying the measures. It would be an error to suppose that a party which ejects its rivals from office on a Budget, has by such an act disclaimed all sympathy with the propositions which it repudiates or condemns. On the contrary, it frequently adopts them as its own, and relying, as such persons have hitherto been fairly able to do, on public ignorance, it not unfrequently assumes the merit of originality in proclaiming a policy as its discovery or property which it has declaimed against with successful energy when it belonged to another. It is difficult to say what the Conservative party would have done in this country had they not freely availed themselves of this simple stratagem. Mr. Disraeli charged Sir R. Peel with the practice, but he knew too well the value of the expedient which he reprobated to decline its utility on his own account when it was convenient to do so. I have little doubt that when Peel succeeded to office in 1841, he intended at some time or other to make his fiscal changes on the lines, or even on larger lines, than those of Lord Melbourne, though he disclaimed any such intention until the contingency of the reform came within what Mr. Gladstone has called 'the range of practical politics.' In short, the Cabinet of 1841 adopted the practice of Idomeneus in Homer, and filled their tent with the spoils of the Trojans, in order to use them in the warfare which was to follow.

The other circumstance was the Report of Mr. Hume's Committee, obtained in May 1840, and issued in August of the same year,—a speed which is remarkable, when one considers the slowness with which such Committees ordinarily act, and when one recalls the singular importance of the Report itself. It 'recommended a revision of the tariff, the removal of differential duties in favour of colonial produce, and the abandonment of all reliance upon protection of the home trade from foreign competition.'* In brief, Mr. Hume's Committee advocated that course of fiscal policy which, commenced tentatively by Sir Robert Peel in 1842, has now become, as far as Customs and Excise duties are concerned, the rule of British finance.

When this Report made its appearance, it informed the public that there were no less than 1150 different rates of duty payable on imported articles, and that the tariff often aimed at incompatible ends. 'The duties were sometimes meant to be productive of revenue, and for protective objects, ends which are frequently inconsistent with each other.' The Report might have stated, with greater accuracy, that in proportion to the success with which the duty assisted the revenue, so it failed to fulfil the purpose of protection, and that in so far as it secured protection to the British producer, so it failed to assist the wants of the Exchequer. Out of 862 articles chargeable with duty, seventeen paid 94 per cent. of the revenue, twenty-nine others paid 4 per cent. more. But, on the other hand, 349 contributed less than £100 a year each, and 147 paid no Customs' duty whatever. It was moreover observed, that the differential duties levied on colonial and foreign produce were virtually no assistance to the colony in many instances; for that the cost of shipment from the foreign country to the colony represented a small proportion of the differential duty imposed against the foreigner, and that therefore certain goods, as for instance coffee, were shipped from Brazil and Hayti to the Cape, and thence reshipped to England, the consumer being thus charged with an extra, and wholly

* Tooke's History of Prices, v. 423.

useless, cost of freight. It was no wonder therefore, as Mr. Tooke has observed, that 'the Report was immediately adopted as a text-book by the large and active party who, at that time, was rapidly rising into notice as the opponents of all corn-laws;' that the leaders of the party, both in and out of Parliament, were not slow to make use of the facts which were laid before them, and that they finally established the free trade canon, as far as applies to production and consumption, as the commercial creed of Parliament. But the Report of 1840 was one only among the signal services which the late Mr. Joseph Hume rendered to his country. Nothing, we are informed, contributed more to the mental conversion of Sir Robert Peel than the publication of this Report. His political conversion was delayed for five years; an illustration, among many others which could be quoted, that politicians accept a demonstrable truth long before they have the courage to initiate the change which turns a demonstration into a fact.

Sir Robert Peel's Customs and Excise reforms in 1842, 1845, and 1846 involved the nominal sacrifice of more than seven millions of annual revenue. In 1848, the so-called West India Interest was ignored, by the equalisation of the sugar duties. These tariff reforms were to some extent supplemented by the imposition of the Income Tax, an impost borrowed from the worst ages of Pitt's finance, but were far more aided by the general growth of industry and opulence, the natural effects of such remissions of taxation as relieved the powers of the nation from the trammels which had been put on its efforts, and of those resources for expenditure with which increased and more effective industry supplied it.

It may be stated then, generally, that the tariff reforms of the last thirty years have taken the following direction. Taxes on the necessaries of life have been almost extinguished. There remains only one, the duty on sugar. Taxes on the most general and defensible luxuries have been greatly reduced, those namely on coffee and tea. Taxes on luxuries which are not necessary in any sense, but are mere enjoyments, more or less mischievous in their physical effects, those namely on alcoholic drinks and tobacco, have been left stationary in amount, or have been increased. Taxes levied on productions have been abolished, such as those on glass, soap, bricks, paper, &c. A slight impost has been put on the succession to landed estate, and on moneys to be expended in the purchase of land; though for reasons which could be easily given, but which are not capable of easy defence, the tax on the succession to real estate is not so heavy as that on personal estate, nor are the receipts from the impost as considerable as was anticipated. Internal taxes, such as stamps and assessed taxes, have not been materially changed, though owing to the rapid growth of wealth, the income which the State has derived from these sources has been greatly increased. But, on the other hand, a fiscal expedient, which was declared in its origin to be merely temporary, and the gross unfairness of which was excused on the ground that it was temporary, and therefore merely a transference of the taxation indirectly paid by an existing generation, has been continued. It is very important to observe that the intrinsic inequality of the Income Tax is more conspicuous when society has accommodated itself to the great fiscal changes which were made during Cobden's early Parliamentary life, and it may be worth while to point out the economical causes of the fact.

When Sir Robert Peel reformed his tariff, and covered his anticipated deficiency by the Income Tax, he could fairly urge that the financial system which he abandoned was constructed so as to mulct all expenditure, of whatever kind it might be, provided only it was made through the agency of a dealer, with a contribution to the Exchequer. I make this reservation, because it was possible for a person, who subsisted on the produce of land, which he cultivated himself, to escape much of that taxation on the necessaries of life which the legislature imposed, either for its own wants or in the interest of protected classes, on the general body of consumers. Food, clothing, the materials of a house, its bricks and timber, as well as the natural and adscititious luxuries of life, were visited by the tax-gatherer. Hence on the remission of many among these taxes, the Government might with some show of fairness argue, We are remitting burdens on production and exchange which tend to multiply themselves in their incidence upon you, the great body of consumers. We relieve your expenditure from numerous, vexatious, and costly imposts. It is not unfair therefore that we should claim a portion of that from which your expenditure proceeds, in other words, impose an Income Tax on you. As the relief is universal, and is proportionate to expenditure, the Income Tax should be universal—at least as far as is possible and convenient—whatever be the source or duration of the income in question. It was on this plea that Sir Robert Peel justified the imposition of an Income Tax on the dividends of public funds. *Prima facie* such a tax was a breach of faith. The British Government borrowed under the following conditions. It debarred the lender from claiming his principal at his discretion. It claimed the right of paying off the creditor at its discretion. It stipulated to pay a fixed annuity to the lender. It would seem then that when it mulcted the fundholder of a portion of his annual interest, it actually lessened the annuity which it had agreed to pay him; that, in short, if an Income Tax of 6*d.* in the pound were levied on the dividend, that the Government had arbitrarily reduced the annuity from £3 to £2 18*s.* 6*d.* But Sir Robert Peel justified the imposition of an Income Tax on the fundholder, by the allegation given above, that the Income Tax was an economical transfer of taxes levied on the expenditure of the fundholder—who resided in the United Kingdom—to the income which he derived. The precedent which Sir Robert Peel gave has been unfortunately imitated, though without the justification and the limitations, by the Governments of Italy and Austria. In those countries, the Income Tax paid on public securities is either a naked confiscation of a rateable portion of the principal, or, in case the impost is temporary, a conversion of part of their public stocks into passive.

Some of my readers may remember that when a Birmingham clerk, a few years ago, appealed to Mr. Gladstone on the inequality and unfairness of the Income Tax, he was answered by an appeal to the extraordinary amount of taxation which had been remitted by successive Governments, and to the consequent relief which the clerk in question must have sustained. The clerk, who probably felt that it was as dangerous to argue with the master of many figures, as the philosopher of old found it to argue with the master of many legions, declined to continue the preposterous combat. But it is not, I think, difficult to point out the intrinsic fallacy of Mr. Gladstone's retort. The relief which the reforms in question gave was immediate, but it was also transitory. The relief was in many particulars on articles of voluntary consumption, while the tax payable on the clerk's income was an involuntary contribution. The profits of commercial freedom are principally appropriated by the producer, the benefits to the consumer are of a different kind. By virtue of a law, familiar to the tyro in economical science, the effect of any reform in taxation on the cost of subsistence is soon distributed, and as population increases and competition for employment gets sharper, is lost to the ordinary consumer. In order to prove his case, Mr. Gladstone had to show that the Birmingham clerk was able to procure the necessaries of life at a cheaper rate than he obtained them before the remissions of taxation were made; that if such necessaries were cheaper, the cheapness was to be ascribed to the reform of the tariff, not to the widening of the market, and to economy in the cost of collecting, transit, and distribution, and that the demand for the clerk's labour, and consequently the income which he received, were not adversely affected by the course of events. There might perhaps be found an argument for the imposition of an Income Tax on the clerk, but there was no real answer given to his question, unless these conditions were satisfied.

The imposition of a rateable tax on such incomes as are included under Schedule D involves three inconvenient and unfair consequences. One of these respects the payer of the tax in his capacity as the recipient of an income, another—extending of course to all persons who receive incomes—on him as the expender of an income, a third affects him in consideration of the circumstances under which he earns his income. The common instinct of men repudiates as inequitable the equal taxation of incomes which are unequally durable. Cobden gave credit to the Government of Lord Derby and the budget of Mr. Disraeli for recognising this fact, and for attempting to palliate its unfairness.* It was, and is, absurd to use the stock argument of difficulty against doing justice in this direction, since Pitt and Peel both adopted such an expedient in relation to the farmer's income tax.

The reason why, in economical language, the equal rate levied on income under Schedule D is unfair to the recipient of the income, as contrasted with a similar tax on what is roughly called realised property, is to be found in the fact that the tax on the latter is a tax on income only, the tax on the former is one on income and capital as well. Every man who is engaged in earning an industrial income may be compared with strict accuracy to a machine on which great expenditure has been incurred in order to bring it to perfection, and which must inevitably wear out at last. To tax the earnings of such a machine on their gross amount, to allow nothing for the cost of manufacture, the capital sunk, the accumulated interest on the process of pro-

* Speeches, vol. i. p. 541.

duction, the risk of the machine getting out of order, the certainty of its exhaustion, and the cost of maintaining its action while it is active, is, disguise it as you may in legal language, simple extortion, from which human nature is sure to attempt, and probably to discover, an escape. It is the practice of financiers to lament over the frauds of those who are liable under Schedule D, to comment on their universality, and to draw sinister inferences from their occurrence. Will they never learn the lesson which experience teaches, that an unjust law does not command respect, and will not, if possible, be obeyed, and that just as fraud is the natural remedy for violence, so is deceit the obvious escape from rapine perpetrated under the name of law? 'To pretend,' says Adam Smith, no mean critic of human nature, when writing of the habits of his own age, 'to have any scruple about buying smuggled goods, though a manifest encouragement to the violation of the revenue laws, and to the perjury which almost always attends it, would in most countries be regarded as one of those pedantic pieces of hypocrisy, which instead of gaining credit with anybody, serve only to expose the person who affects to practise them to the suspicion of being a greater knave than most of his neighbours.'* In the present day the trade of the smuggler is almost extinct, and any person who dealt with the stray persons who call themselves smugglers would be considered rather a fool than a knave, as one who let himself be the dupe of an impostor. The reason is not far to seek. Just financial laws, in which one concern only is before the statesman, that of raising

* 'Wealth of Nations' (Author's Edition), vol. ii. p. 496.

a revenue on the most equitable basis conceivable from imported or excised objects, have succeeded to a mass of statutes the avowed purpose of which was the sustentation of some particular interest which had got the ear of the Legislature, and to the injury of the general public. The trade of the smuggler was the irregular and illegal corrective to a system of legal plunder. In the same way, the frauds or evasions under Schedule D are a practical protest against that most outrageous of all inequalities, an unfair equality. Interpreted rightly, they would result in the condemnation of the Income Tax altogether, or to its revision and recast, upon the principles indicated above. To some extent indeed they have been recognised, in the deduction allowed for life insurance—a deduction by the way which should have been permitted only in the case of precarious and terminable incomes; but what life insurance would ever cover the most necessary, and as regards the public the most beneficent, outlay which those who earn such incomes can make, the education of their children?

The second inconvenience which ensues from the Income Tax is the fact that it can in many cases be shifted. It is only lately that this circumstance has come into prominence, and I am alive to the fact that there is no economical question which is surrounded with greater obscurity than that of the true incidence of certain taxes. It is generally assumed by economists that a tax on general profits cannot be transferred, chiefly because it is assumed that profits tend to, and, as a general rule, do reach equality. But this position is at best dubious, for it must be taken over so limited a range of occupations, and with so many qualifications, that it cannot be allowed as a safe guide to a general conclusion, still less to financial action on such a conclusion. The laws which govern the incidence of taxation, imperial and local, are I believe as follows:—

First, Taxes have a tendency to remain with those on whom they are imposed,—i. e. in order for their transference an effort must be made by the original payer, and a power must be present in him to constrain some other person to acquiesce in their transference.

It is easy to illustrate this position. A tax on consumable articles procured from a dealer will always be paid by the customer, for the demand of the customer puts it into the power of the dealer to transfer the tax, and the dealer will not advance the tax to the Government except upon a very clear understanding that the tax will be repaid him in the price of the article. Here the power of transference is at its maximum. But between such a class of persons, and, for example, the owner of a ground-rent on which a special tax is levied, or the landowner from whose beneficial occupation or letting of land a tithe is payable, and in whom the power of transference is at its minimum, or rather is utterly extinguished, there are infinite degrees of the power which the first payer of the tax is stimulated to exercise.

A second law is, that when a tax is imposed upon any producer or labourer, and this tax is incident upon the bare or customary means of subsistence of such a producer or labourer, the tax is transferred to those who buy the goods or services of producer or labourer.

It was long since pointed out by Adam Smith* that taxes on the mere necessaries of life tend to fall on employers. The case of course is clearest where slavery is permitted and taxes on necessaries are imposed. But what is true of the case where necessaries are taxed is true also of the case where custom has designated a peculiar standard of living as necessary to a particular kind of dealer or labourer. No one doubts that the public pays for the tradesman's shop-front and costly advertisements. It is not less clear that the rent of his place of business, the licence which is occasionally levied on his calling, and the prime cost of his manner of living will be included in the charges which he puts on those who deal with him. Nor is it doubtful either that if he pays an Income Tax he will be strongly tempted to include the amount in the necessary outlay of his calling, and recoup himself by enhancing his prices to his customers. He must do so, by virtue of the law which I have indicated above, in case the Income Tax falls on his customary mode of subsistence; and he can do so over all his transactions by virtue of a rule, which I believe prevails all but universally in retail trade, that the competition of shopkeepers is not for cheapness or dearness, but for custom. Such a rule I presume is well known to be adopted. It is indirectly proved to exist by the facts that dealers spend such prodigious amounts in advertising their wares, and by the stringency with which they bind whole-

---

* 'Wealth of Nations' (Author's Edition), vol. ii. p. 485.

sale dealers not to transact business with private individuals. Now it is manifest that when the smaller dealer finds it necessary to impose all the charges of his calling, Income Tax included, on those who buy his goods, the larger trader has every inclination and every opportunity to do so too. Indeed, so much was expressed to Mr. Lowe by the deputation of London shopkeepers who waited on him in order to denounce the Co-operative Stores of the Civil Service. I need hardly say, that I do not give this analysis of trade procedure with a view to put any stigma on any class of my fellow countrymen. They have a perfect right to adapt their trade and their prices to what the law assists and custom sanctions. It is possible that, under the operation of both law and custom, they are rendered subject to a very sharp competition for the trade which they get on the principles under which it is carried on, and that the wants of the public as well as the interests of the traders would be greatly aided if the number of dealers, increased largely by the competition for custom, were reduced by three-fourths, or even more. But the real purpose of my analysis is to show that under the operation of the Income Tax Acts, classes other than retail traders are constrained to pay a double Income Tax, once in their capacity as receivers of income, and the second time in the act of its expenditure.

The third inconvenience which comes from the present levy of the Income Tax under Schedule D, is that which is derived from the consideration of the circumstances under which the payer earns his income. The possessor of an industrial income, as contrasted with the owner of a spontaneous income, is constrained to select the locality in which he can most conveniently and certainly carry on his calling, while the owner of the other kind of income can consult his own choice as to the region in which he can spend his annual resources. The time of the former is occupied, and he has no leisure to attend to those smaller economics, for the pursuit of which the latter can devote his entire energies. The former is disabled from attempting a number of occupations which the latter can follow. These are not indeed lucrative in any sense, and therefore are not liable to taxation, but they are eminently useful, and may be the means of considerable saving. A parent who has leisure and capacity can undertake for himself, and frequently with great success, the education of his children, a function which the man who earns an industrial income is debarred from attempting, however competent he may be to perform it, and for which he must pay heavily when he delegates it to others; so heavily, indeed, that were it not for school endowments, it does not seem clear how the higher culture could be accorded to many of those who now enjoy it.

It is no exaggeration, I think, to say, that taking all the items into account, house-rent in a town, a necessary condition towards earning most industrial incomes, is five times as costly as equal accommodation is in the country. A man may easily get a house in a village or a country town for fifty pounds a year, the conveniences of which far exceed that for which he will have to pay £250 in London. Add to this rent the proportionate rates levied for local taxation, and that for imperial taxation, and it is easy to see how seriously such an individual's resources are curtailed, how scanty becomes that revenue which Adam Smith declares to be alone taxable, that which he 'enjoys' under the protection of the State, the term 'enjoys' necessarily excluding what he must spend before either income or enjoyment is possible. By a piece of blindness—I do not like to say ignorance—which is almost inconceivable, Mr. Goschen has actually offered the malcontents who voted with Sir Massey Lopes the housetax of the towns in order to form a subvention towards the general mass of local taxation, thus reproducing the precise error for which Mr. Disraeli's Budget of 1852 was deservedly rejected. Talk of a graduated Income Tax with reprobation! The possessor or earner of an industrial income in a town, and especially in the metropolis, pays practically a treble Income Tax when he is contrasted with the fortunate owner of a spontaneous income, who can choose the locality in which he will reside, who can devote all his energies towards husbanding his resources, and who can, if he be competent, save much of the cost which presses so heavily on those who bring up their children as useful and worthy members of society. Setting aside the first two inconveniences and inequalities which I have referred to, admit the strange paradox which Mr. Mill has endorsed, that there is no unfairness in taxing a temporary income at the same rate as a perpetual revenue, on the ground that the former pays only as long as it lasts, and the latter pays in perpetuity, a fallacy which I hope I have refuted *en passant*, and I may fairly claim that any dispassionate person will conclude with me, that the earner of an industrial income can make his means go only half as far as the possessor of a spontaneous income can make his.

I have dwelt at length on the Income Tax, especially in its relation to Schedule D, for two reasons. One of these is to be found in the fact that it was forced on the country in order to save the risk of Sir Robert Peel's financial reforms, was continued in the first instance for reasons such as those which Mr. Gladstone gave to the Birmingham clerk, and has been continued to the present time because financiers have found it to be the easiest process by which the middle classes, or rather a section of the middle classes, may be made to find a portion of the funds for public expenditure. It is sometimes indeed said that were the Income Tax abandoned on industrial incomes, the rich would escape. But no advocate for the repeal of the Income Tax has ever suggested that there should be no Property Tax, and it would not be difficult to point out a number of cases in which the owners of property escape taxation altogether under the operation of our law. I need hardly say that the rich save what they do not spend. In the latter case, they are very scantily assessed on expenditure, in the former they pay and should pay, like the poor, on accumulated and permanent property. In brief, the English Income Tax is an *opprobrium fisci*, it was tainted with a radical fallacy at its first imposition, and the fallacy has been most disastrous as time has passed on.

Another reason is, because Cobden avowed himself an advocate of the movement which sought to abolish all Excise and Custom duties, and to levy all the necessary revenue of the State by means of direct taxation. I shall attempt to point out the motives which induced him to identify himself with a project which has perhaps died out in theory, and which is certainly, to judge from external facts, as far from fulfilment as it was in the time when my friend lent the reputation of his name and the force of his reasoning to the scheme of the Liverpool Financial Reform Association.

After the abolition of the Corn Laws, and the adoption of a Free-trade policy in production and exchange, Cobden purposed to bend all his efforts towards the reduction of public expenditure. I can recall this from my own conversations with him after that epoch, and my memory has been refreshed by similar recollections narrated to me by my friend Mr. Bright. Till he was undeceived by the popularity of Lord Palmerston, and Lord Palmerston's measures,—for the personal popularity of Lord Palmerston, due to his geniality, to his kindliness, and to the invariable support which he gave his political friends and associates, are very different things from his political measures,—Mr. Cobden believed in the possibility of influencing those who had been emancipated by the Reform Bill of 1832, in the direction of financial economy. Mr. Bright, on the other hand, entertained the opinion, and events will prove that he was in the right, that financial economy was an improbable policy until the franchise was carried into a far lower stratum of income and expenditure. Cobden arrived at his conclusion from an interpretation of economical forces, Bright withheld his assent to the cogency of those economical forces from a rational interpretation which he made of human nature.

It has long been a received rule among economists that direct taxation is more irritating than indirect, and that therefore when the former process has been adopted by Governments, or may be forced on them by public opinion, immediate economy is the result. I do not remember that any economist except Mr. Mill has disputed this position, and Mr. Mill has merely suggested that, as the incidence of taxation becomes more clearly understood, preferences for one form or the other will tend to disappear, and the question of convenience only will be before the people. But I venture to doubt my friend Mr. Mill's hypothesis, and for two reasons, one of principle or theory, and one of fact. As I have already stated, I think the incidence of taxation is one of the most obscure questions in political economy, under all circumstances, and therefore one which is likely to be very slowly understood by any body of electors who, contributing to the public revenue, are by their admission to the franchise invited to express an opinion on matters of public policy; though I believe it is more likely to be understood by those who were enfranchised in 1867, than it was by those of 1832. For even if the general principles on which the incidence of taxation can be determined were known, the obscurity of the subject still remains, because the power of transferring taxation—within certain limits—depends largely on the nature of the tax, and even on the intelligence of the individual who forms one of the parties between the primary imposition of the tax and its ultimate incidence.

The other reason is one of fact. Nothing can alter the fundamental difference between direct and indirect taxation, that the latter is on the whole voluntary, the former is on the whole compulsory. Unless indirect taxation is as searching as it was in Holland, a man who is bent on thrift can avoid all indirect taxation; unless a man is particularly shrewd, or the circumstances of his case are peculiar, no man can evade direct taxation. Men it is true may grumble at being mulcted in what they like to do, and there have been occasions, notably in the case of the Gin Act of 1729, in which their discontent is too powerful to be resisted, but they may be irritated beyond endurance at what they are forced to do. Thus, if we can rely on the facts of a very remarkable book which I have lately read, entitled 'Contrasts,'* the limit of local taxation, extended by reckless expenditure on pedantic schemes, has nearly, if not quite, reached the crisis of endurance in London, and is exciting a discontent which may lead to very unpleasant consequences.

The reason of this is plain. No one can be taxed on what he cannot save, and the power of saving from the same income may differ totally. That men are responsible for imprudent marriages I am ready to admit, that they are responsible for the extent of their families after marriage is a dream, and not an over-decent dream, of sciolists. That society, when the laws of the distribution of wealth are not flagrantly violated, as they are in this country, and men are even moderately educated, is not imprudent in the aggregate, can be proved by an induction of overwhelming weight. But the individual who has children is performing the highest duty to society in conferring the

* Strahan and Co., 1873.

best possible culture on his children, by any expenditure however great, provided it be useful, which gives such a culture. One father may save, and bring his children up with the education of clowns and the impulses of animals. Another may spend, and educate his children to be really accomplished, and to be thereby possessed of those permanent resources which make grosser enjoyments simply loathsome. Which of the two has done his duty best by his country? But which of the two has the largest amount of resources with which to contribute to the exigencies of the State? I have the heartiest contempt for the vulgar theory which estimates mental culture by its market value, which values learning by the pay which it earns. It is an error to suppose that in a healthy society general culture earns a direct revenue. On the contrary, the more education is extended, the more learning is diffused, the less is its direct money value to its possessor. Perhaps there was no more learned, certainly there has been no more accomplished nation in the world than the inhabitants of ancient Attica were. But they were withal the most thrifty, active, and energetic. Had it not been for the fatal gift of a foreign empire, and the domestic institution of slavery, they would have civilised the world, and have rendered imperialism and barbarism impossible.

The case is rendered equally clear by examining the question, which was raised by Mr. Macculloch and Dr. Chalmers, as to the effect of loans in time of emergency, as for example of war, when such loans are raised, as they ordinarily must be, within the country on which the extraordinary expenditure is imposed. It is argued, and with perfect cogency, that the capital needed for the loan must be raised out of the existing wealth of the country, from its actual resources. Sometimes, as has happened in France over and over again, it may be obtained from hoards. In a country like our own it would be almost entirely gathered from capital, i.e. the Government as a borrower would compete against other borrowers for a portion of the capital which is seeking a profitable investment in the market. But if it comes out of wealth, why not take it as a tax, instead of taking it as a loan? Why abstract the wealth by one operation, and pay an annual interest on the quantity abstracted, instead of taking once for all the amount which the State needs? It is ridiculous to quote the metaphor of society handing down an estate, which it has been obliged to burden, and that it is fair that the charge should go with the inheritance, for what is the answer to those who say, and say truly, that they have no part in the inheritance?

The answer lies in the fact that the power of meeting such an emergency cannot be obtained by an equal tax on unequal powers of expenditure, that no such collection could be made except from savings, and that the power of saving from equal nominal incomes varies from fifty per cent. or more to zero. Now no one has been bold enough, in modern times at least,—for a graduated income tax was part of the financial system of ancient Athens,—to suggest, in direct reverse to the dictum of Ricardo, that all taxation on property should be proportionate to actual savings. But it is not difficult to see that what is true of a direct war tax and its exceedingly unequal severity, applies in degree to any direct tax, levied on equal incomes perhaps, but on very unequal powers of saving, or, as Adam Smith designates them, powers of enjoyment. A direct tax then must and will be, in opposition to the view of Mr. Mill, one to which the public, whatever be its enlightenment, nay, the more so as it is more enlightened, will be peculiarly sensitive and irritable. Cobden therefore believed that if the weight of taxation were direct, the stimulus to financial economy would be overwhelmingly strong; and it seems to me impossible to doubt, that if its incidence had been that which Cobden anticipated it would have been, his anticipation would have been realised. I have already suggested why such a result would not have ensued from the Income Tax on Peel's basis, and why the extension of such an Income Tax is wholly impracticable, because it would be hopelessly unjust and oppressive.

Another motive which Cobden had before him in advocating the transference of indirect taxation on consumption, to direct taxation on property, was his hope that by these means England would become an entrepôt for all produce, or, to use his favourite expression, a free port. That even under the present very effective bonding system inconvenience and loss ensues in the limitation put on the number of ports of entry, and that a stimulus would be given to imports by the removal of all restrictions on importation, are not I imagine disputable matters. It is also true that, as a rule, the advantage of such a free port to the home consumer is not small, for the freer the entry the lower is the price. But it is clear that such a system tends most of all to the advantage of the merchant and the dealer, that the general result of such a change would be to multiply the number of persons engaged in trade, and to cause an increase of profits in one class of the community, instead of necessarily enlarging the wealth of the whole community. Now it is quite possible for the growth of wealth in one direction to develope no gain to a large portion of the community considered as producers, and to greatly lower their condition as consumers. The importation of foreign goods as a material of manufacture is a positive advantage to all classes. The developement of a mere trade of import and transit need only increase the wealth of the few. But as far as regards raw material, the efforts of the Manchester School have made England a free port with hardly an exception. In 1841 nearly all raw materials were subject to a Customs' duty, nearly all domestic manufacture to an Excise. At present the only customs-paying and exciseable articles are those which constitute the common objects of luxury.

It is a common practice with superficial declaimers on the material progress of the English people, to comment on the growth of wealth as an evidence of general prosperity. But the mere increase of the sum total of exports and imports, a rise in the value of Schedule A, or even of D, is in itself no proof that the mass of the people are better off. That the operatives, as they are roughly called, have bettered their condition, I do not doubt. The demand for their labour has been active and progressive. But the gains of labour have been as nothing compared with the profits on capital, or, to speak more accurately, the wages of manual labour have not increased at the rate of those which have been secured by the persons who afford what economists technically call the wages of superintendence. The rise in the wages of operatives have been set down, as a rule, by the operatives themselves to the operation of trades-unions. I believe that trades-unions have had a great social value. They have taught working-men the advantages of a common purpose, and the possibility of industrial co-operation. Without them the individual workman would have been powerless, a timid slave to that concentration of force which is necessarily possessed by a great employer. They have also assisted in doing away with one hindrance to the improvement of the workingman's condition, the immobility of labour from its familiar or customary place of employment. But it is not by any means so certain that trades-unions have increased wages, though it is possible that they have expedited an increase which was inevitable.

But I have no doubt that in the case of the mass of agricultural labourers, and of many among the unskilled, overcrowded, or underpaid occupations, the economical changes in the English fiscal system, unaccompanied, as they have been unaccompanied, with other necessary internal reforms, have not been equally beneficent. The growth of the railway system, and the consequent transfer of country produce to the towns, has worked very disastrously for the peasant. I am persuaded that, with the solitary exception of house-rent—though this has also risen—the cost of living in country districts has doubled within the last thirty years, and that some articles of food once within the reach of all are now practically unattainable by country people. It is not so much that prices have intrinsically risen, as it is that the country is swept of its produce for the towns. Nor have the towns benefited as much as might have been anticipated. The destruction of the dwellings of the operative classes by the construction of metropolitan railways, and the erection of warehouses in districts once densely occupied by the poor, has been followed by a prodigious rise in the rental of such accommodation as the London and other town poor obtain. House-rent now consumes, in many parts of the metropolis at least, one third the weekly wages of the occupier. Now it is not difficult to see under these and similar circumstances how scantily general prosperity affects a great section of the working classes; how very possibly they are, relatively speaking, worse off than they were thirty years ago. When statisticians make their estimate of the cost of imperial and local taxation *per capita*, and invite us to consider how much more lightly the nation is burdened now than it was a few years ago, they are not at the pains to point out the fact, that the weight of taxation, or the charge on outgoings—for, economically considered, rent is a tax—may be increasingly severe on one class of the community, and increasingly light on another class.

In 1864 the expenditure of this country reached nearly sixty millions, and in his last public speech[*] Cobden commented on the fact in the following

[*] Speeches, vol. ii. p. 370.

manner: 'I do not want any more of this delusion about the reduction or diminution of particular taxes. I want to look at the whole amount of revenue the Government is getting from us. For instance, here is a very customary piece of deception: we are told how many Customs and Excise duties have been abolished, and how many have been reduced, within the last twenty years. Yes; but I look at the whole amount now paid, and I find that, this year, it will be about forty millions sterling more than we ever used to pay before these reductions began. Now I say the proper way to look at that is to see how the whole amount of the income from the tax-payer is reduced. . . . I am sure he (Mr. Gladstone) will perceive that he has nearly finished his career of manipulating the sources of our taxation. He has removed every protective duty, he has reduced most of the other duties. And though I am by no means prepared to say that other Chancellors of the Exchequer may not do a great deal more in giving us direct instead of indirect taxation, yet as regards the question of protection, Mr. Gladstone has finished his work; and therefore any further services he must render us must be in the reduction of expenditure—in taxing us less.'

Mr. Cobden advocated direct taxation as the foundation of our fiscal system, partly for reasons of policy, partly for reasons of justice. The question of justice is easily settled. There are kinds of property equally protected with other kinds of property, and with industrial income. Nay, they are more fully protected by the machinery of Government, and the charges of it, than industrial income ever is; for to a great extent individuals protect themselves. But such kinds of property either do not contribute at all, or contribute very inadequately, to the public treasury. We admit the policy of charging for the use of luxuries, and we tax the luxuries of the people in the duties and excise levied on alcoholic liquors and tobacco, to the amount of twenty-three millions annually. But we levy hardly any taxes whatever on the luxuries of the rich. We put a few, the produce of which is trifling, on certain articles of voluntary use, as male servants, carriages, horses, and the like, though even here taxes are necessarily imposed on similar objects which are used for industrial processes. But by the fact that the use of these objects is purely voluntary in the case of the rich, it is impossible to levy a tax on the use without checking the revenue derivable from them.

The fairer policy is to levy a tax on the possession of property. An enormous quantity of such property escapes taxation altogether, though it is impossible to allege any plea of justice for the evasion. Nor can it be said that such property deteriorates. On the contrary, the most important kinds of it increase steadily and greatly in value. Articles of taste or art, the number of which is limited, rise rapidly in price. The pictures at Petworth are worth a fortune. The Spencer library, consisting as it does of rare early English printed books, would realise a vast sum under the hammer. It is not easy to see why such kinds of property should escape the tax as long as they are transmitted from father to son, or by some other fixed line of descent, while others which are sold under the will of a deceased owner are visited with legacy and probate duty. It is not easy to see why the annual work of head or hand should be visited with an Income Tax, while the growing value of a picture-collector's treasures should be sold without any such visitation at all if they are dispersed during his lifetime, while if they are sold at his death, they are merely liable to the probate and succession duty which attaches to the demise of all personal estate. Furthermore, not only is such personal estate, although it is emphatically superfluous in the fiscal sense of the word, exceptionally relieved, but portions of real estate are valued at nominal sums, even when they are rendered liable to the ordinary rates which are payable from all rateable realty, and to the scanty and disappointing tax known as a succession duty. We are told that taxes on legacies, either of realty or personalty, must be low, in order to avoid *donationes inter vivos*. But I should think that a financier knew very little of his business, if he could not devise a means by which such conveyances, fraudulent in principle as they must be, could be checked.

It is mainly due to the fact that the law, which is carried by the influence of such persons as are the principal owners of this kind of untaxed estate, avoids with such scrupulous care the visitation of the property which, upon all principles of equity, should be rendered liable to fiscal charges, that the demand of Mr. Mill, to the effect that a portion of the unearned increase from land should be appropriated by the State, derives its force. It is an inevitable consequence, when a particular interest claims for itself and secures for itself an unrighteous exemption from taxation, that counter claims are made, which such favoured interests attempt to brand with the name of confiscation. Every tax is a confiscation; the only question is, what kind of confiscation is, under the circumstances, most satisfactory to justice, moral or economical. Put the case fairly. There is a kind of property, which being under the protection of society, grows in intrinsic value, without owing that value in any sense whatever to the personal superintendence or labour of its owner. Its use, whether it be enjoyment or profit, is wholly non-industrial. No possible loss would be inflicted on society were its whole periodical increment appropriated by the State. It might not be wise to visit it with such an appropriation, because it is highly inexpedient to make sudden and radical innovations in the conduct of society, but there is no economical objection to such a procedure. But this is to be also remembered. Whenever public attention is drawn to fiscal questions, and the mass of the people is enlightened as to the true incidence of taxation, as to the many and considerable interests which are very lightly affected by the 'confiscations' of the budget, and as to the fact that enormous fortunes are acquired by the indirect action of population and labour, while labour and population themselves have to be content with a meagre increase, definite opinion, of a very formidable character to protected or favoured interests, is apt to grow with great rapidity and vigour. It is also to be noted, that a limited franchise acquiesces in compromises, a popular franchise sooner or later acquires principles, which speedily ripen into action. At present much property is untaxed or lightly taxed. Hereafter there may arise a clamour that such property as has hitherto escaped should contribute exceptionally to public burdens; that rates paid by occupiers who cause the value, should be paid by landowners who receive the value; that prodigiously enhanced values created by popular demand shall be subject to charges on behalf of those who make the demand; that articles of luxury and display, the use of which and the expenditure on which make the competition for the means of life, now felt so severely by the industrial classes, far more searching than before, shall contribute, as the fortunes of the wealthy Athenian citizens of old did, to the extraordinary charges of the State, to the protection of society, and to objects of general public interest. It may seem a sinister prediction, but I feel persuaded that nothing but the acquiescence, at no distant date, in a genuine property tax, will silence the demand for such fiscal claims as those with which Mr. Mill has identified himself in the programme of the Land Tenure Reform League. *Imitati castora*, the propertied classes may find it expedient to come to terms in good time. Confiscation is an ugly word, but it may be retaliated, for there is no confiscation more gross and more irritating, when it is once understood, than that which leaves untaxed the luxury of the rich, and visits the earnings of the poor with crushing exactions. At the present time, as we are told, the burden of local taxation in large towns which is borne by the working classes has nearly become intolerable, while the rents of a Grosvenor, a Russell, and a Bentinck, no matter how they were originally obtained, are yearly swollen and are regularly untaxed.

Another reason is that of policy. I agree with the principle that underlies Sir W. Lawson's bill. It is, whatever may be the process adopted to give effect to the principle, that a peculiar kind of trade, confessedly open to great abuse, and which is the direct cause of almost all the pauperism and the crime, and of not a little of the lunacy, which disgrace our modern civilisation, should be put under strict control, and that this control should be directly committed to those who suffer from its effects, the ratepayers. That the right of licensing public-houses or of refusing a licence altogether should be left in the hands of those who are indirectly interested in the worst mischiefs of the traffic, seems to me an anomaly, for which it is difficult to find words of reprobation sufficiently strong. Nor can I see what argument can be alleged in favour of the vested rights of such places, unless we are to admit, as a later developement of the principle of compensation, that we are to buy social reforms, as our forefathers did their liberties, from those who, as we aver, had no right to inflict the evil or impose the tyranny. But I have little hope that the moral improvement of the British nation will gain much by coercive measures. The utmost I imagine which restraint will do, will be to promote decency. If the publican were asked to give a candid answer, he would not, I imagine, say that his interests have been very seriously compromised by Mr. Bruce's bill of last session. On the other hand, there is overwhelming evidence that public decency is materially assisted by the control of the new Licensing Act.

The reason is not far to seek. Communities in which tangible and improvable property, such as land is, is distributed, are generally thrifty and sober. Where the masses are debarred by artificial restrictions from its possession, there they are apt to be unthrifty and drunken. The Englishman who shares the passion for visible and improvable property which is manifest in most civilised societies is to a great extent debarred from its possession,—'divorced from the soil,' as Cobden said. The hindrances to the sale of such land as goes into the market (a mere fraction of what should annually go, if encumbered estates were freely disposed of) are prodigious. 'The cost,' says Mr. Macdonnell, a barrister, and the author of a singularly suggestive essay on the land question, 'of transferring land, particularly when all is not held on the same title, is enormous. If the estate is small, the costs may equal the purchase money; and in order to spare themselves the cost of a sixty years' search, persons are often content'—the author might have said constrained—'to take a twenty-five or thirty years' title.'* The author quotes an instance from a work of Mr. Hughes, in which it is stated that in the case of an estate which was sold in two hundred lots, the vendor spent £2000 in furnishing the purchasers with attested copies of the title-deeds. Evidence on this subject is cumulative.

'You may,' said Cobden in February 1846,† when

* 'The Land Question' (Macmillan), p. 27.
† Speeches, vol. i. p. 382.

the downfall of the Corn Laws was foreshadowed, and he was arguing against the dread of the landowners that their estates would become valueless, 'affect the value of silks; you may affect the value of cottons or woollens: transitory changes of fashion may do that—changes of taste; but there is a taste for land inherent in human kind, and especially it is the desire of Englishmen to possess land; and therefore while you have a monopoly of that article which our very instincts lead us to desire to possess, if you see any process going on by which our commerce and our numbers are increased, it is impossible to suppose that it can have the effect of diminishing the value of the article which is in your hands.'

There is abundant information on the character of such a peasantry as has a permanent interest in the soil which it cultivates. In France, in the Palatinate, in Norway, in Bavaria, in Belgium, in a score more instances, the prudence, the forethought, the economy, the sobriety of such peasantries have been commented on *ad satietatem*. It may be that some of these peasants are ignorant and superstitious, but they do not owe these vices to the nature of the occupation, but to the Governments under which they have lived, and to the priesthoods which have been entrusted with the function of deliberately enthralling them. The uniform social virtues with which they are credited are derived from their calling, and will be generally reproduced whenever similar opportunities are accorded.

Unless I am wholly mistaken in the tendencies of the time in which we live and the opinions which are gradually permeating the community, it is impossible that the English land system can last much longer. The exigencies of modern society require that the land of the country should be properly cultivated. It cannot be when it is in the nominal possession of bankrupt landowners, when the tenant is a mere occupier at will, perpetually exposed to the caprice or the rapine of his landlord,—Mr. Macdonnell has given abundant illustrations of both, — and when several important kinds of produce are, under these circumstances, seriously curtailed in quantity. Unless they are stupid beyond conception, English tenant farmers will clamour for security with such energy, that before long they will, unless they be satisfied, relegate the English landowners into the ostracism under which the Scotch landlord finds himself placed. Unless they speedily face the facts which lie inside the agricultural unions, they will discover ere long that the problem of the relations of labour and capital will be even more insoluble in their case than it has been in the case of the operatives, for in agriculture an increased cost of labour cannot be easily met by an increased price. Seven years ago, at the conclusion of my researches into the history of Agriculture and Prices during the thirteenth and fourteenth centuries, I ventured on saying that 'no Englishman who has the courage to forecast the destinies of his country can doubt that its greatest danger lies in the present alienation of its people from the soil, and in the future exodus of a disinherited peasantry:'* and the prediction has been fulfilled before my anticipations.

* Agriculture and Prices, vol. i. p. 694.

I cannot believe that a fiscal system which depends largely on the improvidence and the brutality of the people can have any permanent vitality. Your Chancellors of the Exchequer are satisfied with the present, and perhaps, under our method of party government, need not be expected to take a higher view.

'Nec cultura placet longior annos.'

But although the receipts of the Exchequer are satisfactory, and the cynics of the Press may congratulate the country with the fact of having drunk itself out of the Alabama difficulty (and they might have added, drunk itself into its extravagant expenditure), a calmer review of the source from which these funds are derived is not reassuring. To a nation which squanders its strength in such enjoyments there are two, and only two alternatives—reform or ruin. At the present time the Press, with an affectation of shame at the character and origin of the revenue, felicitates the country on its prosperity, severely lectures the working classes on their habits, and either scornfully ignores, or writes cheap sophistry, on the remedies which have been prepared for the social evils about us, remedies which every other civilised country has agreed on accepting. We do well to keep out of foreign complications, for our fiscal system would stand no strain, the only escape from an emergency being to use that engine of extortion, the Income Tax, the nature of which the public is gradually beginning to see. But the internal and inherent weakness of our fiscal system needs, if it ever can get it, some courage in principle, and more in practice, unless we are to face discontent and degradation in their most formidable shape. It has been well said by Mr. Macdonnell, 'Political discontent is oftentimes another name for the possession of an unsatisfied and lofty ideal of political excellence.'* It is the business of statesmen to obviate discontent by just and timely reform.

* The Land Question, p. 43.

CHAPTER VII.

INDIA AND THE COLONIES.

THIRTY years ago, the trade between England and the East had been finally thrown open to the public, by the abolition of the East India Company's monopoly of traffic with China. Whatever defence might have been alleged for the policy which secured the trade of India to the Company,—and the ordinary apology was that it had incurred the cost of military occupation and government,—no such defence could be alleged for its monopoly with China. The trade, it is true, was of little profit to the Company, for experience had abundantly proved the truth of Adam Smith's reasoning, when he showed that just as the Company succeeded as traders, they failed as rulers, and *vice versâ*. But it was an enormous loss to the British public, as was shown in the rapid decline of prices for China produce when the trade was made free. The abolition of the China monopoly was the extinction of the East India Company as a trading society, for its transactions in opium and indigo were fiscal arrangements rather than trade privileges.

The abolition of the Company's trade involved at some period, more or less remote, the extinction of the Company's political existence. It was clear that the government of a vast dependency, the retention of which involved expenditure, or at least watchfulness, on the part of the British nation, could not be administered by a Committee of Stockholders in Leadenhall-street, but must be brought within direct relations to Parliament. It is true that either because it acted on a sense of its own responsibility in the matter, or because it was naturally jealous of such an *imperium in imperio* as the Indian dependency was, the Houses of Parliament had gradually curtailed and controlled the authority of the East India Directors. Lord Dalhousie was a very different personage from Warren Hastings, both as regards the power which he exercised, and the parties to whom he was made responsible. But even this qualified power must necessarily have come to an end, and it came to an end in 1858. The character of what was called the double government was strikingly illustrated by the Burmese war, which Cobden made the subject of a very important pamphlet, published in 1853, under the title, 'How Wars are got up in India.'* On this occasion—the circumstance commented on happened in 1852—Commodore Lambert, commanding the Queen's ships off the coast of Burmah, took offence at the conduct of the Governor of Rangoon, stormed the fortifications of that town, and ultimately brought about the annexation of a portion of Burmah to the Indian empire.

During the greater part of Cobden's public life, the

* Political Writings, vol. ii. p. 29 sqq.

real question before the British public was not whether the possession of India was or was not a benefit to the British nation, but what was the manner in which a trade, presumed to be exceedingly advantageous, should be carried on for the benefit of the English mercantile classes. The trade monopoly of the Company was extinguished in order to open the peninsula to British traders, and the destruction of the monopoly was an unquestionable benefit, as the destruction of all monopolies is sure to be. But the possession of the Indian empire was justified on the ground of trade. 'We,' said Cobden in 1864,* 'are governing India. The world never saw such a risk as we run with 130 or 140 millions of people near the antipodes, ruling them for the sake of their custom, and nothing else. I defy you to show that the nation has any interest whatever in that country, except by the commerce we carry on there. I say that is a perilous adventure, quite unconnected with free trade, wholly out of joint with the recent tendency of things, which is in favour of nationality and not of domination.'

It is a principle, which Cobden was very fond of illustrating by facts, that the profits of no trade ever were, or ever could be, equal to the charge of maintaining such a trade by force of arms. It is commonly said that the military stations possessed by this country in every part of the world are part, and a necessary part, of the machinery for carrying on such a trade as we possess, and that we should imperil our supremacy in mercantile energy and success if we abandoned such places as we occupy now, or failed, when urged to do

* Speeches, vol. ii. p. 357.

so, to occupy more in advantageous places. Now I can well believe that certain places do promote or sustain certain kinds of trade. I have little or no doubt that a considerable quantity of goods has been smuggled into Spain by means of the possession of Gibraltar. Whether it is creditable to us to have taken a part of Spain from the Spanish people, under circumstances little honourable to our political reputation, to have retained it and so laid a standing affront on the honour of a peculiarly proud and sensitive nation, to have justified its retention on the loftiest grounds of political necessity, and to discover that its chief value consists in its affording a means for committing offences against the municipal laws of a community, analogous laws to which we maintain among ourselves by inflicting very severe penalties on those who infringe them, is a question which may be left for political casuists to debate. There can be no doubt as to how honest people would answer it. But even if this trade be profitable, it is certain that it does not cover the cost of the station, and that even if it did cover the cost, the gain of the transaction goes into one set of pockets, and the charges come out of another set. The profit of all the trade which is carried on in the Mediterranean is far less than the cost of the stations and fleet which are maintained there. But even if the profits far exceeded the cost, the question still remains, is the cost necessary for the trade? The answer is obvious. The American trade with the Mediterranean countries was, before America ruined herself by protection, only second to our own, and this trade was carried on without the assistance of any armed force whatever.

Q

It is stated that India bears the charges of her own government. In a sense this is true, and it has frequently been observed that, as was the case with the Burmese, and later of the Abyssinian, war, the inhabitants of India were saddled with the costs of wars in which they had not the remotest possible interests. But it is unreasonable to believe that the possession of so vast a dependency as India, with the anxieties and precautions which such a possession entails, should be without cost to the British public. The Indian question crops up in a hundred ways. Nearly twenty years ago, we undertook a war with Russia, on behalf of Turkey, and constant reference was made during the time that the war was undertaken in order to effect the consolidation of the Indian Empire. At the present time the march of the Russians on Khiva, and their possible approximation to the north-western frontier of India, is made the subject of very energetic alarms, and equally energetic diplomacy. The bigness of the British army is closely connected with the occupation of India, and the troops are enlisted, drilled, and maintained, as much with an eye to their future employment in India, as to their utility as an arm for home defence. It is true that the very moment they set foot on a vessel which is to carry them to the great dependency they become a charge on its revenues. But I have yet to learn that the previous collection and training of these troops, set down, as far as the rank and file are concerned, at a minimum cost of £100 per head, is borne by the Indian revenues. And similarly, I am strongly of opinion that no small portion of the charges incurred for the navy is due to the contingency of protecting India from invasion or revolt.

Thirty, twenty, ten years ago, those who discussed the economical value of the Indian and Colonial empire, its cost to the British taxpayer, its profit to the British merchant, its advantage to the British consumer, and argued negatively as to its utility from these several points of view, were met by the fulminations of the *Times*, and by the familiar sophistries of that invaluable index of current opinion. In January, 1862, Mr. Goldwin Smith wrote in the *Daily News*:—

'In India we have not only taken up a position from which it is difficult to recede, but assumed responsibilities which we are bound, if we can, to discharge. Whether the dominion of that country, as distinguished from the enjoyment of its trade, for the sake of which our dominion was originally required, adds to our real strength or wealth, seems at least open to doubt. It is indeed something, it is much, to have displayed on that great theatre the qualities of an Imperial race. But when we come to actual advantages, a perennial supply of old Indians spending Indian pensions at Bath or Cheltenham seems the main item on the side of profit; while on the side of loss, we must place a heavy annual expenditure of our best blood, wasted in Indian warfare or by Indian disease, the paralysing sense of our weak point, and the loss of dignity and force thence resulting to our diplomacy in Europe, and not only the Sikh and Afghan, but, in a great measure, the Russian war.

'The crucial question is, whether the English can convert India from a dependency into a colony, by settling in it, taking the place of the Mahometans, its last conquerors, and permanently forming the governing and civilising class. If the climate or any other cause forbids this, the days of our dominion are numbered. No country, much less a poor country as India on an average is, can afford permanently to pay exile price for its establishments. The taxation required to give all the servants of the State double pay and pensions would surely produce revolts; and to be always suppressing revolts in blood would be a prospect which we should hardly desire to encounter. The horrors of the Sepoy mutiny cancelled all the work of our Indian missionaries ten times over.'

This passage was attacked a few days afterwards in the choicest manner of Printing House Square. The statements which the letter contained were spoken of as 'fallacies, which, like comets of short period, give a feeble glare for a week or two,' 'a psychological law' is discovered, 'which causes a certain number of men to fancy themselves capable of great political discoveries,' enumerates among other discoveries the 'alleged inutility of the colonies,' speaks of 'thinkers' and 'gifted persons' as desirous of 'destroying the British Empire,' states that 'Mr. Goldwin Smith advocates the dismemberment of Queen Victoria's dominions as speedily as possible,' warns foreigners that in this country at least 'Professors of History do not count for statesmen,' informs the world, as though it were the administration itself, that 'we declare at once, for the benefit of Americans and Spaniards, Russians and Ionians, Sikhs and Sepoys, that England has no thought of abandoning her transmarine possessions,' and concludes by informing the French Canadians that Mr. Goldwin Smith's effusion 'no way represents the opinions of one class of Englishmen, but only the fancies of one morbid mind.'

It is probable, for the Editor of the *Times* knows his business as well as any other dealer in fashionable articles does, that the views expressed in the article from which I have quoted express with great accuracy what was the general current of middle-class opinion in London, eleven years ago, on the Indian and Colonial question, and on the qualifications of a 'thinker' or 'gifted person' for debating questions of statesmanship, and that it supplied the average man of business in London, the counting-house statesman or politician, with exactly the kind of language in which to express his thoughts at his club in the evening. It is written in better taste than the *Times* was, twenty years before, when it supplied its readers with the metaphor of 'the dying rattlesnake.' But its cleverness is as unscrupulous, as sophistical, as mendacious, as impudent, as can well be conceived. It charges Mr. Goldwin Smith with opinions which he never maintained, and with purposes which he disavowed. The writer and the Editor had of course only one object, that of giving shape and words to current opinion, and both were equally careless about disavowing hereafter the views which they had advocated.

The progress of all political ideas in England has been due to these thinkers. We owe the abandonment of our ancient commercial policy to one thinker, Adam Smith; and with the abandonment of that policy our foremost place in commerce and manufactures. We owe our reforms in the law to another thinker, who was the object of perpetual ridicule during his life,

Jeremy Bentham. For good or ill, the political tendencies of civilised Europe have been leavened throughout by the speculations of another thinker, John Stuart Mill. We owe the acceptance of the principle of toleration in religion, the abandonment of a policy of disabilities against those who would not, or could not, accept a number of speculative opinions on religious topics in connexion with the State, to a number of thinkers who have protested continuously against the theory that the State can enforce particular habits of thought. There is no person who has contributed more to the present stage of public opinion in respect of India and the Colonies, and the radical change which has taken place in the administration of both, than the 'thinker,' 'gifted person,' and 'morbid mind' who was attacked eleven years ago by the Philistines of the *Times*. It is true that these personages have seldom had any direct influence over the policy which they have commended. But they have taught public opinion; and gradually the shopkeepers and country squires, who make up nine-tenths of the British Parliament, and who generally take their colour from their constituencies, have turned opinion into law and policy.

The theory of the relations of this country to India has totally changed within the last ten years. The old defence of the Indian occupation was the advantages of its commerce and the prestige of empire. The public has been disabused of both the absurdities involved in these delusions. England has no advantages in the commerce of India which is not to be shared by any country whatever which chooses to embark in trade. It does not get the profit of that commerce by the fact of its governing India, but by the fact that its merchants are enterprising and its manufacturers know their business. Unless we enacted a Navigation Law in India, and levied different duties in favour of British manufactures, our mercantile superiority in India would not last a day beyond the decline of commercial activity and manufacturing skill. We are governing India with a view to enabling all nations on the earth to use the markets of the country at their pleasure; and as far as the process of government involves indirect outlay on the part of the British taxpayer, we are governing it for the benefit of the whole world at our proper cost. To say that the success of our commerce with India is due to our possessing that peninsula, is as absurd as it would be to say that the modern improvements in navigation are caused by trade winds and ocean currents. The schedule of exports and imports to British India is due to a set of causes which are quite independent of the hands by which the government has been administered. It is possible that the amount would have been as great and the profits as lucrative if the English race had never acquired a permanent footing in the country, though I am willing to admit that it might have been far less if any other country—Holland, Portugal, or France—had conquered it. The value of Indian commerce to this country arises solely from our having established the principle of free trade in India; in other words, from our having deliberately denied our trade any benefit which might have been supposed to be derivable from our political supremacy.

The prestige of the Indian Empire has by this time been fairly discounted. My friend Mr. Goldwin Smith stated it accurately in the passage quoted above. The conquest and occupation of India is a striking example of British energy and vigour. The Seven Years' War, which secured the Indian Empire, was one of remarkable enterprise, and was characterised by remarkable results. Whether the prize was worth, and is worth, the cost of acquisition and government is open to question; but there can be no doubt as to the intrinsic capacity of a race which could undertake and execute such an enterprise, and which could continue the task which it took on itself, especially with such pure and disinterested aims as now characterise the rule of India. If a community undertakes remote and costly undertakings, and having won its immediate object sets to work, as though it possessed a plethora of vigour and activity, to continue the work which is rendered necessary for the success of the undertaking, it gives startling evidence of latent resources. It is very probable that under such circumstances any country might be very cautious in attacking another which can afford to devote so large an amount of strength to a distant object and can bear without difficulty the drain which such a course of action necessitates. From this point of view the Indian Empire adds to the prestige of Great Britain, and if evidence of military capacity is valuable, can be pointed to as a legitimate ground for inferring the strength of this country.

But prestige is an affair not only of capacity, but of actual power at any given moment for any sudden emergency. Hence it cannot be doubted that to scatter the military resources of a country over a host of distant dependencies is a source of weakness and not of strength, besides being formidable on the ground of expense. In modern warfare, it appears that the concentration of force is the chief cause of success, not its dispersion. Hence it is not too much, I think, to say, that no continental country—such as France or Germany or Spain—could have maintained a permanent empire over distant races by annually drafting off large bodies of their native soldiers in order to secure the military possession of the country. We can contrive to do so, because we have the enormous advantage which is given us by the barrier of the sea, and which enables us to dispense with an army *en masse*, and even of a portion of our small professional army. But to say that there is any military prestige (by which I presume is meant any deterrent effect on a possible enemy) in keeping a hundred thousand British soldiers in India is an absurdity which needs only to be stated in order to be exposed. There is yet another fact in connexion with this question. The public defence of the United Kingdom is maintained by voluntary enlistment, by a militia—to which as yet the ballot has not been applied—and by the subsidiary force of volunteers. The last of these, by no means popular with the regular forces, because it hints by its existence at a possible reduction of the professional army, appears to be stationary. If the voluntary enlistment of the militia men should fail to supply the quotas demanded at the War Office, the military authorities can put the conscription into force. But the relations of labour and capital, especially in the agricultural districts, are becoming more and more unsatisfactory as time goes on. It is very improbable that numerous recruits will be forthcoming hereafter. Labour is moveable, is migrating from under-paid to well-paid districts, is discovering better conditions of life in the United States and Canada. The pleasures of the Scotch deerstalkers and the calamities of Ireland have rendered Scotland and Ireland almost barren to the recruiting sergeant and the crimps. Mr. Cardwell's scheme of depôts is an experiment, the success of which is likely to be dubious, but the purpose of which is to gather more of what is becoming scanty. Now in such a dearth of the raw material for a professional army, the competition of enlistment for India is a severe strain upon the resources available for enlistment at home, and is an indirect tax upon the British public, for it cannot be doubted that the cost of the rank and file will be soon enhanced.

It would carry me beyond the limits of the subject which I have before me to attempt an exposition of the process by which public opinion in this country has undergone such a change as it assuredly has undergone on the Indian question. It has been changed too concurrently with the great growth of commerce with India, with the development of Indian resources, and with the success of Indian finance. Primarily Indian commerce owes its rapid start to the circumstances of the American civil war. Not only was the native growth of Indian cotton, previously all but valueless, stimulated by the extraordinary demand for this material,* but all other textile materials, notably jute, were subjected to a sudden and urgent demand. The progress of the

---

* Between 1860 and 1864 the rise in the price of Surat was from £37 per ton to £167, more than 450 per cent.

country was greatly assisted by Government works, which have really been the chief cause of the permanent improvement of India. There is indeed no reason why, if the natural resources of the country are properly developed, India should not become as wealthy as any other country which possesses great natural advantages, and has found out the means by which those advantages may be brought to market.

Angrily as it was opposed at first, and severely as it was criticised afterwards, I am disposed to believe that the internal government of India has derived great advantages from the change which threw open the Civil Service of India to public competition. I dare say that the old Service, taught in no very effective way at Haileybury, had some very solid administrative traditions. But such traditions may be as often obstructive as they are convenient. It is possible that some of the appointees to Indian office may have been uncouth and rough-mannered, and lacking in the polish which the old training was said, though not without reclamation, to have afforded. But there is generally something in a man who owes his advancement to fair work, and there is hope of diligence and originality when he is freed from the habits of a clique. At any rate it is certain that the general administration of India has improved under the change, and that much moral good is likely to ensue from the admission of the natives to the government of their own country.

The remarkable movement in the Lower Provinces, which appears to have coupled a new religious system with an effort after social reform, is, I make no doubt, destined hereafter to facilitate that habit of self-government which a more enlightened theory of the Indian question desires. Centuries of oppression have made the Hindoo, we are told, the most pliant and the most obstinate of races. He has submitted without a murmur to a change of masters, and has obeyed with alacrity the most harsh and rigorous despotism, having of course developed during the process the faculties of cunning and deceit to perfection. But he has clung with the utmost tenacity to the traditions of his ancestry, to the distinctions of caste, to grotesque ceremonies, to an iron and relentless routine, from which escape was impossible, because ceremonial defilement was social degradation. It is true that at times an internal reform has been attempted upon Brahminism. It appears that the mission of Buddha had for its central tenet the repudiation of caste, and after a struggle, carried on no doubt with the ordinary ferocity which characterises theological quarrels, that Buddhism was vanquished in its own home. The researches of Mr. Hunter have led him to the conclusion that the worship of Jugganath in Orissa has had a similar origin, the desire to deliver the outcasts and degraded members of Indian society from the thraldom of the Brahminical rule, though here the means employed was not a speculative creed, but an enthusiasm. The promoters of the new movement, called Brahmo-Somaj, have the advantage of some sympathy on the part of the rulers of India, and the assistance of those leaders of European thought, whose tenets, to a far greater extent than is imagined in St. Stephen's and the Offices, have leavened the wealthier and more enlightened classes of India.

I am certain that, at the present time, public opinion

looks on India as a possession which the English nation may occupy for a long time, but which cannot be held perpetually by a foreign administration, especially as that administration cannot take part in the soil. We are in it, but not of it, and we must reverse the whole precedents of history if, being such a Government, we are able, perhaps I may say we remain willing, to continue the functions of its administration. In the meantime, it is our interest and our duty to aid the natives of the country in acquiring the faculties necessary for the administration of their own affairs. We must carry out those projects of internal communication by which peoples are made to understand the common interests and reciprocal benefits of mutual trade. We must expedite all means by which civilisation may be spread through the agency of primary schools and higher culture. We must study the circumstances under which a sound system of finance can be established in the country. We must familiarise the people with a rational code of law, and with its just administration. We must make the people learn that an army should be a police, whose operations are preventive rather than military, and which is intended to protect property. We must permit, and even encourage, the habit of debate on questions of public policy; for while obedience to law and order is the duty of all subjects, the criticism of Government and its acts is the right of all free persons. It is hardly necessary to say that it is an obligation on Government to repress with the utmost severity any harsh or insolent conduct towards the natives on the part of European officials. It is a common mistake with coarse natures to believe that brutality and haughtiness are marks of high spirit, that scrupulous courtesy and habitual justice will be mistaken for timidity. It may not be easy to get rid of hereditary distrust, but it is certain that the distrust is deepened when rulers take advantage of their position to affront their subjects.

The real danger to the future of India lies in the risk that the British nation, when it comes to understand the task which lies before it in the government and developement of its greatest dependency, may grow weary of the labour. Hitherto India has not been an unattractive field for enterprising men among the middle classes,—those classes which have wielded power in England between 1832 and 1868,—for the professional and trading elements in English society. It is not equally clear, when the household voters become alive, as they may become alive, to the sacrifices which the retention of India demand from the British public, that they will acquiesce in a system which drains money and labour from this country, and receives nothing in return but a few places for civil servants and an administrative career for a few high officials. At the present time, the interest taken by Parliament in Indian affairs is exceedingly languid. The financial statement of the Indian Secretary will hardly command a house, however brisk and epigrammatic is the speech in which the facts are announced; for under the present constitution of the House of Commons, and in its ordinary temper, no attention is given to any case in which some interest is not threatened, or in which no interest beyond that of the public good can be served. It is in this way that the English Parliament has deteriorated so much of late years,—has got the credit of being a theatre for men who, having gained mercantile success, aim at social promotion. It may be an excellent thing to crowd the Legislature with ambitious men of business, aspiring lawyers, and discontented officers. But it will be a serious thing if the greatest dependency of this country, now assimilating itself to European habits of thought, comes to the conclusion that its rulers will not spare an hour to its most urgent affairs. And, conversely, if the Legislature is apathetic, and the people get to think that the possession of India is a dead loss as well as a dead weight on the resources of the country, there is some risk lest members of Parliament may be educated up to a dislike in place of apathy.

The politicians of the Manchester school had a great and material interest in Indian affairs, because they were fully alive to the danger—as was afterwards abundantly verified—of depending on the Northern States of the American Union for the chief supply of cotton consumed in the Lancashire mills. The crisis which they dreaded came at last, and though it entailed much suffering on the cotton districts, it forced the Indian Office and the Indian Administration to do something for the means by which the transit of native produce could be effected. Before it came, they attempted by all the means in their power to induce the Governments of the day to assist them in averting a great national calamity from a class of persons who had done so much to develope the mercantile and manufacturing greatness of England. It is possible that, had steps been taken, much of the loss and distress of the cotton famine would have been averted. Believing that the supply of cotton under a system of slavery must always be insecure, Mr. Bright got a committee appointed on the subject of the cotton supply, and he says that 'but for the folly of a foolish minister, the House would have appointed a special commission to India'* for the purpose.

I cannot, in quitting the subject of India, do better than refer my readers to the statements contained in the collection of my friend Mr. Bright's speeches which I made five years ago. Mr. Bright devoted great pains to the subject, collected all the information which came in his way, studied the facts which were to be found in Government papers and the publications of authors, and lost no opportunity of inculcating his views on the present and future government of India. These views he shared with Cobden, and there can be no doubt that together they did much to bring about a healthy public opinion on the subject, for the reforms which Mr. Bright indicated referred as much to the general administration of the country, as they did to the supply of an all-important raw material for a special Lancashire industry.

If the progress towards a rational interpretation of our relations to India and the military outposts occupied by this country is so obvious; if the issue of the Abyssinian war, scandalous and contemptible as were the causes of that expedition, marks the close of the policy of annexation which has been pursued by this country for two centuries; if there is reason to believe that we have nearly seen the last of such occurrences as the Lorcha case, the burning of Kagosima, and the inchoate Mexican expedition; if public morality has made such progress that English administrations will pause before they recall the practice of the Palmerstonian epoch, still more marked is the alteration in public opinion on the colonial question proper.

* Bright's Speeches, vol. i. p. 273.

THE COLONIAL SYSTEM.

The colonial system, as Adam Smith saw, was part of the mercantile theory; of that theory which was gradually exploded between the period in which cash payments were resumed and that in which the principles of free trade were admitted to be the policy of this country. The first breach in the mercantile theory was the abolition of all restrictions upon the exportation of the precious metals, the last was the abolition of all Customs' duties which varied with the origin of the commodity. For a long time the English people had to pay a fancy price for sugar and coffee, ostensibly, and it is to be feared hypocritically, in order to exclude the produce of slavery from the market, really in order to secure protection to the planters in the West India Islands. Similarly, the British public freed inferior Canadian timber, in order that the transatlantic colony might have a monopoly in the home market. These duties were the last fragments of a reciprocity system, under which colonial produce possessed advantages in the home country, and the colonies were understood, on the other hand, to exclude all manufactured goods of other than British origin from their ports. Translated into economical language, the mother country and the colonies were at the pains to adopt a policy which was either superfluous or mischievous; the former, if each of the producing countries supplied such goods as could compete with other products in point of price and quality, the latter if English manufactures or colonial raw material were inferior in quality or higher in price than those of foreign origin. The fact was that the English manufacturer enjoyed no actual advantage, for the growth of English manufacturing industry was

R

such that English products could undersell those of most other nations; but the colonist did enjoy an advantage, as a very considerable and a very lucrative monopoly was accorded him by the protective operation of the English tariff. It was a natural, but an inconvenient result of the old reciprocal system, that the colonist imagined it was advantageous to England, and thereupon, when it was abandoned, the greater British colonies fell into the trick of 'protecting native industry' by putting heavy import duties on British manufactures.

The questions which were raised eleven years ago by Mr. Goldwin Smith, and which, as I have stated above, were replied to by the invective of the *Times*, the indignation of colonial politicians, and the criticisms of such English advocates of so-called colonial interests as Lord Bury, were exceedingly simple. They were in brief as follows. When the privileges of self-government are accorded to a colony, when it is allowed its own discretion in making laws, subject to the veto of the Colonial Office,—a veto which is really almost abandoned, or at any rate is nothing when compared with the veto which the irresponsible part of the British Parliament uses against the responsible and representative side of the same Parliament,—is it not necessary that the colony should undertake its own military defence, at its own discretion, and at its own cost? Are we not suspending one of the most important factors in the political education of a nation, when we make it responsible for our foreign policy, and undertake the duty of its defence? Are we not, supposing the statement be true that our power is watched by eager and insidious enemies (for the topic was debated when we were carefully kept in a state of periodical panic by the politicians of the Palmerstonian school), incurring enormous risk by scattering our military resources, and by offering an infinite number of points of attack? Would not the relations of our colonies to ourselves be more honourable, more close, and more safe, if we treated the colonists as responsible beings? Such were the topics raised by Mr. Goldwin Smith. I speak with some confidence on the subject, not only because I was on intimate terms with the writer of those remarkable letters, which were afterwards collected into a volume under the title of 'The Empire,' but because I took an active part in the controversy which the discussion of the subject provoked.

To those who are unacquainted with the tricks of political controversialists, and particularly those of the partisan Press, the irrelevancy of the issues raised by the critics of Mr. Goldwin Smith would seem incredible. Thus the advocates of a reform in our colonial relations were charged with a design of dismembering the empire, while if the questions stated above had any meaning whatever, their object was to prevent the dismemberment, to say nothing of preventing the disgrace, of the empire. As long, for example, as the foreign policy of Canada is dictated by the Foreign Office in London, Great Britain is peculiarly vulnerable on the Canadian frontier. As soon as it is understood that the foreign policy of Canada is one for which Canada is alone responsible, and the foreign policy of Great Britain is one for which her colonies are not responsible, those colonies are totally freed from British complications, and the United Kingdom can retain her defences intact.

Or are we to say that the reasoning which insists that the privileges of self-government must be coupled with the responsibilities of self-government is a policy of dismemberment? As well say that a family is dismembered, if when a son is grown to such mature years as to be able to carry on a trade or a profession on his own account, his father tells him that he must be prepared to undertake the responsibility of his own acts, and pay the debts which he incurs.

Again, it was stated that the advocates of this reform made light of the advantages of the colonial trade. To this charge the answer is easy and obvious. Colonists do not deal with us because they are colonists, but because our goods are cheaper or better. It is true that, being Englishmen, habit may induce them to make use of manufactures with which they are familiar, and of whose quality they may be assured. An Australian or Canadian does not purchase English goods merely because they are English. If he pretended that he did so he would be laughed at for a sentiment in which his neighbours would detect something else. To imagine that an Australian farmer grows wool or a Canadian lumberer lops and fells timber out of an occult sympathy with a community on which he is reputed to be politically dependent, is to credit him with irrational folly. He would sell timber or wool to a Dutchman or a Frenchman with as much alacrity as he would to one who speaks his native language; with more alacrity if Dutchman or Frenchman paid him a better price for either. Political sentiment has no place in business transactions, as the Stock Exchange and the Chamber of Commerce know very well.

So far is it from being the case that the British colonies have a peculiar predilection for the manufactures of the mother country, that the larger colonies have done their best to curtail the dimensions of the colonial trade. In a word, they have adopted protection. They have committed an economical folly in doing so, a greater folly than we should commit if we were to revert to our former practice, gross as it would be in our case. It is not difficult to see the origin of the heresy and its justification. The first and principal is that it is the easiest and most convenient way of raising a revenue. It is perhaps not easy to collect a direct tax in a sparsely peopled country, though the United States have done so with success. Of course when a duty is levied on an imported article, and no corresponding internal tax is imposed on the same article when produced at home, the duty operates as a protection to the home manufacture. But the defence for the colonial tariff is not by any means its motive.

It is one of the principal difficulties in the adoption of a sound system of finance, or indeed of any other reform, that a change to a right course not only injures existing interests, however indefensible may be their origin and however mischievous their continuance, but is very slowly appreciated as a real benefit by the public. Nothing illustrates this fact more strongly than the very different attitude occupied by the manufacturers and the agriculturists in the days of Adam Smith, and that which they took during the epoch of the Anti-Corn Law agitation. In the eighteenth century the British farmer exported corn, and was therefore a free-trader. In the nineteenth he could not supply the inhabitants of these islands with food enough, he was brought into competition with the foreign producer, and he became an intractable protectionist. In the eighteenth century the manufacturer was so wedded to protection that Adam Smith spoke of the prospects of free trade as an Utopia. In the nineteenth the extraordinary developement of manufacturing industry gave him the command of the markets of the world, and he became a free-trader. There were of course advocates at all times of what is proved to be economical wisdom, but the risk seemed too considerable to the majority, and the reform was impossible till the occasion arose.

Two classes of persons, both possessing considerable influence in colonial towns, are advocates of colonial protection. These are the capitalists and the artisans. The former are allured by the prospect of high immediate profit, the latter by that of good wages. Neither of them sees that extra profit will attract competitors to the calling, and unless immigration is checked, that the rate of wages in the protected calling will fall by the competition of other labourers. Least of all do they see that a colony in which capital is scanty is the last place where it should be diverted into unproductive channels, or that a distant region possesses, in the cost of carriage and the expense of agency, a natural protection against the foreign or home producer, or that when the change to free trade does hereafter take place (and it is certain that the mass of consumers will not ultimately submit to the exactions of a protectionist policy), there will be very serious distress in those occupations which have hitherto relied on the assistance of a tariff for their profits.

Another charge levelled against the advocates of a colonial reform was that of hostility to colonisation, and thereupon to the relief of a superabundant population. The charge was absurd from every point of view. The adoption of a system by which the dependency assumed the duties as well as the privileges of political independence has no more to do with the practice of emigration than the solar system has. The Colonial Office has never assisted colonisation or emigration. All that it and the Board of Trade have done is to put some hindrance in the way of emigration by most properly insisting upon an inspection of emigrant ships. The British Government has never colonised except with convicts. Nor does voluntary emigration relieve a superabundant population. The voluntary emigration from Great Britain has induced, and is inducing, some of the gravest social questions upon us, for it carries off the most enterprising and ablebodied of the population, leaving behind, it is to be feared, very inferior stocks, and making room for a very doubtfully valuable immigration from Ireland and Germany. No emigration relieves population unless it takes away a whole section of the community.

The answer to the question whether the colonies are really important outlets for emigration is very easy. Do they receive the mass of emigrants? Is emigration checked from countries which have no colonies? The answer to both these questions is a negative. The largest number of emigrants from the United Kingdom seek the United States. Only a few go to Canada or Australia, though the former of these colonies offers a very advantageous career, and is near, the prospects of the latter are exceedingly bright. The reason why Englishmen and Irishmen choose the United States is partly to be found perhaps in the fact that the machinery of settlement is easier and the climate more attractive, partly because the more adventurous emigrant prefers institutions which contrast markedly with those he leaves. Men quit England as much because they dislike its social system, as because they wish to better themselves. Again, there is as copious an emigration from Germany as there is from the United Kingdom, though Germany does not possess an inch of land out of Europe. But though the emigration from this country is purely spontaneous, and bears no relation whatever to the Colonial Office and its relations to the British dependencies, it is to be regretted that some pains have not been taken to relieve the population in this country in one direction. The colony would very properly repudiate the expatriation of a criminal class to their shores, and would as likely resent the adoption of any machinery by which a portion of our adult pauperism could be transferred to them. But they seem willing enough to admit destitute children, who run great risk of being drawn into pauperism at home, but who would get a good start and become very useful members of society in a colony like Canada or Australia.

The enquiry into the relations of Great Britain to her colonies was stimulated by the circumstances of the American civil war. It is possible that there is a brood of filibusters in the United States which has always looked on Canada as a perpetual convenience for inflicting an injury or an insult upon England. It is probable that there is a party in Canada which does not particularly object to the maintenance of a spirit of unfriendliness between the Union and the Dominion, either as a stimulant in party politics, or as a means whereby advantageous negotiations may be entered into between the colony and the Colonial Office. But the American Government has always discouraged by all the means in its power those adventurers who have sought to bring about an embroilment with Canada, and the Colonial Office has generally been induced to decline imperial guarantees for colonial loans. But the opinion of the public has gradually veered round to that which was advocated with some energy by certain English writers eleven years ago, and which was met by very strong and not very fair remonstrance on the part of others who pleaded for the existing state of things. We have informed the inhabitants of the Cape that we have made up our minds not to encourage them in making war on the Caffres. We have repudiated the protectorate of the Orange Free State and the Transvaal Republic. We have withdrawn our troops from New Zealand, and have assured our colonists that they must manage the recalcitrant Maoris at their own cost and in their own manner. The change has had the happiest results. We have remitted Canada to the defence of its inhabitants. We have not, it is true, formally announced to these colonies that they must undertake the responsibility of their own foreign policy, but the line which we have taken virtually amounts to such an intimation. The colonies are apparently not suffering from the consequence of the increased dignity which is consequent on the recognition of increased duties.

The British Parliament, undoubtedly with a view to conferring solidity on the settlements, to which it was about to give the boon of full political responsibility, passed an Act constituting the Dominion of Canada. Politically I think that Act was an error, and that the policy which we should have adopted was to invite the several states which were to constitute the Dominion to debate and agree upon the terms of union. There is of course little doubt that the scheme was fully discussed by the parties concerned, and that the dissatisfaction loudly expressed at the time by Nova Scotia was more superficial than real. But there is always some inconvenience clinging to a constitution which has been framed from without instead of being developed from within, some risk that the machinery may get out of gear, and that the dissatisfaction which may be felt at any disappointment in the working of the system may be charged to the framers of it. If no such inconvenience does arise, the judgment of those who framed the Dominion Act is proved to be sound, as far as the particulars of their procedure seemed open to challenge, but the question of policy still remains, and is still liable to debate.

Cobden strongly entertained the view that colonial interests would be best secured if the colonies were left to their own defence. 'We are just now,' he said in 1861,[*] 'getting into a discussion with respect

[*] Speeches, vol. ii. p. 331.

to keeping an army for the defence of our colonies. Very soon that discussion will ripen—as all discussions in this country are apt in time to do—into a triumph of the true principle, and the colonists, who are much better able to do so than we are, will be left to defend themselves, or, if they call upon us to defend them, will have to contribute towards the expense.' But even long before this time, when Lord Russell had in 1850 instituted those changes which give the colonies 'the right of framing their own constitutions, of levying their own taxes, of determining their own tariff, and of disposing of their own waste lands,' though Cobden gave his hearty approval of the project, he coupled his approval with the following observations:* 'Is this country to give to the colonies as complete independence, nay even greater independence, than the separate States of the American Union possess, since they cannot dispose of an acre of waste ground, nor touch their tariff,—are the people of this country, I ask, to be called upon by the same Prime Minister who gives the colonies the right of governing and taxing themselves to pay and maintain the military police which occupies those colonies? It is utterly impossible, under the altered circumstances arising out of the policy of the Government towards those colonies, that any minister with a head on his shoulders, after declaring what I have heard declared with reference to Australia, the Cape of Good Hope, New Zealand, and Canada, can permanently impose upon the people of this country the charge of maintaining the military police of those colonies. It is but

* Speeches, vol. i. p. 504.

a military police, and not an army kept up for the defence of the colonies from foreign attacks; for this country charges itself with the expense of defending the colonies in the case of war. These military establishments are maintained 10,000 miles away. We send out relief at an enormous expense, and that to maintain a police which the colonists are better able to pay for than are the people of this country.'

The words in which Adam Smith characterised the colonial system of his day are true of the same relations in our own. 'The rulers of Great Britain have for more than a century past amused the people with the imagination that they possessed a great empire on the west side of the Atlantic. This empire, however, has hitherto existed in imagination only. It has hitherto been, not an empire, but the project of an empire; not a gold mine, but the project of a gold mine; a project which has cost, which continues to cost, and which, if pursued in the same way as it has been hitherto, is likely to cost immense expenses, without being likely to bring any profit.' * The construction and consolidation of such an empire might tax the energies, but it would establish the reputation of a statesman.

They who have taken the strongest objections to the condition in which the colonies were a few years ago—twenty-two years ago, when they were entrusted with the management of their own affairs, and allowed the freest action in connexion with their tariffs, their domestic legislation, and the land comprised within the geographical limits of the colony; or ten years ago,

* Wealth of Nations (Author's Edition), vol. ii. p. 549.

when they were allowed almost an unlimited discretion in drawing on the British Exchequer for aid in their wars against native races—have never looked with other than satisfaction on the growth of the English race, and have always desired its legitimate extension. They have done so, not from that blind and silly patriotism which sees nothing but perfection in English institutions and the English character, and which reflects with insular or provincial scorn upon other traditions and habits in other countries. They have seen that it was inevitable that the emigrant Englishman would utterly repudiate, in his new home, social facts and customs which are supposed to be deeply engrained in this. The first settlers in the New World attempted an Established Church, revived the persecutions from which they had suffered at home, and eventually extirpated the malignant thing root and branch. It was the solitary and transient error into which they fell. From the very first they repudiated an hereditary aristocracy. Lords Say and Brooke, during the evil times which found a remedy in the action of the Long Parliament, turned their attention to those settlements of the West which formed the cradle of the American Republic, and thought of emigrating thither. But they claimed the rights of an hereditary peerage. The colonists were anxious to conciliate their powerful friends, but they stood firm against the principle of transmitted nobility, answering through Cotton as follows: 'When God blesseth any branch of any noble or generous family with a spirit and gifts fit for government, it would be a taking of God's name in vain to put such a talent under a bushel, and a sin against the honour of magistracy to neglect such in our public elections. But if God should not delight to furnish some of their posterity with gifts fit for magistracy, we should expose them rather to reproach and prejudice, and the commonwealth with them, than exalt them to honour, if we should call them forth, when God doth not, to public authority.'* The puritan minister gives in the most courteous, but most decisive manner, the fundamental objection to an hereditary legislature. It is to be regretted that the Colonial Office has seen fit to stimulate the morbid vanity, perhaps the jobbery, of certain colonists with the grant of baronetcies—all I presume, in the way of hereditary distinction, which it could venture on conferring—and the establishment of a colonial order of knighthood.

Similarly the British colonies, though the emigrant carries out with him his *jus Anglicum*, do not adopt that number of laws which put such serious inconvenience on those who remain at home. As they have no Church establishments,—the attempts made to create the system in the Canada Reserves and the Jamaica State Church have been abrogated or rescinded,—as they have no hereditary nobility, so they have been able to dispense with the unfairness of primogeniture, and the mischievous protection which settlements of estate accord to particular families. They can solve the problems of society under a new and an equal set of conditions, and find no necessity for succouring imaginary rights with preposterous safeguards. There

* Bancroft's History of the United States, vol. i. p. 388 (quoted by Mr. Goldwin Smith).

may be, and probably is, much vulgarity and bad taste in the bustle of these new settlements, but they are free from that incomparably worse vulgarity which characterises English society, and under which wealth and rank are adored and insolent.

The satisfaction which those who have always advocated colonial independence feel arises from perceiving that the best parts of English civilisation will be developed under the most favourable circumstances in those new regions. In the old world society is constantly being drawn back into those struggles which are not indeed reproduced with the ferocity of the middle ages, but in which the same intolerance and arrogance are latent. Western Europe is still engaged in the contest which began with the war of the League and the Huguenots in France, which inflicted the sorrows of the Thirty Years' War in Germany, and which forced England into the struggle which lasted from 1643 to 1688, along with its unspeakable misery and pollutions. The pretensions of sacerdotalism in France, in Germany, and in the United Kingdom may be merely echoes of those war-cries which once threatened European civilisation with utter ruin, but they come from the same spirit, and they aim at the same object, the degradation of mankind and civil government under the craft of the priest. In the colonies of British origin, that struggle is absolutely over, that page of history is finally closed. In alliance with these sinister influences, the spirit of feudal insolence is still striving to stifle the growth of a sound social life, whether it consists in the political progress of the nation, or in the natural distribution of wealth.

The age of violence has almost passed away in the old world. The wars of the Barons in England, of the Public Good in France, were the result of feudal privilege. But the struggle after social equality led to the Revolutionary war, to the reaction of the Holy Alliance, to the diplomatic system of modern Europe. Germany suffers from Junkerism, Spain from Carlism, France is even now in great peril from the intrigues of those Monarchists who are wholly intractable, while the progress of social reform in England is arrested by the persistent advocacy of indefensible interests at the hands of an irresponsible aristocracy. From these contingencies our colonists have saved themselves by refusing to allow social inequalities within their political system. One social inequality was indeed permitted in past times, the institution of slavery. To get rid of this, the United States had to endure the waste of life and wealth entailed by the great civil war. Had it not been for slavery and a privileged class, this country would not have been stained with the disgrace of the Jamaica massacre, and with the ignominy which attended the escape of those who perpetrated it.

It is no false patriotism to say, that whatever may be the blemishes of our social system at home, and however much the plan of our civil government is disfigured by the interests which strive to hinder the machinery of Parliament, this country has furnished the precedents by which the objects of popular government may be secured. Those institutions have been transmitted to the colonies of English origin, and are allowed free scope within them. If under circumstances of more secure equality, improvements have been made on the form of the original instrument of government, if wiser laws are enacted, and order is more certainly established, material progress more surely developed, the policy of the Colony will react on the mother country. As long as the growth of English institutions was limited to the British islands, men might pause before they changed them, and imperilled the positive good which the present certainty affords, in a search after the advantages of an uncertain future. But if the same race tries, and with incontestably good results, certain political experiments in a distant region, the wisdom of following the same course at home is challenged by the authority of successful precedents. The British colonists adopted an extended franchise, and there is no doubt that the example was not lost on the politicians of the Old World. They secured the independence of the voter, and the decorum of the contest, by the use of the Ballot in Parliamentary elections, and the precedent of the Australian Colonies, nay even their practice, was recommended and accepted by the British Legislature. The rule of absolute and unconditional religious equality, the expediency of maintaining civil equality, the grant of secular education, with free religious teaching, and the necessity of keeping the process by which land is transferred simple, are principles in the Colonies. In a short time they will be urged with overwhelming force in the home country, and will be accepted. The sections of the English race act on each other, and nothing shows how alien to the sympathies of the English people are the traditions of a feudal aristocracy and a dominant church, than the fact that no British Colony has thought of voluntarily reproducing either, and that when it has been enabled to deal with the latter, it has invariably and speedily demolished it. Now it is not quite safe to say that the political action of the Colonies is un-English.

On the other hand the Colony derives considerable advantages, even from the clumsy and informal relations between it and the mother country. It would take too long time to point them out, except succinctly. But, as the Colony follows substantially the same law, it has the benefit of those precedents by which the English courts detect the purposes, and remove the ambiguities of English legislation. It can use the convenience of that part of our diplomatic organisation, which is least open to objection on the score of utility and fidelity to public advantage, the consular service. It shares in the security which the more enlightened policy of our own time is effecting through the growth of a better theory of international relations. It has the great boon of perfect free trade with the mother country, a boon which it has not estimated at its proper merits, or met with a corresponding enlightenment.

The independence of the British Colonies is the best condition under which they can work out their own destinies. But their severance from the country of their origin would be an evil. The question is—what are the circumstances under which a real federation could take the place of their present relations? From Adam Smith's time to our own, various projects of Colonial representation in the Imperial Parliament have been ventilated. But the British Parliament is already of unwieldly bulk, is divided into sections which severally care very little except for sectional interests, and which give a hearing with difficulty to any questions which do not deal with their interests. It is to this vice of the British Legislature that the cry for local Parliaments on definite or limited topics is due, and by which it is justified. The tendency of the times is more and more towards a federal system, and therefore the possibility of Colonial representation in an Imperial Parliament, much of whose time is occupied in private legislation is progressively remote, and progressively distasteful. As long as Parliament deals with such matters, it is not easy to see how Colonies whose social system and many of whose fundamental laws differ from those of the home country, would have to be admitted into a Legislature which is still occupied with problems which have been long since settled in the Colony. Even now the claim for a local Parliament on behalf of Ireland is assisted by the facts that Ireland has been relieved of a State Church, and has an exceptional Landlord and Tenant law.

I cannot pretend in the compass of an article like this, which only purposes to deal with the changes which have been induced on the relations between Great Britain and her Colonies during the last thirty years, to discuss the terms of the federation. It is sufficient to indicate that they grow out of the changes which have been made, and out of the necessity of reviewing a relation which has been so materially modified. There is indeed no precedent in political history on which that statesman may rely who takes in hand this, I venture on declaring, the greatest and most important work which can be undertaken by courage and forethought. It would be well, if they who declaim about the unity of the British Empire, and insist on saving it from disintegration, would devote their attention to discovering the means by which a real union between its parts should take the place of a loose and uncemented aggregation.

CHAPTER VIII.

PARLIAMENTARY REFORM.

COBDEN entered into the House of Commons nine years after the first Reform Bill was passed. That Reform Bill was a compromise, arrived at only after a severe struggle, and the threat of a revolution. It was impossible to retain some of the boroughs which possessed the Parliamentary franchise before the Bill. There had been a project, it is true, for buying the franchise of these places from those who had become possessed of them, and Pitt, when he contemplated a reform of the representation, lent his sanction to this plan. At the time of the Reform Bill, the principle of compensation, in other words, that practice of Parliament by which the nation is compelled to pay exorbitantly for reforms, when the object of these reforms happens to have great influence with the Legislature, had not reached its later development, under which, for example, the public has had to compensate the officers of the army for breaking the law. Perhaps too public indignation rendered it impossible to bargain on the terms. At any rate, on this occasion 'the rights of property' were sacrificed to the public good. The Duke of Wellington, however, actually called the unreformed Parliament, the perfection of human wisdom.*

<small>* Cobden's Speeches, vol. i. p. 11.</small>

The gain of the Reform Act of 1832 was so enormous, that the generation which succeeded to the old system did not entertain a very lively sense of the deficiencies and inequalities of the measure. In order to save some boroughs, a huge cantle of the county was sliced out and added to the village which still retained the franchise. In order to secure the territorial interest of the landowners, Parliament endorsed the Chandos clause, by which the landowner's tenants at will were emancipated, while almost all other occupiers in the counties were debarred from civil rights. The large cities were admitted to the privilege of representation, but in such a manner as to prove that the Legislature had the strongest determination not to approximate to anything like numerical representation.

Before the Reform Bill of 1832, the House of Lords was the dominant power in the Legislature. Its members nominated, in the vast majority of cases, the so-called representatives of the boroughs. But they had less power in the counties, where the freeholders thought and acted for themselves. It is difficult for our modern experience to conceive a case like that of Middlesex, which returned Wilkes three times over in 1768, and by overwhelming majorities. But a century ago, there were freeholders, who could not indeed save the country from despotism, but who could remonstrate pretty loudly. They have been extinguished by the great Continental War, and under the operation of primogeniture and deeds of settlement.

The hereditary branch of the Legislature has occupied a wholly altered position since the first Reform Act. The unreformed Parliament did not pretend to represent the nation, and therefore there was no anomaly in an hereditary chamber making laws for the people, and refusing laws which the people needed. With rare exceptions, the character and capacities of those who sat in the House of Commons were inferior to those of the Peers. The Protests of the Upper House before the Reform Bill constitute a valuable body of State Papers. After that epoch they are far less interesting and important. Those of the former epoch are characterised by breadth and generosity of sentiment, those of the latter are often angry, shallow, and reactionary. In the anti-reform epoch, the debates of the Lords were often long and animated. They have now sunk into an occasional declamation. Of old the Lords had a policy, not perhaps always wise, but generally broad and intelligible. At the present time, they confine themselves to petty hindrances, and apparently to petty spite.

It is a common practice with Parliamentary reformers to advocate some modification in the constitution of the Upper House. There are those who think it wholly useless, and recommend its abolition. There are those who consider that it has a useful function in checking rash legislation. There are those who cannot discover any service which it does beyond that of sustaining indefensible interests, and that it only earns the poor praise of thankfulness from the interests which it saves from merited condemnation.

The gratitude, they say, of those who thank Heaven for the House of Lords is not the joy of the righteous, but the congratulations of culprits whom justice has failed to chastise.

The constitution of the House of Commons, and its relations to the Administration of the day are in themselves an effectual bar to any hasty legislation, even if it were not the practice in England to debate every question long, and accept the true answer long before action is or can be taken in the Legislature. When the public mind is made up to the change, the Upper House is notoriously unable to resist. Some ardent spirits urge the Peers to take a firm stand against innovation, but their Lordships always succumb. The fact is, the measure comes, backed by all the forces of the Government within the Lower House, and public opinion outside. All Bills which pass the Commons, pass by the assent and with the responsibility of the Government, unless of course the Government is, in direct contradiction to the spirit of the constitution, in a minority, for no individual or body of individuals can pass any Bill to which the Government of the day shows a decided resistance. But on the other hand, a minority has great powers of hindrance, which it does not use the less, because the process of its power is not apparent. It can and does talk Bills, even Government Bills, out. It can prevent the passage of Bills on which a strong Government has made up its mind, and on which public opinion is matured, and it does so every session, for the forms of the House, and its standing orders lend themselves to these expedients. Nor is the memory of constituencies over keen on the short comings of their representatives. It does not therefore appear that the House of Lords is preeminently useful in effecting the delay of public business, when the object of the business is a rash or premature change.

There is a usefulness in the House of Lords which is not very frequently recognised at the present time, but which is very real. When the law or the customs of a country permit the accumulation of wealth in few hands, and particularly that kind of wealth which, by its character or its prestige, confers great influence on its possessor, it becomes necessary, in order to preserve the balance of the constitution, to neutralise the effect of such a concentration. The universal testimony of history shows the mischievous effects of an oligarchy, whether one gathers one's precedents from ancient or modern times. Social progress is arrested at an early stage, when an aristocracy is permitted to rule a people and a despot rules both. The history of the Roman republic and empire is an illustration. Every event in it is a political lesson of the clearest kind. A militia of farmers gradually subdued Italy, and transformed itself into an opulent aristocracy. It was not indeed a close aristocracy; for though the representatives of the first founder of a family had great advantages by virtue of their descent, they were not necessarily entrusted with legislative or administrative functions, and it was possible for new men to rise to eminence. But the Roman aristocracy first enslaved, then ruined the world, and were themselves constrained to submit to a military despotism, the most wasting and barbarous conceivable, and the traditions of which are even now stifling the political progress of the Old World.

The wisdom or policy of the Athenian constitution invented expedients by which to check the political influence of excessive wealth. It levied special taxes on that which it conceived to be an overplus, compelling large fortunes to contribute to the extraordinary exigencies of the State. It does not seem that this practice provoked any profound dissatisfaction in the objects of the charge, but that rather wealthy men vied with each other in doing service to the State. The Government of Athens also adopted the practice of ostracism. It sent the person whom it thought dangerous to public liberty, or perhaps public morals, into a kind of honourable banishment, putting no loss upon him beyond that of a temporary but enforced absence from his native country. It may be said that the practice was rarely adopted. But this does not mean that it was less effectual. The validity of the custom must not be measured by the frequency of its occurrance, but by its motive and its effects. An identical system prevailed at Syracuse.

The Italian republics treated their most restless citizens in a similar way. The Government derived all its powers from the people, and the nobles of, for example, Florence were excluded from the administration. Hence, when it was considered expedient to neutralise the influence of an overwealthy or overpowerful citizen, he was ennobled, and thus became a political cipher. Neither Athens nor Florence had hit upon the device of a representative Chamber elected by the people, and an hereditary Chamber composed of the nobles. Had they done so they would have discovered the safeguards which are provided for the British constitution in the House of Lords. To abolish this House, and to suffer its members to become candidates for seats in the Lower Chamber, would be, under existing circumstances, to transfer all the power of Government in the first instance to the great landowners, and to provoke at no distant date that political Armageddon which is even now menacing the future. But no one would advise that the English nobility should be disfranchised utterly, should be debarred all political rights. It is better, therefore, to leave them where they are most harmless, and where, as events progress, they will wield less and less of real power. It may be hereafter necessary to limit the power of veto which they possess, and which they occasionally use vexatiously and factiously.

Nor can the House of Lords be reformed. Any radical change in its constitution would be either futile or reactionary. It might, indeed, be made an elected Chamber, similar in most particulars to the American Senate. But while the administration is responsible, but yet possesses such vast and undefined powers in the Lower House, a second Chamber appears to be superfluous. In the United States the President's ministry is not at all responsible, and the President hardly at all. President Buchanan committed manifest treason against the Union, and did it with impunity. President Johnson defied the Legislature, and his impeachment was a *fiasco*. But suppose the Upper House in Great Britain were made elective, of whom should it consist? Is the nation to choose a limited number out of the existing body of peers? To give the peers such a power as the Scotch and Irish peerages have would be to bring matters to a dead lock—the result would be very much what there is now, except that there would be a mischievous and absurd phantom of representation in the Upper Chamber. Or is it to choose peers as it will? Then the inconvenience to which I have referred above will arise, and, for a time at least, the Lower House will be swamped with a party of the Right, which an extreme radicalism will be invited, indeed compelled to displace, and ostracise. It is impossible to construct a popular representation out of a privileged class. The perils of France are an exhaustive comment on such an attempt, for the legal equality of all classes in France is no bar to aristocratic reaction, and intense social bitterness.

It has been suggested that the hereditary Lords should be reduced in numbers by some process of co-optation, and that a number of life peers should be added to the roll. Such a suggestion is one of the most reactionary character. If the persons added to the list are nominated by the Crown at the instance of the Prime Minister for the time being, they will occupy an inferior position in the House as the Bishops do; will be made to feel their inferiority as the Bishops are, and be expected to limit themselves to specialities as the Bishops are. If, as some have proposed, the supplementary peers are to come from the House of Commons, that persons who have served a constituency for fifteen or twenty years, or a Government for five or six, should escape from the storms of a Parliamentary election into the haven of the Upper Chamber, and hold a seat there for life, still greater difficulties arise. The popular Chamber must and will direct the policy of the nation: is it expedient to deprive it of the counsels of those who have had the longest experience in public life? The inconvenience which arises from having Ministers of State in the House of Lords is increasingly felt in the delay of public business, and in the slowness of official replies: is it wise to adopt a change which will make it necessary to seek for an increasing number of Ministers of State in that inaccessible and desultory House of Parliament? Or supposing these difficulties to be slight or superable, the project would be reactionary. It would make one of the branches of the Legislature more irresponsible than before. At present the peerage is debarred from using its extreme rights under the constitution, because it knows that its position is an anomaly, and its privileges an usurpation; but if the Legislature formally grants a new constitution to the Upper House, it recognises, under all the sanctions of law, powers, and authority which are hitherto mere customs, and bestows them upon persons who have been controlled by constituencies, and are now formally emancipated from their old responsibilities. If such a Chamber were like the present House of Lords, its existence would be wasted; if it became an active body, its powers would be discretionary. We should, in fact, establish a Long, a Versaillist Parliament by our own act.

It has been said further that such a House, being composed of able men, would appropriate to itself all the dignity and authority which is now possessed by the House of Commons. Were this likely to ensue it would be a powerful argument against the change, because it would tend to take the Legislature more and more away from popular control. But the risk is, I think, imaginary. A safe seat is seldom occupied by an active man, for the security of his position tends to make him indolent or fastidious. Besides, where the

purse is there is the power. Now, no one would
suggest, I imagine, that the House of Commons should
relinquish its control over taxation and public money
to a Chamber composed of cooptated peers and retired
members of Parliament. If the power is to reside still,
then, in the Lower Chamber, it is certain that the
Lower Chamber will continue to attract the most competent men to it, and that a seat in it will remain the
principal object of ambition to those who wish to take
part in public life. Nor is there reason to believe that
the public would retain any great interest, or even confidence, in those who elected to retreat from a responsible into an irresponsible body. Pitt was the most
popular minister which England ever had, but when
he became Chatham he needed all the popularity he
had won in order to reconcile the English nation to his
Peerage.

The mere fact however that projects for the reconstruction of the Upper House are debated, and are
even contemplated by the Lords themselves, the circumstance that they have abandoned the use of prox-
ies, a peculiarly irritating form of voting on the part
of an assembly which should, at least, debate on
matters of public interest, and the concession of the
principle that the Bankruptcy laws should apply to
the Peerage as it does to the Commons, are evidence
of the growth of public opinion on the rights and
privileges of a body of whom Cobden said that 'they
never lose their calmness and self-possession upon any
domestic topic.' This change is of course due to the
fact that the public has been engaged for the last
thirty years in discussing principles as well as details.

But the nation has been constrained to do so, because it is formally told that only when public opinion is made up, does a question pass from the region of abstract sentiment into the arena of practical politics. Men do not enter upon a justification or defence of their tenure until their title deeds are called in question, or think of providing themselves with allies until they are roused by the threats of an enemy.

There is no finality in political warfare, and in political compromises, but there may be languor, and after a point is gained, there may be a cessation of hostilities, more or less prolonged. The first Reform Bill stormed the outworks of privilege and led to several social changes. I do not think that an unreformed Legislature would have ventured on Poor Law Reform, for it had always been asserted that the liberal maintenance of the poor was the compensation for enclosures, for the loss of the commons and for other privileges formerly enjoyed by the peasantry. On the other hand, it is unlikely that the abolition of the Corn Laws would ever have been extorted from an unreformed House of Commons, in which the great towns of Manchester, Birmingham, and Leeds were unrepresented. But again, grotesque and absurd as the system of representation was, and governed as it was by two dominant powers, the great landowners and the great merchants, the old House of Commons had not given way to that vice which is so characteristic of its successor, the representation of special interests, and the growing tendency to ignore all interests which are not represented within it. It has often been commented on, that while the Reform Act left the freemen, the least satisfactory and the most corrupt element in the boroughs, it extinguished, for a time, those householders in several of the towns, who had contrived to retain their franchises, and so that it really limited the suffrage in certain localities.

I have elsewhere observed that in the first instance, Cobden did not exhibit any marked anxiety to assist in passing beyond the compromise of 1832. He thought probably that the purposes which he had before him, such as those of reduced expenditure, of peace, of improved international relations, of education, of free-trade in other directions beyond that in foreign food, might be expected from the action of a Parliament composed of 'the middle class.' He might, remembering the facts of his free trade campaigns, and the honest but mistaken hindrances which the Chartist put in his way, have conceived that the mass of the working classes would be an obstacle to the reforms which he saw were necessary for the material progress of the English people. In the same way, he had a momentary hesitation in throwing the weight of his influence into the cause of the Northern States at the commencement of the civil war in America. His hatred of violence, his feeling that war was a barbarism, which could not effect as much good as it inevitably did harm, were so strong that, for a time, he inclined to the belief that it would have been better if the North had acknowledged the independence of the South. But in each case the hesitation was only temporary. He supported in a speech of great vigour Mr. Hume's motion of June 20, 1848, which averred 'that the House as at present constituted, did not fairly represent the population, the property, or the industry of the country; that great and increasing discontent had thereupon arisen in the minds of a large portion of the people; and that it was therefore expedient, with a view to amend the national representation, that the elective franchise should be extended so as to include all householders; that votes should be taken by Ballot, that the duration of Parliaments should not exceed three years, and that the apportionment of members to population should be made more equal.' These were not all the objects which Cobden included in his scheme of Parliamentary Reform. He was favourable to the charge which should put the necessary expenses of elections on the constituency, he thought it perfectly fair and reasonable that representatives should receive a modest salary for their services, he had a rooted dislike to fancy schemes of voting, such as the minority and the cumulative vote, and he appears from a passage in one of his speeches to have been favourable to a claim which has been brought forward since his death, the admission of single women to the Parliamentary franchise*.

The unequal distribution of the franchise, and the notorious enslavement of the constituencies in certain counties and boroughs to the direct influence of nobles and other great landowners, were the obvious and constant topics of which the advocates of Parliamentary reform dwelt. In order to secure their influence in the Lower House, by controlling the votes of the electors, the great landowners strove to accu-

* Speeches, vol. ii. p. 475.

mulate all the land which came into the market, and took care to leave their tenants the minimum of liberty in their occupations. The ancient freeholders were extinguished, and faggot freeholders were created in order to neutralize what little independence might be left. Thus to take the example of Bucks, well remembered as the county from which numerous freeholders rode in arms under Hampden more than two centuries ago. There is one village, Hartwell, in which fifty-one faggot freeholders are created out of a rent charge on the estate of a Mr. Lee, most of which are or were held by Conservative Fellows of the Oxford Colleges. Dod's Parliamentary Companion, gave, perhaps still gives, with perfect frankness, the fact that in many boroughs the members are the nominees of some neighbouring grandee or that the electors are totally under the influence of some eminent personage. There is probably no country in the world which could supply so shameful a record. No circumstances more thoroughly justified discontent. It was clear that when Mr. Bright commenced his campaign, the concession of an extended franchise, the redistribution of political power, and the protection of the voter by the Ballot would be mere questions of time.

I have already adverted to the primary cause of discontent, in the growing conviction that unrepresented interests were uncared for in the House of Commons and that inadequately represented interests were negligently considered. It is easy to multiply evidence on this score. The artisans of the manufacturing towns secured a Factory Bill, through the energy of the present Lord Shaftesbury, and by the good will of Lord Russell's first Government. No such consideration has been shown for the agricultural labourers, and in the opinion of these labourers it will not be shown till household suffrage has been extended to the counties as well as to the towns. Even now the Legislature seems to be unaware that the franchise is so overpoweringly in the hands of the working classes, that they can, if they please, give their own colour to legislation. It is wonderful that a Parliament elected by household suffrage should have introduced those clauses in the Mines Regulation Bill which put the charge of proving the safety of the Mine on the miners, that it insists on the same condition in the case of a ship, which its crew has reason to believe unseaworthy, on the sailors; that it has enacted the provisions of the Criminal Law Amendment Act, a piece of exceptional legislation which rouses the liveliest indignation in the minds of artisans, and that it has talked out Mr. Plimsoll's Bill, which, even though the member for Derby may have given way to exaggerations, provides a remedy for possible evils and wrongs of the most terrible kind. The sense that the House of Commons never deals fairly with unrepresented interests, is the real basis of the agitation for the grant of what are called Woman's Rights. It is believed, and probably with reason, that the Commons would have passed a far more satisfactory Married Woman's Property Bill, and the Lords would not have ventured on mangling the imperfect measure which the Commons passed, if women had possessed a direct voice in the constitution of the Legislature. Similarly it is likely that the great injury which is done to women, many of whom have to earn their living, in excluding them from callings for which they are perfectly qualified, and in refusing them any share in the great educational endowments of the country, would not have been continued, had women been able to make use of their votes in Parliamentary elections.

It has been alleged that the extension of the franchise would be followed by a movement on the part of the working classes to relieve themselves of such taxation as they now endure, and to put it on the richer classes. It is a stock practice with the *Times* to charge any speaker who adverts to the origin of a particular tax, or to the compromises by which land has been relieved of its burdens at the cost of the general community, or to the character of the taxation borne by the working classes either directly or indirectly, with a wish to stimulate the masses to relieve themselves of all their burdens at the cost of their richer fellow countrymen. But I do not find that speakers advocate these views, or that the working classes endorse them. The real difficulty lies in that ignorant patience with which the working classes endure taxation, not their taxation as compared with that borne by those who are better off, but the extravagant public expenditure which weighs upon them. This however may be said: If the working classes ever do attempt to transfer the charges put on them to the shoulders of the richer classes, they will merely retaliate on the richer classes the treatment which they have themselves received, for, from the Restoration down to the tariff reforms of Sir Robert Peel and Mr. Gladstone, the policy of the influential classes was to relieve themselves at the expense of the poorer classes. Besides, it cannot be doubted that if Adam Smith's dictum is right, 'that the liability to taxation should vary with the power of enjoyment, heavier taxes than are now levied upon property would be justly imposed, however distasteful they may prove to those who have hitherto been so conspicuously favoured in the imposition of public burdens.

The conviction that, in a House of Commons composed of rich men, justice will not be done to the interests of the working classes, has led to a movement which is extremely natural and perfectly legitimate, but which will, I think, be of very dubious success; that which is known as the movement for the direct representation of labour. I have no sympathy with those who would dislike to see working men, or rather persons elected by working men from their own order, in the national Legislature, and I feel a profound disgust at the prejudice or jealousy, if it be real, which induces working men to withhold their votes from their own brethren. The only doubt which may be entertained is whether men, ordinarily untrained in controversy or debate, or at least conversant only with one side of great social questions, will not find themselves at a disadvantage when they come to cope on the floor of the House with the trained advocates of those interests to which working men frequently believe themselves normally placed in antagonism. It is as though a man were a litigant in a cause, and that a difficult and important one, and instead of accepting the services of an advocate, determined on selecting one of his own profession or calling for the business. But be this as it may, it cannot be doubted that the persistency with which working men advocate the direct representation of labour is indirectly a serious charge against the equity and honour of Parliament as at present constituted; is proof of the discontent men feel at the manner in which representatives use their position in order to further their personal or professional interests; demonstrates how great is the distrust which electors entertain towards candidates who make the loudest professions of integrity; and how, in sheer desperation, they are insisting that the Member must be a delegate, because he has not the honesty to be a representative.

Cobden advocated the extension of the franchise to householders. He intended to include lodgers, for he quoted with satisfaction a decision of the Court of Common Pleas, by which lodgers inhabiting a house in which the landlord did not himself live, and from which they contributed to the poor-rate, were householders within the Act, provided their occupancy was of £10 annual value. These conditions were necessitated by the language of the first Reform Bill, but were of course not essential to the principle upon which such a lodger should be enfranchised.

After several abortive attempts, some of which probably were not honestly intended to face the demand for an extended franchise, the Conservative Government of 1867 conceded household suffrage, with however a vexatious rate-paying clause which was speedily abolished. What Lord Derby's Government really wished to do, and what, on the other hand, a section of the House of Commons, familiarly known as the tea-room party, compelled them to do, can easily be discovered from the contrast between the resolutions moved by Mr. Disraeli on the evening of February 11 and the Reform Bill as it received the Royal assent. The changes of tactics comprised the 'Ten Minutes Bill' of February 25, based on the resolutions of February 11, the resignation of the three members of the Cabinet on March 2, the introduction of a new Bill on March 18, the abandonment of the measure to the House of Commons on March 26, the instructions to Mr. Coleridge on April 6, the Tea-room defection on April 8, and the stages by which the Bill reached its third reading on July 15. But the events are too fresh to need further illustration.

The question whether it was proper to confer the franchise on the adult male population or on those who inhabited houses was one which Cobden argued not to be one of right, but of expediency, for he held that there was no natural right to the franchise, but merely a legal right. Of course there are individuals in all societies who have no legal rights to action because they are as yet unable to exercise these rights, or are permanently disqualified for sufficient reasons. But I must demur to the position that anything which is essential to the full development of the individual is not a natural right, though it may be legally denied from necessity or caprice. Children have natural but not legal rights. Criminals have natural as well as legal rights, however much they may be narrowed, except when they are adjudged to have forfeited both through the magnitude of the offences which they have committed. It is frequently said that all natural rights are the creation of law and society, and this no doubt is true if the right is merely considered from the point of view of its being secured with due limitations by the police of law or society. But to extend this statement so as to make human institutions the origin of personal right is to raise an abstract, a logical entity, a product, which for convenience sake is treated as a person, under the name of the State or Law, into the place of a cause or an agent. The State or the Law, unless society is to be governed by the arbitrary discretion of a unit, or a corporation, must justify, and constantly justify, the limitation of that discretion which an individual naturally exercises. It often does so for wholesome reasons, but it has much more often done so for the selfish interests of a narrow section in the community. It may be right, it is always necessary, to limit human freedom, but the power which limits is always on its trial. Now I cannot conceive any right more permanent, more intrinsic, more inalienable, than that of the individual to discuss, criticise, and, within certain very intelligible bounds, to resist the law under which he is made to live. But the resistance itself must be legal, i.e. it must conform to the conditions which are essential to the safety of society. It must not change law by force, it must change it by opinion, and in the absence of any power by which opinion may be valued, it must effect the change by courting opinion. And if it be urged, as it is constantly assumed, that this is to allow the many to control the liberty of the few, I reply, that there is no other means by which society can hold together, that when the many lay down the law, they are always checked from excess by the risk that the law which they must obey will react on themselves, and that power in the hands of the many has never and can never be tyrannously exercised, while power in the hands of the few will always be and has always been exercised tyrannously over the many. Now if there be a natural right, it is that of resistance to tyranny, of repudiating the doctrine, and enforcing the repudiation, of the inherent right of one man over his fellow man. If there be no natural right, slavery is the inevitable lot of the weak.

It is obvious to see how this affects the franchise, and how necessary it has been that men should affirm their natural right to a voice in their own destinies. The power which the machinery of modern legislation gives the permanent administration of any country is far more searching than anything which has ever been possessed by ruder organisations. Now it is believed that the system of parliamentary representation, for reasons already alleged, is regularly turned, unless very effective checks are put upon it, to the sustentation of particular interests. But the exaltation of one interest is the depression of another. If that other which is depressed happens also to be voiceless, if it is made deliberately dumb, can we trust to equity to raise it, to plead for it? We are told that we cannot, and experience confirms the statement. To take an instance. Up to within the last eighteen months the English agricultural labourer was voiceless and unfriended. He has found a voice, and he has a few friends. But his voice is that of a plaint, not of a power, and he is very surely convinced that he will only get a fair hearing for his plaint when he has made himself a power. If Parliament were an ideal, in which the members were, like a jury, sworn, and, being sworn, bound to give a true deliverance on all questions at issue, the largeness or smallness of the franchise might be of little import. But Parliament is a crowd of eager ambitious men, who do as much for their own interest as they dare, and do as little for that of others as they can help.

There is however a question of expediency in connexion with the franchise, and its extension to those who are not householders. Is it desirable to confer the right of judging on questions of public policy on those who may be imprudent, to withhold it from those who are probably prudent? If it be proper to allow a vote to those who may be ignorant, is it just to refuse it to those who are probably well-informed? There are many persons belonging to the middle-classes who defer the cares of a household and family till they have earned sufficient to start themselves safely and comfortably. Is it judicious to refuse that to prudence and forethought which is granted to others who may be reckless or unthinking? It is a common complaint among London artisans, and the complaint will probably be heard in other large towns, that one of their number will take a house, and sublet it to his fellow-workmen, who are too cautious to undergo the risk, and that while he, under the household franchise, gets a vote, the others have great difficulty in registering themselves under the lodger franchise. So it is notorious that young men belonging to the middle classes live to a very large extent in lodgings, and put off their marriage to a much later period than that at which a class occupying a lower social position, and possessing an inferior education, have contracted theirs. Some of these persons possess a fancy franchise, that of the academical vote, the least valuable perhaps, as it is the least defensible, of all franchises. But the vast majority of those prudent and fairly educated persons are disfranchised, and this solely because they show some common sense.

During the whole of his parliamentary career in the House of Commons and to the country, Cobden gave his support to the Ballot. He did so for two reasons. He held that the Ballot secured decorum at elections, and that it conferred a necessary freedom of action on the elector. The polling day was a scandalous saturnalia, the franchise was in many cases a farce. The votes of honest and fearless electors were neutralised by coercion and bribery, and men were taught to consider that the exercise of a great political right, and a great public duty was a property in which they might traffic. The Parliament which insisted on maintaining these scandals, the members who owed their existence in great degree to these scandals, affected to punish the offence by which they profited. The punishment of Great Yarmouth, in which the many were sacrificed to the few, was as justifiable as it would be to put penalties on the victims of a fraud, and to let the doers of the fraud go scot free. It was even more unjust, for it chastised those who had taken no part in the transaction, who had neither offered nor taken bribes, and who were powerless to check unscrupulous agents. But the House of Commons was never in earnest to put down bribery, for it almost invariably decided that the dispossessed member had known nothing of the transaction. Now it is clear that in such a case it was bound to make a striking example of the agent, who not only was guilty of an offence against the electoral law, but of the still graver offence of attempting to compromise the character of another man, by pretending that he was acting under a principal's instructions. It really never did so. But as the House of Commons did not mean to stop bribery, the 'legitimate influence' of wealth, and coercion, the 'legitimate influence' of property, there was no remedy but the Ballot.

I presume that no one imagines that a secret vote is the most heroic way of recording an opinion. The best men will always give utterance to what they believe and to what they have made up their minds, and it would be far better if all men were willing and able to give free utterance to their convictions. If the majority of men arrived at positive convictions on public questions, and avowed their opinions without hesitation, the course of reform would be easy and rapid. But no sensible man expects that his fellow creatures are a race of sages and heroes; that they all will arrive at a true comprehension of all the social problems which are before them, and will all have the courage of all their opinions. Such wisdom and courage are the rarest of gifts. Still less will he imagine that others who have had the opportunity of effecting indefensible usurpations upon their fellow countrymen, who are aware that these usurpations are indefensible, and that they are therefore menaced, will abandon what they have obtained without a struggle, a struggle in which they will use every weapon which corruption or force may grant them. And if he becomes conscious that he is juggled out of his own franchise by the baseness or weakness of others, it is only natural that he should welcome a process which makes his opinion a power, because it takes away temptation and ensures the independence of secrecy to those who vend or yield their votes under an open system. The ballot is a refuge from great evils. Its merit lies in its defensive character. If there be any blame in adopting it, the blame lies with those who force its adoption. An honest candidate for a seat in Parliament may dislike the Ballot because it renders his prospects dubious, when he might reasonably wish to anticipate the likelihood of his success or failure, but he would have supported its adoption, and will guarantee its continuance, since he is convinced that it is the security for the independence of the voter; an honest elector may feel shame that he is constrained to give his vote secretly, but he will remember that the real shame should rest with those who have made compulsory silence a necessary means of protection. The House of Lords must be convinced that their attitude to the country is one which cannot be defended, or they would not have avowed so plainly their disgust at secret voting, or have trifled with the patience of the nation, when they limited the duration of the Act.

For these reasons, and for reasons like these, the large majority of speculative Liberals urged the use of the Ballot as a necessary security for political liberty, long before the Legislature adopted it. The objections urged against it by partisans and wire pullers were below contempt, and deserve only the notice that they were the remonstrance of imperilled and indefensible agents. But there were objections taken to it of a more solid character by men whose political motives were above suspicion, and whose attachment to public liberty had been uninterruptedly conspicuous. Foremost among these was Mr. Mill, who resisted its adoption during his short parliamentary career for reasons such as those which have been referred to above. Now it is never easy to determine the respective merits of two processes when either course of procedure involves certain inconveniences or mischiefs. The mind of each person who attempts to estimate them is swayed by the feeling which he has about the loss which the adoption of the one, and the rejection of the other involves. Retain open voting, and there is a field for political courage at a crisis, but you subject a constituency to the coarse influences of wealth, and the insolent pretensions of rank. Adopt secret voting, and you have the advantage of decorum, you give a check to bribery, and you secure the voter's discretion. But you run the risk of taking some of the life out of political action, and of losing some of that courage which is most valuable when it resists openly.

The Septennial Act of 1716 was passed because the Government of the day dreaded a Jacobite reaction, and therefore feared to face the constituencies at the general election of 1717, which must have been held according to the terms of the Triennial Act. There was even a project[*], as Mr. Hallam informs us, of prolonging the life of the first Septennial Parliament in 1720. The

[*] Hallam's 'Constitutional History,' vol. ii. p. 399.

Act passed after a sharp contest, and was strongly protested against in the Lords*.

There is of course no magic in numbers. It is true that the rule of a triennial election was one of the best acts of the Long Parliament, the mutilation of which was early effected by that venal crew of placemen and pensioners which sat during nearly the whole reign of Charles II. The guarantees for a triennial election were obtained in an Act of 1694, William having vetoed a Bill of the previous year, so that the Act of Parliament which George the First's ministry modified had been in existence for only twenty-two years. It is also true that the resistance to the Septennial Bill came, for the most part, from the Jacobites, against whom the friends of the Hanoverian succession had good reason to be upon their guard. Moreover, though it was really *intra vives*, there was something unpleasant in a Parliament deliberately prolonging its own existence, just as there is in the continuance of a House which has enlarged the franchise, or has introduced a radical modification in the process by which votes are recorded, and may therefore, if the reform was needed, be supposed to represent public opinion imperfectly.

The origin however of the Septennial Bill may be left to constitutional antiquaries. The real interest to us, is the effect of so prolonged an existence on the conduct of public affairs. *Prima facie*, the trust is too large. 'We do not appoint †,' said Cobden, 'people to be our stewards in private life for seven years, we

---
* Lord's Journals, April 14, 1716.
† Speeches, vol. ii. p. 481.

do not give people control for seven years over our property.' He went so far as to suggest that Parliaments might be elected on the system of municipal councils, that one third should go out every year. The principal objection alleged against frequent elections is the cost of the process. There are those who think that this is a powerful argument in favour of them, because in this manner the evil complained of would cure itself.

The average duration of Parliaments since the passage of the first Reform Bill has been three years nine months and nineteen days. This calculation omits the interval between a dissolution and a re-election. Including this time, the average period is four years. In practice then, Parliament may be said to have sat under a quadriennial custom. It has been usual too for no Parliament to exceed six years, and only two Parliaments since 1832 have continued as long, or almost as long as that period.

The chief objection to the Septennial Act is that it tends to make representatives too independent of their constituents. To some extent this mischief is obviated by a custom which has latterly sprung up, and has become nearly universal, of subjecting the representative to the annual ordeal of an address and a vote of confidence. But there is no mechanism by which the defection or bad faith of a member may be punished. It may fairly be said, indeed, that instances of tergiversation are rare. But on the other hand, those of growing distrust are common, and it is difficult to account for the growth of such a distrust except on the ground that the representative very inadequately expresses the sentiments of his constituents. Besides it seems to be taken as a rule that the representative should take the colour of his opinions from his constituency, should be educated by them, should be generally conservative till they urge him onwards. But if this be the case, the argument for more frequent elections becomes overwhelmingly strong. Nor does it seem that a recurrence to the triennial practice would lead to rapid change. Governments are always strong enough to check rash or even wise legislation, and extreme views find favour with few constituencies. Besides, frequent elections assist the political education of the people, and bring them face to face with great questions of principle. The ignorance of the mass of electors on political and social questions, even when they are most powerfully interested in the subject, is profound. What, for example, would be the attitude of ratepayers to the question of local taxation, if they understood the true incidence of a tax paid by the occupiers, and knew the fact that at present the great landowner's rent is free of imposts, while the contributions of the tenants actually give the landowner the power to levy an additional rent on the outlay of the occupier.

It is a common complaint that the House of Commons is too much under the control of the Administration, because the Prime Minister can advise a dissolution at his discretion. Such a state of things is partly due to the fact that members of Parliament are rarely returned on the ground of their intelligence or capacity, but by reason of their professed allegiance to a particular politician, and his party; partly to the fact that the expense of an election is so enormous, and that therefore the threat of a dissolution is a powerful check to the disobedient or refractory; partly to the circumstance that a Parliament may be prolonged to six years if matters are made agreeable to the Administration. The House is too obsequious to the Administration only because it does not contain in itself the elements which would enable it to assert its own dignity. The mere limitation of the duration of Parliament to three years would not enable the House to make the Ministry its representative, instead of its master, but it would contribute something to that result, and the constituencies in the end will do the rest.

In nearly the last letter which he wrote, Cobden advocated the distribution of the country into districts, each of which should return one member. It does not follow that these districts should be numerically equal, or that the English people should adopt the constitutional rule in the United States, in which representation is merely relative to population. But there is a difference between such a system and the glaring inequality of our present practice, under which sixty-three members are returned from a number of electors, which in the aggregate does not equal the voters in each of the three boroughs of Glasgow, Birmingham, and Manchester. Though Cobden would have urged an approximation to the principle of equal electoral districts, he was more interested in that of the single member for each constituency. This in his opinion was the best means by which the representation should be real, and the candidate put into a genuine relation to his constituents; by which those compacts or arrangements

ELECTORAL DISTRICTS. ELECTION CHARGES. 291

for the settlement of the representation in counties and boroughs could be avoided; and by which the claims of those who urge minority representation and cumulative voting could be satisfied, without reverting to those innovations in the constitution of Parliament, which appeared to him to cause great mischiefs, even if they cured small evils. It is I think impossible to doubt, that ere long the redistribution of the representative system will become a practical question. It is inevitable as soon as ever the county franchise is extended and made identical with that of the boroughs.

One of the most important reforms in the representation, and one most urgently demanded, is that which would transfer the charges of the election from the candidate to the constituency. Such a reform would render it possible to extirpate the last relics of bribery, and to eliminate the merely vulgar rich man from the House of Commons. People affect to lament that under the present system, in which many nomination boroughs have been annihilated, and the existence of the rest is threatened, that the opportunities for poor men of ability to enter the House have been greatly straitened, and we were invited to comment on the fact, that had it not been for the nomination borough of Richmond, the House of Commons might have lost the services of Sir Roundell Palmer. Still, Sir Roundell Palmer sat for Plymouth at the elections of 1847 and 1853, and does not appear to have ever been rejected by that constituency. But in the first place the seat of a nomination borough is rarely filled by a person of ability, but generally by some relative of the proprietor; and next, the House of Commons and it only is to blame for the expense which attends on elections. To the candidate the cost is prodigious; to the constituency, even if it remained at its present amount, it would be trifling, and if it were cut down, as it assuredly would be, were the charge put on the constituency, to the lowest necessary amount, it would become infinitesimal. Some years ago I was at the pains to calculate the cost of the county elections of 1865. The cost of 50 county seats contested on that occasion amounted to an average of £5836. But if these costs had been distributed over the contested counties the charge would have amounted only to a rate of 3½d. in the pound; if over all the counties contested and uncontested to about 1½d. Such a calculation of course includes the charges of agents, the erection of polling places, the conveyance of voters, all of which should be made unlawful, if the nation is to have a free and impartial Parliament. One of these items alone, the conveyance of voters at the charge of the candidate turned what was once the cheapest constituency to contest—the University of Oxford—into the most costly, and necessitated the adoption of the system of voting papers, an expedient by which the country clergyman is hurried into supporting the party of the squire.

It is surprising that the country gentlemen, (who, whatever may be their faults, are infinitely superior to the upstarts who ape politics with a view to a rise in social life, and whose Toryism is a mere advertisement,) do not see that they are gradually excluding themselves, by permitting the existence and the growth of these expenses, from political life, as well as making their own political opinions inconceivably distasteful to the

electors whom they have hitherto led. At the present
time, it is very difficult for the country party to find a
candidate out of their own body who is willing and
able to contest a county. They have, and will have to
turn to those settlers among them, who have nothing
whatever but their wealth to recommend them. It is
more surprising that constituencies do not see that
they never will be represented by men who have purchased their seats, that the men who have bought their
way into the House will use their place in Parliament
for private and not for public ends, and that the special
discredit of Parliament, that it cannot and will not
look on public questions according to their merits, but
as they affect the wealthy, the privileged, and the really
represented classes, is due to this cause and to this
cause alone. It is yet more surprising that they do not
see that this determination on the part of the present
House to let no one in except by a golden key, is irritating to the utmost those who are foremost in the
struggle between labour and capital, that it is widening
the gulf between class and class, setting them doggedly
against each other, provoking heartburnings, stereotyping discontent. It is sometimes said that the
transference of the expense from the candidate to
the constituency would stimulate adventurers to aim
at a seat in Parliament. But it would seem that the
worst kind of adventurer is the man who gets into the
Legislature in order to subserve his private interest
or ambition, and of these the House of Commons
has had abundance for the last century and a half.
It is more reasonable to conclude that if the constituencies are at the expense of getting their candidates

they will take care that they have worth for their money.

On this topic Cobden's opinion and practice coincided. He was returned for the county and the borough for which he sat from time to time, at the cost of those who honoured themselves in electing him. The borough of Rochdale, for which he was returned during the last six years of his life, boasts that since it became a borough it has always adopted the honourable course of conducting the contest on behalf of a Liberal candidate at the charge of the electors. But it was Cobden's opinion also, that a candidate should receive a moderate salary for his attendance at the House of Commons. There are inconveniences attending such a course, and notably, a danger which Mr. Mill has dwelt upon, that it is inexpedient to make politics a career or a profession, for that such persons as devote themselves to such a calling would be apt to be unscrupulous. To this indeed one might make an immediate rejoinder. Does one escape the presence of such people under the existing system? But, giving the objection its value, it seems that the advantages exceed the inconveniences. At present a member of Parliament is tempted to sacrifice the purposes for which he has been sent to Westminster in order to advance his private or personal interests, and he is justified in doing so by the circumstances of the case, and the concession of the public. In many cases the member is tempted, in order to improve his fortunes, to lend his name to commercial undertakings, which occasionally bring him present gain, to the serious injury however of his reputation, and sometimes of his fortunes. In order to allow lawyers and merchants to be present in the courts or in their counting-houses during the day, the House acquiesces in the preposterous practice holding its sittings after dark, and in the dubious propriety of continuing them after dinner on to the short hours. A day sitting, and the despatch of public business is impossible with an unpaid parliament, and a bore has his rights against it. But were the members in receipt of a modest salary, they would understand the value of the time for which they were paid, and resent its waste. It may be added that the object which many working men have at heart, and which many members of Parliament say that they desire to see, the direct representation of labour, as it is made impossible by the costs of elections, so it would still be difficult, if such representatives had to sit at their own cost. In short, the temper of the times is repudiating unpaid services because it distrusts them, is demanding a paid magistracy, because the unpaid is apt to be partial, and is seeing cause to distrust unpaid representatives because it imagines that it cannot and will not get honest work out of them.

To one of the novelties of Parliamentary representation, which during his life was still a mere theory, but which has been partially adopted in the last Reform Bill, Cobden always made a firm opposition. The representation of minorities was partially carried by the efforts of a few 'philosophical Radicals,' among whom Mr. Mill was conspicuous, and by the assistance of the Conservative party. The motives which influenced these discordant elements were as opposite as the parties were who framed a temporary alliance.

Mr. Mill wished that every body should have a hearing, and especially a hearing in the House. Hence he accepted and advocated Mr. Hare's plan, the chief feature, and indeed the chief recommendation of which is that it would enable a candidate to appeal to the whole country, to receive votes from any constituency, and thus to collect from all quarters those suffrages which might be recorded in his favour. This it is manifest, is not minority representation, but a means by which the opinion of the majority could be consulted and registered. It has the defect of difficulty, it has the merit, if it could be carried out, of reducing the local nobody to his true dimensions, and thus probably of weeding the House of persons who have no true place there. But on the other hand the general candidate would be apt to be the migratory orator, and in some few cases perhaps, the man of culture and information. In the present state of the nation, when education is so very scantily extended, when the middle classes read little besides newspapers and novels, it is far more likely that the men who are best known would be very far from being those who best ought to be known. It is open also to the objection that it would submerge all local feelings, and thereby weaken instead of strengthening political interests. It would be difficult also to resist the impression that the most popular candidate should be the leader of Parliament, for the election would partake of the nature of a class list, or a selection to places in the civil service by open competition. It would tend to measure a man's reputation by the extent of his popularity or notoriety, not by those qualities which may be supremely useful, but are occasionally very unobtrusive, and I may add, unpopular. And, what is something to the purpose, it would be a complete reversal of a practice which has become a part of British life, and which is capable of such modifications as may make it a sufficient instrument of legislation, and in which to some extent the influence of large numbers is not wholly dominant, and it would substitute in its place the system of numerical representation carried out in its most rigorous form, and in a manner which would demand very considerable enlightenment on the part of the public in order to prevent very unsatisfactory results.

The representation of minorities is a very different affair. In the first place, it will be seen that the adoption of this expedient, unless the House of Commons were made vastly more numerous, only succeeds in representing some of the minorities. In the next place the minority in this country is abundantly over-represented at present, and therefore to grant minority representation under the present circumstances of the distribution of political power, is to confer on the minority more of that of which they have already too much. The Conservatives saw this advantage at once. They hoped to neutralise the representation of the great towns, to which three members were to be given, and they did so with all but two, where by clever strategy the attempt was foiled, but where of course the unrepresented minority is still unprovided for. They wished also to facilitate arrangements and avoid contests in the three-cornered counties, for wherever an arrangement can be made, the nominal opponent of the Conservative party is never over zealous, while the proper position of a representative who is, under such circumstances, returned unopposed, is not nearly so well understood either by himself or by his constituency. Under the Ballot it will be all but impossible, however powerful the majority may be, to prevent a candidate from being returned by some fragment of the opposition, because it never can be known how the majority are to husband or distribute their forces. Now that two of the candidates should be returned by three-fourths of the electors, and the remaining candidate by one-fourth or one-fifth, is minority representation with a witness, but a great and glaring wrong to the majority.

The fact is, the whole theory seems to me to be derived from a misconception of the functions of constituencies and representatives. In the first place a representative is returned by many varieties of opinion, not of course discordant but frequently disparate. So numerous are the facts on which public opinion is exercised that there are always persons who devote themselves and their energies with exclusive attention to one topic or a few, and who attach themselves to a candidate whose acquaintance with the subject proves that his mind is made up on this or that point, and who can give reasons for having made up his mind. Assuming that different individuals in the constituency are interested in one subject or more, upon which political action is feasible, that person whose views can embrace the largest quantity of such subjects, and can treat them most exhaustively, tends towards associating to himself the largest number of political sympathisers, provided the constituency is reflective and intelligent. Next, again assuming that the constituency is concerned with the character and capacity of its representative, and is indifferent to the circumstances of his rank or wealth, the numerical majority of a constituency should be attracted to a person who can form a judgment as to the best means by which the aims which he avows, and by which he is in harmony with his constituents, can be effected. Now as a rule, all electors with whom the direction in which they exercise their franchise is a duty as well as a right, are generally enough agreed on ends; they simply differ as to the means by which these ends can be carried out. All respectable persons wish that their fellow countrymen should be sober, prosperous, treated fairly in matters of taxation, governed by equal laws. The traditional parties merely represent the forces under which in a general manner, rivals for popular support suggest that these ends will be effected, and allegiance to this or that party is exacted simply as a pledge that the representative will use the means which his supporters believe to be best to the ends which they have before them. If a constituency can thorougly trust the man of its choice, it needs exact no such pledge from him whatever, but has simply to learn his mind on the great questions of the day, and trust to his action. The restriction therefore which is put on a minority by the selection of a majority resolves itself, under the circumstances which have been assumed, into a limitation as to the agency by which admittedly beneficent ends are to be effected. In so far of course as personal or selfish interests influence a majority—and it is pretty certain that such interests will prove their own bane—a minority may be mischievously compromised, for a time at least, by a majority. But this leads one into the process by which men are educated into political opinion, and it is in this that I think the attitude of those who advocate minority representation misunderstand the function of a constituency.

The representative system is not intended to extinguish the habit of forming political opinion, (the best kind of social education which men can get,) but to assist it as well as to enable it to ripen into action. Now I can understand no process by which a sound political opinion can be formed and tested except by the representation of the majority. Opinion is not formed by mere reflection, it must be matured by debate, for social questions are so many-sided that it is very hard for any man to avoid prejudice, if he does not try to view the facts of the case from the experience of his fellow men, as well as from his own. Let each man secure by minority representation—of course it is really only possible to a limited extent—the reproduction of the tenets he accepts in a representative, and his motive for debate ceases, he has no need to attempt to win others over, he may be perfectly satisfied with having given his voice. But as long as the majority rules and the minority submits, it is the business of the minority to criticise the judgment of the majority, to impugn its validity, to try to convert it to a different way of thinking. Were a complete system of minority representation possible, political thought would stagnate, and political opinion cease to make progress. The operation of the Press, the significance of public meetings, the discussion of political topics, the associations of those who favour this or that social change, depend entirely on the relations of a majority to a minority, on the necessity imposed on the former to hold its own, on the anxiety of the latter to supplant its rival, and turn it into a minority. Take away the motive of political debate and you arrest political knowledge. Diminish it, and you produce a partial effect in the same direction. Does anybody doubt where political knowledge is at the lowest ebb? It is in those constituencies where the system of arrangement, the precursor of minority voting, has been longest practised. But that person best understands the true social interests of his countrymen who stimulates their natural inclination to discuss social questions from every point of view which can be taken of them, not one who advises them to commit a strong prejudice to the exposition of a representative of it.

The system of minority representation was an experiment, and I think a crude and ill-advised one. When first proposed in the House of Commons it was rejected.* It was afterwards inserted in the Lords, and was finally accepted by the Commons, for the reasons which I have given before, because the Conservative party foresaw that it would neutralise the great constituencies, and because the philosophical Radicals imagined it to be just. But I am strongly disposed to think that the English people is gradually coming to the view which Cobden strongly advocated, and which by the way gives the fairest prospect of minority representation, that of parcelling the country out into electoral districts, based pretty much on the old lines, and giving each district one member.

* See Bright's Speeches, Reform xiii.

CHAPTER IX.

COMMERCIAL DIPLOMACY.

THE earlier years of Cobden's political career are identified with the struggle after free trade, i. e. the vindication of commercial liberty as a matter of principle, and the application of the principle to all processes of production and exchange. As I have already shown, Cobden was equally alive to the further application of his principle in the other two economical circumstances of distribution and taxation; that his doctrine of 'free trade in land' was adopted in order to serve the ends of a natural distribution, and that his adhesion, in a general way, to the principle of direct taxation was equivalent to a declaration that the rules and hopes on which British finance are founded are indefensible in theory and unsafe in practice.

But the later years of Cobden's life were devoted to a purpose which, to the mind of many, seemed to be a policy which was either external to free trade, or even repugnant to it. Free trade, it was alleged, simply removes obstructions to the discretion of the individual, in disposing either of his labour or his property; and the State, when it adopts free trade as the maxim of its action, is merely concerned with the removal of such obstacles in the way of individuals or associations as hinder the development of free exchange. It does not restrain the action of any, and by implication it assists the action of none. It does not prohibit bargains, but it does not, on the other hand, aid the act of bargaining, for it admits that the wisdom of self-interest in the individual is far more active and accurate than any faculty which would be developed under the assistance of a Legislature or an Administration. And if it declines to help enterprise, still less does it, under such circumstances, make itself a party to any engagement which might check action, or prohibit its discretion. But a commercial treaty necessarily involves restrictions. It is simply absurd to negotiate on the principle that one party is to have unlimited freedom, while the other is tied by conditions. No arrangement can be entered into which does not involve the surrender of some liberty on the side of both contracting parties.

The critics, therefore, of that commercial diplomacy into which Cobden entered in 1860, and which had for its fruits the commercial treaty with France, and ultimately with other countries, adopted two forms of objection to the preliminaries of the treaty, which they conceived were fatal to its soundness, or at least to its consistency with the rules which its originator and author had so powerfully vindicated during the whole course of his public life. They inculpated the treaty on grounds of fact, and on grounds of principle. The whole theory of commercial treaties was identified with the worst fallacies of the mercantile system. These instruments had been used in order to further political alliances of a mischievous kind abroad, or to sustain special interests at home. The annals of England are full of diplomatic documents which, while they commended themselves to the political passions or military projects of one party in the community, stimulated an interested body, which discerned its own immediate advantage in the creation or sustentation of particular treaty stipulations, but to the detriment of the public good, and to the ultimate profit of no one. If there be two truths which have been demonstrated conclusively, they are, first, that there is only a very limited period during which protection assists private industry, since competition soon puts an end to the exceptional emoluments of the favoured calling, while the injury and loss to the public commence at the very moment that the protection is accorded; and, second, that the reversal of a protectionist policy is always difficult, because far more loss is effected on the protected industries by a return to the principle of economical freedom, than profit had been secured during the time that the protection was granted. Evidence on this subject is cumulative and overwhelming.

Among the earliest of those diplomatic engagements, which are partly commercial, partly political, and which were negotiated because the country secured the latter end, and appeared to secure the former, are the treaties which the Plantagenet kings of the fourteenth century entered into with the Low Countries. The weavers of Ghent cultivated the English alliance, and stipulated for peculiar privileges in the English wool market. There is, I imagine, no reason to doubt that according to the policy of the time, it was the interest of the Flemish burghers to gain the assistance of England against their feudal lord, and that it was equally the interest of the English wool-growers to have a free market for their produce in the Flemish towns. In other words, the advantages of the treaty could be secured, and would be secured, without the interposition of any formal instrument, and therefore this ancient treaty was either an injury, or a superfluity; the former in case the interests of trade did not dictate its provisions, the latter if trade would have been carried on equally well without it. Similarly the negotiations which, under the name of the *Intercursus magnus*, are reported to have finally destroyed the hopes of the Yorkist party in the fifteenth century, were nothing more than a recognition of those relations which might have been fairly left to natural causes, since it was certain that if no hindrance were put on the parties who might traffic together, traffic would certainly be originated and sustained.

Nothing better illustrates the source of economical fallacies than the eagerness with which the mercantile classes have always grasped at the grant of the favoured nation clause in commercial diplomacy. When the prospect of a monopoly in a particular market is offered, the bait is snapped with instant eagerness. But commercial history is full of proofs that no advantage whatever attends the monopoly. The merchants who constituted the East India Company soon found that the profits of their trade monopoly would not give them a dividend, and were constrained to find a revenue from the taxes which a conquering despot can lay on his slaves. The Dutch adopted, as is well known, even more stringent measures to secure their trade monopoly, for they actually bribed the natives of the Spice Islands to root out all spice-bearing trees, and regularly burnt a portion of each year's harvest in order to keep up the price. But the Dutch East India Company was a commercial failure. It absorbed the savings of the Hollanders, and reduced the rate of interest to a lower point than it has ever been reached in commercial history. It was to their commercial policy, and not to their system of taxation, as Mr. Macculloch has most absurdly argued, that the low rate of interest among the Dutch was due; for heavy taxation raises the rate of interest by perfectly obvious causes. But the Dutch threw all their savings into the abyss of the monopoly trade with the East, and, as was proved at the outbreak of the French revolution, devoted the deposits in the Bank of Amsterdam to the same visionary end. Shrewd traders as they were, they had not learned the simple rule of business, that numerous transactions at a small profit are more gainful than a few transactions at a great profit.

The type of our commercial treaties was that negotiated with Portugal by Mr. Methuen in 1703, under which the British Government agreed to admit Portuguese wines at two-thirds the duty levied on French wines, in return for an arrangement under which English woollens were freely imported into Portugal. As usual, this treaty, which has been criticised by Adam Smith,* contemplated political as well as mercantile objects. It hoped to create an interest in the

* 'Wealth of Nations,' vol. ii. p. 122 (Author's edition).

Spanish Peninsula, which should be adverse to that of France, and it offered a bait to the woollen manufacturers of this country. Furthermore, it was supposed likely to assist in the importation of specie into Great Britain, then, and for a long time afterwards, a primary object in commercial legislation. 'The treaty,' says Adam Smith, 'was considered to be a masterpiece of the commercial policy of England.' He devotes some pains to proving that it was delusive and wasteful. It was reasonable, therefore, when men had before them the recollection of this and many other abortive efforts in commercial diplomacy, that they should look with grave suspicion on all negotiations which had or seemed to have the same direction. No good had ever come of such undertakings; they belonged to an era in which Governments thought themselves wiser than men of business are in their own callings, and this delusion had been happily exploded.

I have already suggested the principle which was alleged against such and similar expedients. 'If,' it was argued, 'the trade between England and France is good for England, the English merchant will speedily embark in the trade. The Government intends to do away with the differential duties on French wines and brandies. To this we offer no sort of opposition. We are free-traders, and in the interest of both producer and consumer, we disclaim all forms of protection whatever. We are willing to abandon, if need be, any industry whatever, of which it can be proved that it is unable to subsist in the absence of some fiscal aid. It may be that the silks of Coventry and Macclesfield, hitherto protected, may not be able to compete in the home market against those of Lyons. Be it so. We have no wish to preserve that which cannot bear the healthy climate of pure competition. But we have unlearned the old lesson, that it is the business of law and government to assist importation. Our maxim has been, take care of the exports, and let the imports take care of themselves. We can do so with perfect confidence. If we can sell our goods, we sell them for other goods, and we get all the advantages of a commercial treaty without its wearisome restrictions, and its delusive advantages. A commercial treaty is an economical heresy, got rid of with difficulty, but got rid of entirely. To go back to it, is to reverse a policy which has been generally accepted, because it has been uniformly approved.' It was, I presume, from this point of view that Mr. Lowe condemned all treaties of commerce when he said that 'the plan for negotiating foreign treaties of commerce is the mother of the heresy of reciprocity as against free trade[*].'

I shall take occasion to show hereafter, how notably the treaty of commerce which Cobden negotiated differed from the type of those which Smith condemned, and which Mr. Lowe probably had before him when he uttered this adverse criticism on all such instruments. But for the present it is better to confine the subject to the general topic of commercial diplomacy.

Many of my readers may be aware of the circumstances under which Cobden negotiated the Commercial Treaty of 1860. But they must be briefly recapitulated. In 1859 Mr. Cobden had been nominated,

[*] February 28th, 1870.

in his absence, to the office of President of the Board of Trade, under Lord Palmerston; an office which he declined. In January, 1860, he was appointed Plenipotentiary to negotiate a commercial treaty with France. Mr. Gladstone's Budget was introduced on February 10. The circumstances were favourable to a change in the financial system of the country; for by the extinction of the Long Annuities, an annual charge, amounting to nearly £2,500,000, was remitted. It was in connection with these facts that Mr. Gladstone resolved to equalise certain duties which pressed upon French produce, and which, being differential, offended against free-trade principles, and to abolish certain others altogether for similar reasons. In connection with these changes in the British tariff, Cobden undertook to negotiate certain reforms in the French tariff, with the sympathy and assistance of the Emperor of the French, and of his minister, M. Rouher.

The Emperor of the French had adopted free-trade principles, and had thus conciliated many of those who were, of necessity, politically opposed to his theory of government. He was intelligent enough to see the advantage which a policy of free trade would give to the country which he governed, and he was strong or bold enough to undertake a policy which was in accordance with these views. His predecessor, Louis Philippe, had exactly the same estimate of the advantages which would ensue to France under a free-trade *régime*. After the Repeal of the Corn Laws, when Cobden was recruiting his energies by a continental tour, he was invited to Neuilly by the King of the French, and fell, at the King's suggestion, into a train of reasoning, by which he showed how great a boon free trade would be for France; dwelling in particular on the advantage which a free importation of iron goods and cutlery would be to French households and French agriculture. 'It would be so,' said the King, 'but, *ma foi*, these ironmasters are our masters.' Napoleon, either because the situation was modified, or because his own Government was stronger and more popular—the events occurred just after the Italian war, and the cession of Savoy; circumstances which flattered French ideas of glory and ambition,—felt himself competent to cope with the ironmasters, and other protected manufacturers.

There is no country in Europe to which free trade is more natural and more advantageous than it is to France. The country produces certain articles for which, as civilisation and refinement extend, there is an almost unlimited market. In articles of taste the French artisan fears no rival. He seems to possess a faculty of investing the most homely materials with the most attractive forms, and to be equally capable of the most graceful and the most grotesque ideas. By a happy accident in art, he is as logical as he is imaginative, and can express the best conceptions of his fancy in the simplest and the most effective methods. It is true that this power follows him into politics, and unfortunately makes him a doctrinaire and a despot, because he combines, in the most remarkable manner, the gift of individuality and the vice of egotism. There is hardly an educated Frenchman who is not agreeable and intolerant.

The success of the Frenchman in art follows him

into those branches of agriculture in which art is most effective. It is very possible that he grows fewer quarters of wheat to the acre than the English agriculturist does, that his stock is greatly inferior to that on a well-managed English farm, that his tools and other implements are rude, and that his knowledge of the process by which machinery can be made to supplement labour is by no means perfect. It is a common practice to sneer at the ordinary agriculture of the French peasant, and to compare the miserable menage of the small proprietor's homestead with the handsome appointments of an English tenant. But the French farmer wastes nothing, and spends nothing uselessly. Moreover, where he can turn his labour to effective results he has absolutely no superior. Thus he has a perfect genius for making wine.

During the time that the commercial treaty was in progress, Cobden told me that he conversed with M. Rouher on the singular capacity which the French people had for manufacturing those lighter beverages, in which the greatest possible amount of delicate flavour is combined with the most persistent power of lasting in sound condition; and that, as France seemed likely to have no rival in the art, her power of extending her wine trade was practically unlimited. He said that M. Rouher replied that he saw no possible rivalry in any other country but Hungary. The recuperative powers of France are now being exhibited. The value of her exports steadily increases, while she is thrifty in importing. The return of the particulars in which this growth of trade consists is not given, but it is more than probable that it is derived from the increased demand for French wines, and the increased price of the article. She is recovering herself on what Adam Smith calls the balance of production and consumption.

But favoured as France is in climate and soil, and in the peculiar genius of her people, nature has not been bountiful to her in mineral wealth, or in mechanical invention. The coal measures of France are few and poor. Her mines are not productive. She has every reason for exchanging those products of her soil, which the skill of her inhabitants can so successfully manipulate, for those foreign products which she can procure from other nations with such ease, and in such abundance. She is pre-eminently an agricultural country, and when the agricultural products of any country represent great wealth in small compass, and answer to the demand of a wealthy and increasing body of customers, the arguments in favour of free trade in such a country are cumulative and irresistible. That there should be any demur to the acceptance of free trade can be due only to the fact that interests which never ought to have been created, because they do not naturally exist, oppose a beneficent policy. It is possible that certain French manufactures, which are supposed to be imperilled by the adoption of free trade, would not only survive the shock, but would thrive under a healthy system of competition, and that the evidence afforded by the results of the Commercial Treaty of 1860 is sufficient to remove or abate many of the alarms which were honestly entertained when the experiment of a modified free trade was originally attempted. But even if it were found that some manufactures must be abandoned in order to effect the general good of the country, it cannot but be that minor and unimportant interests should give way to the great advantage which an agricultural country invariably discovers in the extension of its markets.

The changes in the English tariff contained in the Budget of 1860 was made the occasion for Mr. Cobden's commercial diplomacy. On that occasion the English Legislature did not, as in other commercial treaties, proffer a monopoly to the French producer, or bind itself to customs' charges which would in any degree whatever curtail its trade with other nations. But it stipulated that it would not hereafter, during such time as the treaty might last, entertain any scheme for fiscal alterations which should qualify or alter those relations between the United Kingdom and France which are contained in the treaty. The chief advantages which France gained by the treaty were the adoption of the alcoholic test on wine, and the substitution of a low duty for a high one, the equalisation of the customs duty on French spirits with the excise or other tax on home and colonial alcohols, and the abandonment of the duty on silks and other small articles of French manufacture. The English Government also bound itself to impose no export duty on coal. In connection with these changes the French Government engaged to admit English manufactures into France under moderate *ad valorem* duties. It is true that changes which the English Government was bent on making were the basis of negotiations on which certain concessions were demanded from France, and that, strictly speaking, there was no reciprocity whatever in the Treaty. It is also true that the English Government, by means of Cobden's diplomacy, assisted the Government of the French Emperor in imposing a free-trade policy on a rural population which was generally indifferent to the change, because it was ignorant of the beneficial results which would ensue from it, and on reluctant manufacturers who might have been alarmed for their monopoly and were professedly fearful of their very existence. Hence it has been said that the negotiations of 1860 were carried on rather in a missionary than in a diplomatic spirit, and that the principle by which they were guided was grotesque and out of place.

It may be admitted at once, that if the success of diplomatic finesse consists in overreaching the Government of one among the intriguing States, and that the whole of those international relations which proceed from embassies are simply the machinery for finding the gain of one nation in the loss of another, the commercial diplomacy of Cobden was absolutely alien from ordinary diplomatic traditions. But it is, I submit, equally clear that the distinction is a condemnation of political diplomacy altogether, and that, if the difference holds, those politicians are in the right who argue that diplomacy is a standing nuisance and a danger. But it is just in so far as these relations wherein the government of different countries are founded upon natural equity, that they are tolerable, and in so far as they bring about feelings of international amity, afford guarantees of peace, and disabuse the public mind of such prejudices or delusions as may lead to grave international differences, in so far, if you please, as they are based upon what is called the missionary spirit, that they are useful, and will be lasting.

All restraints upon the free intercourse of nations are virtually acts of war. They are attempts, more or less openly avowed, to show that it is expedient not only to keep one's neighbour at arm's length, but to cripple his resources or injure his interests. The real purposes which they intend may be disguised under a variety of pretexts, may be the mere defence of selfishness. There is perhaps no country in which a greater number of ingenious and plausible excuses have been alleged for these acts of hostility than have been in the United States, where reasons are brought forward for a protective policy by persons whose abilities make it all but impossible to believe that the opinion or the argument is a genuine conviction. Thus we are sometimes told that it is expedient that a Government should develope all classes of occupation or industry; sometimes that a nation should be wholly self-supporting; sometimes that a limited period of protection is necessary in order to secure the existence of an important and legitimate industry; sometimes that the American manufacturer cannot compete against the pauperised labour of the Old World; and a variety of other reasons equally irrevelant and unsound with these which have been quoted. It is fortunate indeed for the progress of civilisation that these errors or sophistries carry with them a practical refutation in the decay of trade, in the rise of prices, in the depreciation of labour, in the curtailment of real wages, and the temporary exaggeration of trade profit.

Now, that a statesman, who has the ability to refute these fallacies, and the opportunity to give practical effect to his refutation, should undertake a negotiation with a foreign Government in order to induce such a change in a fiscal system as will be wholly beneficent, is, I submit, a clear gain to mankind. To make light of the effort and to nickname it, is, I think, as shortsighted as it is malignant. The intercourse of nations should be one of mutual benefit; and it is a mere relapse into the selfish theory which up to fifty years ago, characterised the trade legislation of Europe, to be indifferent to the wisdom or folly of foreign fiscal systems, and to acquiesce, as though it were a fiscal maxim of deliberate prudence, in the dogma that we may be intelligent for ourselves only; or, in the jargon of trade, should take care of the imports only, and let the exports take care of themselves. On grounds of public policy, and on grounds of general advantage it is expedient that we should seek to extend the area over which free trade is accepted, and bring other nations into the same mind with ourselves. Negligence in this direction gives a colour to the ridiculous, but oft-repeated statement, that the English nation has indeed gained its advantage in free trade, but that this system is suited only to the peculiar genius or destiny of the English people. It is superfluous to say that what is found to be good for ourselves is good for other communities also. It may be proved that the beneficence of the change is incomplete, as far as regards ourselves, until other nations have entered on the same policy.

Diplomacy has not disdained to negotiate on subjects where mere morality is concerned. The English nation led the way in renouncing slavery, in putting an end to the slave trade, and in making the suppression of the traffic the object of unceasing negotiation. It carried out a reform in its own colonies, though with the certainty of a great cost to the nation, and with a prospect of great loss to the colonies. It appears to have cut up the institution root and branch from motives of humanity only, and in the interests of the negro. It is true that society is inevitably brutalised wherever slavery prevails, and that the economical progress of a community is arrested at an early stage wherever labour is degraded. But it does not seem, when the English nation resolved on this reform, that it was anxious about the morals of the planter, or considered the condition into which labour might be brought by the influence of the custom of slavery. But from the time that we undertook to abolish and uproot slavery, we have never tired of those diplomatic efforts which have ultimately enlisted the sympathies of the civilised world. Now if it be worth while to struggle after conferring freedom on labour, it is equally reasonable to labour on behalf of freedom for trade. The policy which holds human creatures in bondage is doubtlessly more odious than that which deliberately uses the powers of the Legislature in order to mulct the consumer, that it may satisfy the greed of the producer; but it is exactly of the same stock as the outgrowth of slavery is. To fetter the discretion of the man who purchases goods in order to satisfy the necessities of his life, only differs in form from restraining the labourer in choosing the market for his labour, and from the possession of his natural wages. If it be wise, just, right, to direct diplomacy to use all its efforts and address in uprooting slavery, is it less just and wise and right to attempt by the same means to secure to all men the fullest enjoyment of what they earn and spend?

The course of that commercial diplomacy which Cobden undertook was rendered difficult by the temper of the time. That the Emperor of the French was sincerely anxious to maintain amicable relations with England is, I believe, indisputable. But he was surrounded by a vain, impulsive crowd of military and political adventurers, whom he might be obliged to conciliate. We know that he gave way to them at last, and to his cost. He had undertaken the restoration of Italian liberty, and he had won Solferino and Magenta. But he suddenly checked the progress of his own arms, and wished to establish an Italian protectorate which he might direct. How he was baffled by the astuteness of Cavour and the daring of Garibaldi is matter of general history. But as if to give a sinister interpretation to his Italian Campaign, he had demanded Savoy and Nice as the price of his assistance in Lombardy, and his connivance at the aggrandisement of the Italian Kingdom. The cession of these Italian provinces was an excessively unpopular and, as events proved, an imprudent act. Thenceforth it was clear that he intended, as opportunity offered, to aim after the territorial enlargement of France at the expense of his neighbours. The English people shared the general distrust, and listened to rumours as to the ultimate designs of the French Emperor on Great Britain.

While he was negotiating the treaty with Cobden, he was credited with the project of constructing a vast navy which should transport an invading army in a night to the shores of Sussex or Dorsetshire. Lord Lyndhurst and Mr. Horsman denounced the danger and the man. So serious were the difficulties that Cobden more than once thought of throwing up his commission, and abandoning a task which seemed to be hopeless in the presence of such excited alarms.

The system of Napoleon's Government added to his unpopularity in England. Men knew the story of the *Coup d' Etat* of December 1851 only imperfectly, and they entertained pretty generally an impression that France was a country which could hardly be governed on constitutional principles. But the English people has a profound belief in parliamentary government, and looks on despotism, however it may seem justified by circumstances, with suspicion and hostility. It does so with some reason, for a despotism gives all the appearance of concentrated power, and does not betray at first sight its inherent weakness, its corruption and want of genuine public spirit. Within the experience of the present generation three great European despotisms have collapsed, two of which had, up to their fall, powerfully attracted the imagination of mankind. There were very few persons who anticipated the conclusion of the Russian war, of the war between Prussia and Austria, of the war between Germany and France. Yet in each case the cause of the collapse was the same. Hence, during the negotiation of the French Treaty, persons asked how so sound a Liberal as Cobden was could transact business with a ruler of Napoleon's type. Cobden's answer was obvious. He asserted that, were he a Frenchman, he should be as ardently in opposition to the Emperor's Government as any French Liberal could be, but that Napoleon was the head of the French nation, and that there was no reason why he should not try to do benefit to the people of both countries because he did not sympathise with the policy and projects of the personage who wielded supreme power in one of these countries. He even thought Lord Palmerston to be as mischievous a man as Napoleon. I have reason to know that when M. Chevalier allowed himself to support the Mexican expedition, he found that he had put Cobden's friendship towards him to a strain which it could not bear.

Apart from the material advantages which the French Treaty would give to British manufacture and trade, Cobden saw in it a guarantee of peace between the countries. I do not envy the gratification which a particular class of men feel, or the exultation with which they express their conviction that efforts after a better and more amicable relation between Governments are visionary and Utopian, and bid us survey the history of the civilised world during the last twenty years. If, as is now generally admitted, there is not any defence whatever to be alleged for the aggressor in all these wars—with the solitary exception of the war of Italian Independance—it is easy to see how, after a time, very adverse and menacing criticism will be employed against those political institutions which render such wars possible. The impression, that monarchs exist by making wars, may be understood hereafter with a stern significance. But meanwhile the commercial intercourse of nations renders quarrels between them increasingly difficult, because it checks all inclination to the exaggeration of imaginary wrongs. It is the business of a true statesman to aid in effecting such relations between communities as to give the guise of civil war to any rupture between the amity of two races or two governments. Cobden did not indeed allege that close trade between two nations removed the possibilities of quarrel, but he held, and held with reason, that it assisted in the explanation of disputes, and made actual warfare increasingly difficult or remote, that it helped to disarm the professional soldier, and check diplomatic intrigues.

The extension of international trade tends to develope two other guarantees of international amity. It assists in proving the necessity of an international law of commerce, and an international currency. That these reforms will commend themselves to the exigencies of modern society, as they do to the judgment of all intelligent persons, may be safely predicted. That the jealousies, which have hitherto prevented the adoption of such reforms, are due to the old policy which strives to isolate the interests of European nations and to trade on their differences is manifest. Just as there are professions which are imperilled by the concession of salutary reforms, so there are forms of government and parties which believe that they can maintain or justify their existence only by upholding an indefensible policy, or by withstanding a necessary change. It was to the credit of the princes of divided Germany that, with few exceptions, they saw the necessity of a united Zollverein. That there should be a rate of exchange between the currencies of civilised countries is as great a barbarism as a rate of exchange was between London and Edinburgh. Similarly it is in the highest degree expedient that legal process for the recovery of debts between the inhabitants of this country and other civilised communities should be as easy and as obvious as it is between the subjects of any one country. It would be well indeed for us if we could borrow parts of the French law of bankruptcy, and better still if we could cultivate that nice sense of commercial honour, which is one of the most generous characteristics of the French merchant. In any case, it is certain that the closer are the ties which bind together the commercial intercourse of nations, the more lively is the anticipation of the inconveniences which would ensue from a rupture, and the stronger are the guarantees of peace.

The formal development then of such international relations as Cobden contemplated in the diplomatic negotiations which are identified with his later activity, is part of that high political education in mutual duties and mutual benefits which must be, in time to come, the process of modern civilisation. The true student of political philosophy has a feeling which is almost contemptuous towards forms of government. He is a stranger to that enthusiasm which some men call loyalty, and equally a stranger to that passionate hatred of dynasties and institutions which some men call a love of freedom. He is at war with no institution, with no privilege which is not noxious. He reserves his ardour for the solid freedom of unrestricted employment, exchange, enjoyment; provided employment, exchange, enjoyment, are innocent. He does not dislike things because they are, but because he sees they ought not to be. But there is one principle with which he always does battle. It is that which justifies an economical falsehood on the ground that it serves a political good. He knows that this is a sophism as detestable as it is false, as delusive as it is dangerous. He is aware, whether his investigation of history has been narrow or extensive, that he can trace all the rivalry, the feuds, the bloodshed which have disgraced the annals of civilisation, and constitute the every day life of barbarism, to the doctrine that nations have disparate and not reciprocal interests, and he is well aware that while the doctrine of free trade is one of the forms in which this true reciprocity consists, it is only one of the means, though the earliest and the most powerful means, by which public morality may be developed, and immoral ambition frustrated. In a sense then, an economist may accept the title of a missionary, and may perhaps win more for peace and good-will among nations than many who have usurped a sacred name, and have given little warranty for their claim in the results of their teaching. They who knew Cobden can confirm my statement, that in the ultimate victory of his principles, of which indeed he never doubted, the smallest consequence which he foresaw was the distribution of the benefits which Nature accords through the machinery of free trade; and that he dwelt with peculiar satisfaction on the conviction that in the freedom which he loved and for which he laboured, lie the highest hopes of morality and civilisation.

It is possible that the avowal of these purposes would have led to the charge that the work which Cobden undertook was visionary and Utopian, and would have even discouraged many who went with him from active co-operation in the transaction. For the majority of men it was expedient to show that the interests of trade would be furthered by a relaxation of those restrictions which had formerly prevailed, and that the form of a commercial treaty was a guarantee against the reversal of a policy which had been once adopted. These anticipations were justified on grounds of reason, and have been confirmed by experience. It may be desirable at this point to show at length what are the economical consequences on the producer and consumer in each of two countries which trade together when one of these countries has adopted free trade, and the other still clings to the policy of restriction or protection.

Mr. Mill has argued that the value of articles exchanged between the inhabitants of any one country tends to be determined by the cost of production, while the value of any article which is produced in a foreign country is, on the other hand, determined by the cost of its acquisition to the country which produces it in exchange. I do not feel satisfied with the distinction which Mr. Mill has made, and I fear that it has made his interpretation of the process of international exchange needlessly obscure. The truth appears to be that the two factors are co-efficient of the product under all circumstances, but that in interpreting the circumstances of international trade, the latter is more dominant and more visible. From this point of view then the value of French goods in the English market is not decided primarily by the cost to which the French manufacturer or agriculturist was put in order to supply them, but by the cost to which the English merchant or trader was put in order to procure them. As a consequence, as Mr. Mill observes with perfect accuracy, 'the circumstances of trade may be such that the English consumer may obtain French goods at less cost than the French consumer may be put to when he obtains them in his own country.' Now if it can be shown that such a contingency is not only possible but probable under a system of protection or restriction, the policy which brings about such a result is a sheer waste of national resources.

The condition of the French consumer of English goods was intelligible enough. If the duty levied on foreign manufactures was prohibitive, he was constrained to pay the French manufacturer whatever the necessities of his case and the state of competition among manufacturers could exact. The latter limitation is I believe a decreasing quantity, for, as I have elsewhere observed, the tendency of modern habit is to agree on prices, and compete for custom, that in short, what has been said of railway enterprise, is in a modified form true of manufactures, that where combination is possible, competition is at an end. In England it appears that such a result has been arrived at in many great branches of industry, that associations regulate prices by their interpretation of demand, and that the chief business of the individual manufacturer and trader is to obtain as much business as he can by soliciting orders or by advertisements. If such a habit is growing in foreign countries, protection operates at once to enhance price and to lower quality. It is manifest that protection would be superfluous if such a consequence did but ensue. It is not seen with equal clearness that it is mere extortion if such a consequence does ensue.

The waste of wealth involved in the compulsory purchase of articles manufactured at home of inferior quality and higher price is nowhere seen so plainly as in the United States. In that country the purchasing power of money, in all articles of secondary necessity and great convenience, is lower than in any other civilised community, while it ought to be naturally higher. Clothing, tools, agricultural implements, hardware, and a variety of other analogous articles, are excessively dear, for reasons which will be obvious to any one who has given the least attention to the laws which regulate price.. Even under the circumstances, domestic industry is not always protected or fostered. The tariff of the United States puts a duty which is almost prohibitive on foreign damask linen. It may be doubted, however, whether the Union weaves a yard of any but the commonest kinds of this material, as I have been informed by a considerable and intelligent manufacturer of linen damask. The consequence of this policy is that all the superior advantages which America affords in its abundant and varied soil, and in the high rate of wages which it offers to labour, are lost in the artificial enhancement of price. Nay, the very purpose for which these restrictions are enacted is frustrated. The American Legislature wishes, no doubt, to develope and strengthen its iron manufactures. The resources of the country are such that without any assistance whatever, it ought to supply the civilised world with an unlimited amount of pig and wrought iron. It is probable that it does not export a ton of either, and it is certain that it cripples its domestic industry by the enormous duties which it levies on the foreign article.

As a consumer, the inhabitant of a country which has adopted free trade is not injured by the adoption of a protective tariff in the country with which he deals, he may even be a gainer from this point of view by the unwisdom of his neighbour. The price of American wheat is not raised a single penny per quarter by the restrictive tariff of the New England manufacturers. The protection accorded to the French manufacturer does not raise the price of Bordeaux wine. Nay, in both cases the tendency is to lessen the price of the articles sold. The reason of this is to be found in the ordinary conditions of trade. Producers wish to sell. It is very rarely the case that financiers find it possible to exact an export duty, and when they could attempt it, they find it highly unpopular to do so. Unless the article is one which cannot be procured elsewhere, the effect of an export duty is to divert the trade into some other direction. Even if it cannot be procured from some other locality, an economy may be induced in its use, or some substitute can be found for it, and in any case the export duty tends to exclude from the market that produce which is obtained under the least favourable circumstances.

Now it will be manifest that a dealer sells to the least advantage when the articles for which he can exchange his goods are artificially limited in number or heightened in price. The Illinois farmer and the Bordeaux wine-grower wish, for example, to sell their corn and wine to a British merchant. Under the best conditions, they would exchange their produce for a selection of those British manufactures which they could dispose of to the greatest advantage in their own country. But the law interposes. It prohibits the purchase of one article, and it narrows the market for the other by artificially enhancing its price. Under these circumstances the corn-grower and the wine-grower are constrained to take less out of a narrower number of articles, and thus sell at a greater disadvantage than they would if the market were free. Now if Mr. Mill's position be sound, that the cost of foreign produce is determined by the cost of acquisition, it may very well happen that the price of such foreign produce, as has been obtained in exchange for articles of inferior quality or of less amount, may be actually lower in the importing country than it is in the place of its origin or growth. The case is still stronger if a country declines to sell for anything but gold or silver. Here it narrows the purchasing power of its goods to a minimum, and does its best to diminish to a minimum also the value of that which alone it agrees to take in exchange.

From this point of view, therefore, the British consumer may look with indifference or even with satisfaction on the follies of his neighbours. Here the maxim, take care of the imports and let the exports take care of themselves, has a foundation of reason. We may say: 'the industry of other countries supplies, nay presses upon us, a variety of useful or convenient articles. The laborious and enterprising owners of these goods are of so beneficent a disposition that they deliberately place themselves at a disadvantage in dealing with us. They want to sell. They must sell, for what we can use is to them a superfluity. Under the impression that they are supporting and sustaining native industry, distributing employments, and making the nation self-contained, or for some other equally visionary objects, they are willing to forego the natural advantages of our market, and to acquiesce in a loss where they might make a gain. We find it to our advantage in trading with these simple folk, who are willing to barter on so singular a basis.'

But of course the trade of two countries not only considers the convenience of the consumer, but the advantage of the producer, and here the restrictive tariff of another country does lay a loss on those with whom it deals, as well as inflicts a far greater loss on its victim. To buy you must sell, to sell you must produce, and if restriction were universal, trade would be annihilated. It may happen, as in the case which was cited above, that an intended prohibition becomes nothing but an enormous tax on the unfortunate victim of an enlightened or paternal government. But even in this case the market is narrowed. The American public may keep a dozen damask mills at work in England, each with its three hundred to five hundred Jacquard looms going. But if the tax were abandoned or lowered to a reasonable impost, the demands of the American consumer might stimulate fifty such mills into activity. There may be a million Americans clothed in English broad cloth, purchased at a ridiculously high price, whereas if the restriction on the importation of this article were remitted, five times as many might exchange a ragged or ill-made fabric for a stout and sound one, and thereby call into a productive industry an increased number of British workmen. Now that which wakens and extends industry is beneficent, while that which checks and narrows it is hostile.

I have already adverted to the fact that the immediate benefit to themselves as manufacturers and traders, which the agitators for free trade in corn contemplated and insisted on, was not a lowering of wages. On the contrary, they predicted, and with a success which falls to the lot of few prophets, that wages would rise if free trade were accorded. Nor did they anticipate a lowering of agricultural prices. They did not expect that corn would be cheap under a free-trade régime, but rather that it would cease to be liable to sudden and violent fluctuations in price. But they predicted, and with perfect success, that there would be an abundant compensation for any loss on corn by the exaltation of the price which other agricultural products would command, owing to the increasing numbers and the increasing prosperity of the people. As a matter of fact, the only article which fell in price was wheat, for the causes referred to effected a rise in the price of oats and barley, as is proved by the indisputable evidence of the tithe-charge averages.

What they did anticipate, and what ensued, from the principle already laid down, was an extension of their industry by the exchange of manufactured goods against corn. They knew that there were plenty of foreign corn-growers who wished to sell, and they saw of course that in order to sell they must buy. They foresaw that the change which they instituted would bring this country within the range of a perpetual harvest, would stimulate industry everywhere, and thereby increase the security and the opulence of mankind. It was not to be expected that they were indifferent to, and ignorant of, their own interests, any more than those among their critics were who ridiculed the free-trade gospel, and spoke with scorn of the homely but convincing axioms on which the reform was founded. Nor did the advocates of free trade consider simply the profits of the employer or manufacturer. They knew that high profits mean as a rule high wages, and that if they were attempting to effect a change which should give the manufacturer an epoch of prosperity, they would assuredly and inevitably fill the home of the labourer with plenty. Now beneficence is not less beneficent because it makes its appearance under the form of thriving business and active industry. I cannot conceive that any person of intelligence would have failed to see the importance of opening foreign markets to British produce, unless he had been at once led by phrases and ignorant of the conditions under which international trade can be successful.

A considerable portion of British trade has been and is carried on with nations which have not arrived at that stage of civilisation which believes in the efficacy of protective tariffs and differential duties, and which seems to affect communities in the same way that certain diseases are endemic among the children of civilised races. Had however the products of British industry sought and found a market only among those communities which are imbued with the notion that our profit is their loss, that free trade is a growth which is capable of existence only in the British Isles, that it is an error to transplant it into other regions, and that protection is the normal law of political and social enlightenment, we should have been very stupid or very patient if we had not made every effort to disabuse foreigners of so foolish and malignant a delusion. It is because we have a market where those fancies have not yet been developed or taught, that we are comparatively indifferent to the obstructions which more enlightened governments have put on our commercial interest with them. But that the advantage of both parties would be consulted in the extension of free trade principles, and that the control of trade is a mean and malignant sophism, is or ought to be plain to every man but a monopolist or a doctrinaire.

I am ready enough to admit that a commercial treaty is not the highest manifestation of economical intelligence. But it may be the best under the circumstances. Men must walk before they can run. They must be taught their alphabet, and con words of one syllable, before they can read an ordinary sentence with fluency. If it be once granted that the adhesion to a protective system, which still vitiates the legislation and checks the amity of other nations, is a vice and a loss to the community which adopts or allows it, and a loss and hindrance to those who are debarred from free trade by its provisions, it is surely expedient to adopt any means which the practice of diplomacy permits in order to mitigate or abate the mischief. It would be best if we could persuade all nations that they can gain nothing, and must lose much, by maintaining those regulations which experience and reason have shown to be generally injurious, and most of all injurious to those who fancy them a benefit. But it is still a good if we can induce them to travel a little way on the same road with ourselves, to realise in some degree what the facts are, and gradually to see that what they thought to be an evil was an unmixed benefit. The education of nations is something, even though the process stops short of absolute enlightenment. What should we say of a man who declined to teach a child anything whatever, on the ground that he saw no prospect of carrying his pupil through all the arts and sciences? The English people have accepted free trade as an irreversible position, the abandonment of which would amount to the sacrifice of a science; do they play false to their principles when they induce, or seek to induce, other nations to accept the science temporarily as an hypothesis?

There is a radical difference between the old commercial treaties and that which Cobden negotiated and which has served as the type of analagous engagements. The former were based on monopolies, and were of the nature of alliances entered into with a hostile meaning towards those who were excluded from the alliance. To this form of treaty there was it is true an exception in the treaty concluded between Great Britain and France in the year 1786,* and which might have been the precursor of similar arrangements, had not the war of the French revolution broken out shortly afterwards.

* See Macpherson's 'History of Commerce,' vol. iv. p. 111.

By this treaty the wines of France were to be admitted at the same rates with those of Portugal, or, in other words, the distinctive clause of the Methuen treaty was abandoned.

The treaty which Cobden negotiated, and which was the first of a series, bound the contracting parties not to raise their tariffs. France was perfectly well aware that England had given up all differential duties, and would therefore admit all other nations to the arrangements which were made with France, and England was also well aware that immediately on the completion of the treaty, France would be ready to negotiate with other countries on the same basis as that taken in the English treaty. Both parties therefore solemnly disavowed the old notion of exclusive advantage, the one by virtue of a principle which she had now finally adopted, the other because she was willing to admit all other countries to a share in the compact. The natural results followed. England negotiated similar treaties with other European countries, and France followed in the same track.

The practical justification of the treaty, even if it be treated as a compromise, is to be found in the growth of commercial relations with France. This country, we are told triumphantly, is the home of compromise, and it is perhaps not unreasonable to ask those who boast of such a practice, as the height of political wisdom, to allow some scope for their principle in international relations. There is an apology for the compromise in the fact that the relaxation of the old restrictions led to violent recrimination on the part of those interests which were supposed to be imperilled, and that experience taught that the fear was empty, and that no legitimate French interest was endangered. On two points, indeed, the English public was, or affected to be, alarmed. It was objected that the treaty provided against the imposition of an export duty on coals, and that the English plenipotentiaries had neglected to secure the remission of a prohibitive export duty on rags in the interest of the paper makers.

It need hardly be said that the former of these was a visionary objection. If it was founded on the alarm at the exhaustion of the motive power of machinery, the quantity exported, as compared with that consumed at home, was so small that it hardly bore on the question. If it was based on a political reason, and implied an objection to supplying a possible enemy with an important munition of war, the answer was twofold, first that such an alarm would apply to every article whatever which might be made hereafter available for belligerent purposes, and next that commercial treaties, like other treaties, exist only in time of peace. And lastly, if it referred to the propriety of maintaining the power of levying an export duty, as a fiscal resource, it is sufficient to say that export duties are never expedient and rarely profitable, and that they press with severity on that part of the supply which is raised under the most unfavourable circumstances.

The charge of negligence as regards the export duty on rags was more subtle, but not more solid. That the French Government retained the tax in order to support a particular domestic industry is indisputable. That such a policy is theoretically and practically unsound need not be demonstrated. If it were effective it inflicted—in the case that under the conditions of trade French rags would have been exported—a loss on a very poor class of the community, rag collectors and dealers, in order to confer a problematical benefit on paper makers. The real grievance was therefore slight to the English manufacturers, and great to the French rag dealers. It is moreover clear that the restriction excluded the collector of foreign rags from the French market, because the purpose of the regulation was that of cheapening the raw material, and no one will sell, it may be presumed, in a market where his goods are artificially depreciated. If, therefore, it was effective, the loss was local; if ineffective, the restriction was nugatory.

The fact is, that the cry for cheap material in aid of the manufacture of paper arose at a time when the supply of this material was affected by the enormous increase in the consumption of paper products. Now it is impossible that a great and growing demand can be satisfied from a secondary and therefore limited material. The supply of rags increases no doubt with the growth of population, but the demand for paper grows in a far more rapid proportion. Hence the question was a momentary one, pending the answer to a much more important enquiry. In the dearth of what was once mere waste, and what is now insufficient, what fibre can be found which will afford a supply, practically inexhaustible, as the material for a product, the demand for which increases so rapidly? The first answer, as is known, was Esparto grass. This, it seems, is inadequate to the demand, and jute has been suggested. Latterly, it appears that paper pulp will be afforded in sufficient quantity from the wood of certain non-resinous trees. But, in any case, the relation of rags to paper has ceased to be of vital importance, for no possible supply of this material would meet the requirements of the manufacture.

We are now in a position to estimate the result of Cobden's labours in negotiating the Treaty of 1860. After a short time a great international arrangement was entered into between continental communities, the basis of which was that Governments were to be precluded from raising duties on articles of foreign manufacture. The advantage of the limitation became obvious, and therefore many Governments were eager to avail themselves of it. It was seen that each country was better off, by being able to sell in the most advantageous market, though, by a perversity frequently commented on in these pages, such Governments were slow to allow the converse of the position, that if it was good to sell in the most advantageous market, it was good also to buy in such a market. But as each of these countries was added to the list of associates in this effectual protest against monopoly, the difficulty of extricating itself and recurring to the old vicious system of protection or restriction became greater, the benefit of the reform became more manifest, and the civilised world was being converted to free trade piecemeal, but progressively, and simultaneously. The engagement indeed, as all honest engagements should be, was for a limited period, but the obligations of each state were renewable at different dates, an arrangement which had the effect of making the treaties permanent, or at least continuous; since, in case the treaty (for example) with England were abandoned by France at the conclusion of the term for which it was entered into, that between Germany and Italy, or Italy and France endured, as well as that between England and Italy, Germany, or Austria. Hence the consequence of the relinquishment of the treaty with England might injure the English producer, for it drove him to adopt a roundabout trade with some one of the countries with which his treaties remained intact, but it gave no assistance to the French monopolist, whose hostility led to the abandonment of the treaty, or to the French doctrinaire, who, like M. Thiers, was too old to learn a truth, and too opinionative to be ashamed of his ignorance.

The efficacy of these tactics in assisting retrograde financial action was never seen more clearly than in the difficulty which they were to M. Thiers. This statesman, whose abilities and patriotism are beyond dispute, entertained and tried to enforce the most mischievous financial projects. His favourite tax was that on raw material, an import which has been assailed by all reason, and repudiated by all experience, as the most wasteful and the most disastrous which can be inflicted on the industry of a nation. Taxes on raw materials necessitate a return to rigid protective duties. But while protection is sure to annihilate foreign trade, a tax on raw materials, apart from any protective import, or concurrently with it, is certain to destroy home production altogether. But, on the other hand, M. Thiers resolutely rejected a tax on personal effects, and *bond fide* income, on the ground that it was ill adapted to French habit; though the French people have always acquiesced without murmuring in a heavy tax on real estate.

It will be in memory of my readers that the Commercial Treaty of 1860 formed a powerful obstacle to the projects of M. Thiers. It is true that this treaty had nearly expired, and that it was in the power of the French Government to denounce it. It must be admitted that the English Government showed great willingness to acknowledge the difficulties in which the administration of French finance was put; and though they gently pointed out the error into which the late President was running, they made no great stand for the principle on which the treaty was founded. Perhaps it was felt to be almost impossible, in the face of the vast financial difficulties in which France was involved, to reject the entreaties of M. Thiers. But some of the language used by a member of the present Government, and not the least able member either, proved that one person in the Administration had no sympathy with the commercial diplomacy of Mr. Cobden, that he could impart the atmosphere of his opinions to the Premier, and, still more conclusively, that he neither understood the bearing nor saw the importance of Cobden's Treaty. Mr. Lowe imagined that the essence of Cobden's Treaty was reciprocity, and he explained reciprocity as the antithesis to free trade. Now the Treaty of 1860 was not a reciprocity treaty, for France did not accept free trade in the same measure in which England had accepted it. But, if it had been a reciprocity treaty, it need not have been hostile to free trade, for it is quite possible for two nations to enter into such a reciprocal obligation as involves the mutual acceptance of free trade doctrines. Cobden's Treaty was an arrangement by which a true reciprocity of free trade was made a question of time, and this the *Times* newspaper has grudgingly recognised.

The difficulty in the way of M. Thiers was, that even had the treaty with England been abandoned, the protective system which he wished to restore, and in which he most erroneously imagined the recuperative powers of France to reside, would have been no nearer than before. The English treaty was near expiry, but France had negotiated other treaties of a similar kind, and under similar provisions, with several other nations, who were not willing to submit to a sudden abandonment of these obligations. As long as any of these were in force, the policy of M. Thiers was impracticable, and before matters were finally settled, or indeed could have been, the administration of M. Thiers came to an end. It may be a political misfortune for France, that the late President was ejected from office, but it is certain that his resignation was an unmixed financial boon.

There were three countries with which it might have been possible to have extended these relations. These are Russia, the Iberian Peninsula, and the United States. All these countries are producers of raw material on a very large scale, and all are greatly interested in the English market. It is not too much to say that the greater part of the income of the Russian nobility depends on the opportunity which England gives for the purchase of Russian corn, flour, and hemp. Similarly, Spain and Portugal are producers of wines which are still, from long habit, or from their intrinsic merits, permanent favourites with the English public. The United States supply, and on an enormous scale, two important kinds of agricultural produce, cotton and corn. But though, for reasons already given, free exchange is of the greatest interest to all three nations, the first and the last are, as yet, resolutely bent on protection, and are vindicating, with passionate folly, the privilege of injuring themselves.

Spain has her grievances. One is mercantile, and consists in the fact that the alcoholic test is the basis of the English customs duty. I see no intrinsic difficulty in *ad valorem* duties, and great justice in the arrangement, if it be of possible adoption, though it may give a little more trouble to custom-house officials. But there is no doubt that were such a change effected, it would be easy to make it the basis of those concessions which would bring Spain within that international association, the true object of which is to break down monopoly, and to determine taxation simply on the basis of revenue necessities. There is however another hindrance, and a political one, to amity between Great Britain and Spain. It is the retention of Gibraltar. The first occupation of this place was as disgraceful as that of Metz was, and the scandal of the acquisition is not obviated by the fact that it has been secured to us by treaties. I have elsewhere stated what Cobden's opinion was of the value of Gibraltar to ourselves, and of the value which its cession would be to Spain.

It is not easy to say what prospect commercial diplomacy has in Russia. We are informed on all hands that the purposes of that country are to establish a strict monopoly for Russian manufactures, wherever she may command or influence men, and we are told particularly so by alarmists. But if those who must have an increasing influence in the policy of that empire become alive to their own interests, it will be speedily found out that a protective policy is the worst prospect which can be put before the emperor, the nobles, and the peasantry.

The United States may be safely left to discover their own errors. The case is well nigh desperate when Mr. Carey, the apostle of monopoly and protection, of high prices at home, and a crippled trade abroad, detected a crowning mercy in Cobden's death. But a good cause, it may be confidently asserted, never fails for want of efficient advocacy. Already we see the beginning of the end. In order to escape the tyranny of the slave-owner, the Union made a compromise with the tyranny of the monopolist. But it is in the nature of a compromise that it should be temporary, and we already hear that men are marshalling themselves for the second struggle through which the Union has to go, the struggle of Free Exchange against Protection, and in which light and darkness must again contend, as they contended before in the great fight between Freedom and Slavery.

CHAPTER X.

EDUCATION.

VERY few practical politicians know anything about education, whether it be primary or technical, or what is called the higher culture. An education debate in the House of Commons, or for the matter of that in the House of Lords, is a mere wrangle between the partisans of sectarian privilege and the advocates of religious equality. In the case of primary education, the perennial dispute about the respective merits of denominational or secular teaching is more than usually complicated. In the first place, there is the question whether it is the business of the State to provide religious instruction, either directly, through grants from the national exchequer in aid of denominational schools, or indirectly, by remitting the struggle to educational boards, who are to be entrusted with one of the worst forms of permissive bye-legislation conceivable— the discretion, as the majority shall determine, as to the payment or non-payment of school fees in sectarian schools. In the next place, there is the question whether in the matter of national education it is desirable to utilise sectarian zeal, perhaps as the most thorough way of supplying an admitted want, perhaps as an expedient for relieving the tax-payer, either wholly or partially, from the tax or rate which, in the absence of voluntary contribution, must be exacted from those who are able to pay. There are those who think that the State is no more bound to provide the machinery of education at the public cost, except in cases of total destitution, than it is to provide food, clothing, and shelter to any but those who come within the legal definition of pauperism, and that therefore it is only right and proper that, if it be necessary to aid the non-destitute poor towards the education of children, no safe plan can be found except that of voluntary charity. Again, there is, not indeed freely expressed, but unquestionably felt, and very generally felt, a conviction that a system of general primary education should be connected with definite religious teaching, because it is hoped that the religious tone imparted, or supposed to be imparted, by this method, will be a powerful check to that spirit of discontent or innovation which it is believed might, in the absence of such training, grow and make itself inconveniently conspicuous.

The most grotesque statements are uttered, and the most irrelevant topics are introduced, in connexion with the dispute about the process of national education. At one time we are warned against the State abandoning the maintenance of a creed, as though the State were more religious than the persons who compose it, or as though, while the mass of the people admit the teaching of Christian doctrine, there were any risk that the inculcation of this doctrine would be abandoned, whatever may be the limits which the State assigns to its own agency; or as though, in case the community were averse or indifferent to Christian opinion, any guarantees taken by the State would secure the maintenance of dogmatic beliefs. The Established Church again, in connexion with this topic, is sometimes spoken of as a national institution of the widest possible character, and thereupon obliged to duties which it cannot neglect; and more frequently as a sect, which possesses rights which it would be utterly unfair and ungenerous to curtail. The most contradictory statements too are made, as to who among the sects were the originators of national education, as though, when it is recognised as the duty of the Legislature to take in hand the primary education of the young, and to see, in some way or another, that children are taught, it signified one jot who were the parties that attempted the satisfaction of an obligation which was not yet recognised by the State, or as though such parties had a right to compensation after their mission had ceased. Again, it is said that unless the child is assisted to religious teaching by the machinery of common or primary schools, he would receive none in his own home, and it may be presumed none from the various active religious bodies, who are as a rule exceedingly zealous in attracting disciples to their organisation. We are told that it is grossly unjust not to allow a parent who pleads, *in forma pauperis*, for relief from the payment of school fees for his children, to choose the particular school to which he shall send his child, as though it were not the essence of public charity that the recipient should accept and not make conditions, and as though the refusal on the part of the State to assist special beliefs out of public taxation were equivalent to refusing the parent all opportunity whatever for obtaining religious instruction for his child. It is incredible that arguments like these are alleged in order to show how an indifferent attitude can be held on the part of the State towards various religious sects. They are alleged, either consciously or unconsciously, with a view to sustaining the interests of the National Church, either from a belief that it is the only sound form of religious opinion, or because it is thought to be a powerful aid towards a Conservative policy. The proof that the former motive exists is supplied by the all but unanimous hostility of Nonconformists to the payment of fees in denominational schools, that of the latter in the equally unanimous dislike of Liberal politicians to clerical control over the teaching of the young. Among the wealthier classes it is the practice to insist on a pretty uniform negation of all religious teaching in such day-schools as they institute for their own children. For a similar reason, whenever boarding-schools are generally popular it is generally necessary that the religious instruction imparted in them should be colourless. It is understood that proselytism in public schools is not to be attempted, and it is clear that a creed is colourless when its professor is practically debarred from recommending it.

So with technical education. There is not the slightest justification for grants of public money in aid of that education the possession of which secures the person who receives it wages for his services. To teach a person the art of a practical miner at the public expense is to provide comparatively cheap labour to those who own mines and wish to work them, and to reduce the earnings of those who learn the art of practical mining at their own expense. To grant subventions to the teachers of medicine out of the sums voted in Parliament, is to favour one class of teachers or one class of students at the expense of other teachers and other students; for it is an axiom in political economy, that assisted education lowers the wages of those who receive the education, and use that education in order to earn a livelihood. The only kind of education which the State should aid is that which confers great public service, but which, owing to peculiarities in the character of the service which it bestows, cannot receive the ordinary remuneration for utility in the world's market. It is the duty of the State to assist certain kinds of learning or research, but it is not the duty of the State to impart at the public charge that kind of knowledge which commands a ready price in the labour market.

The Legislature is equally inexperienced or ill-informed in relation to the higher culture. It knows nothing or next to nothing as to whether educational endowments have any value whatever, and, if they have a value, what is the best way in which they may be made useful. The question which it has been principally debated and has ultimately settled, is whether the Universities shall be secularised or not. It has secularised also the minor endowments of the Colleges, but it has still assigned much of the most valuable part of these endowments, and all the highest offices in the Colleges, to the clergy of the National Church. It has thereby given an opportunity to the clergy to do their best towards reversing the policy of religious equality which Parliament has insisted on, for a clergyman would be hardly faithful to his calling if he did not seek to use every occasion in his power in order to support and extend his opinions among the persons with whom he may be brought in contact. To enact that no member of the University shall make any declaration whatever as to his religious belief or profession, in order to enable him to take a degree, and to insist that after they have taken their degrees, a number of such persons shall make the various declarations which are necessary, in order to qualify a graduate to become a clergyman, is a contradiction which one never meets with except in a Legislature which prides itself on being practical and which affects a profound horror for abstract and necessary principles.

Thirty years ago, the Legislature made a small grant in aid of national education. Its assistance was chiefly to the National Church, for a generation back Parliamentary grants in aid of the Establishment were not infrequent. For some time, dissenters were unwilling to accept State assistance for their schools, though they were zealous enough in extending, under their own tenets, secular education to all whom they could reach. As is constantly the case with the Civil Service estimates, the slender stream of the education vote rapidly became a broad river, and the Nonconformist party found that they would be heavily weighted against the wealth of the Church and the votes on behalf of the 'National System of Education,' unless they put in their claim on behalf of a share in the bounty of the Exchequer.

The schools belonging to the National Church were put under the supervision of a body of clerical inspectors, who, in the first instance at least, were approved by the Bishops, those of the Nonconforming and the Roman Catholic bodies were visited by lay inspectors. The general superintendence of the system was annexed to the Privy Council Office, and assigned to the Lord President of the Council, a nobleman who rarely possesses any qualification whatever for the office which he fills. In practice, of course, the management of the department was left in the hands of the permanent chief officials, as is unfortunately the case with most public offices. Gradually, as the spirit of resistance to ecclesiastical zeal or intolerance, as the feeling is variously designated, was developed, certain provisions known by the general name of Conscience Clauses were enforced with greater or less success on behalf of Nonconformists.

Such a system of education could never have become national in the true sense of the word, and despite its modifications under Mr. Forster's Bill, never will be. It is either the business of the State or of the sects to teach secular knowledge. If it be the business of the State, the functions of the teacher of religion and of the schoolmaster must be separated. The former must have his opportunity for imparting religious knowledge, will indeed have it, for the temper of the three or four nations included in the United Kingdom is strongly religious, and apart from the deeper feelings of belief, identifies, and rightly identifies, the religion of the Reformation, and of several successive and internal Reformations, with civil liberty and moral progress.

There does not then appear to be any reason why persons should be alarmed, as they sometimes, on various grounds, affect to be alarmed, at the risk which religion may run if the State undertakes the secular instruction of the people; or why they should assert that, if the State teaches secular education, education will be secular. The education of the people will never be secular in the ordinary acceptation of the word, unless the clergy of various creeds abandon all attempts to teach religion to the young, or unless parents repudiate altogether the offices of the clergy, and the religion which they profess. Both these contingencies are in the highest degree improbable, I may even say, impossible. There has never yet been a civilisation without a religion, and in my opinion, there never can be one. There has been no agency so powerful for civilisation as Christianity. I may go further, and say that the true foes of civilisation are those who ignore the practice of Christianity, however much they may ostentatiously profess its creed.

On the other hand, national education may be left, as it practically is left, to the sects. Under these circumstances it is not difficult to predict its failure, and to forecast the reasons of the failure. The business of a minister of religion is to make proselytes and to inculcate dogmas. With him secular knowledge is quite subsidiary to theological uniformity. It is necessarily so, for if he were more interested in the latter than he is in the former, he would be unfaithful to his office. If proof of this were needed, it is to be found in the repudiation of what is called 'common Christianity' as the basis of school training. Such a project of a common foundation of religious belief has failed in Ireland, and its failure in England is only obscured by the fact that Irish sectarianism is more outspoken, more bitter, and more contemptuous than English controversy is. I am speaking simply of abstract or dogmatic belief. The morals of Christianity are part of, or rather identical with, universal morality. Most of the Christian virtues, diligence, submission, kindness, truthfulness, cleanliness of speech, courtesy, and the like, are part of the essential discipline of a school, and can be ignored in no place of education, however secular may be the teaching conveyed.

Now to expect that zeal for one thing will necessarily and habitually provide another thing, still more that they who long to gather proselytes will effectually undertake the work of a national and universal education, is the simplest of credulities. The framers of the Education Act did not, I imagine, anticipate that the machinery of the Act would really provide for the education of the people. They probably believed that more would be educated, when the assistance given by a dispassionate Government to passionate religious feeling was graduated by numbers and efficiency, and when therefore the various sects were constrained to fight for existence. They hesitated, though the conditions were completely reversed when the Legislature had once acknowledged the duty of providing the means of national education, to supersede the existing machinery. They adopted the policy, which is becoming more and more general, of delegating the decision on rival systems to a local committee, and thus of getting rid of an awkward question in the House itself. Such a process is

no doubt a ready means for assisting in the formation
of local opinion, but the opinion is formed at the cost
of much bitterness, and perhaps of energetic intolerance. But it is futile to imagine that a national
system of education will be developed under such a
process. Perhaps the city of Oxford is an exceptional
case, but, as is said, chiefly from the representations of
the clergy and their associates, the city of Oxford
chose a School Board which was almost entirely clerical,
in order to avoid a fresh Rate. The School Board has
been in existence for nearly three years. Naturally,
its object was to preserve the Church schools, and to
prevent the creation of any other. Of course it has
a certain number of paid officials. But it appears to
have wholly failed as an instrument for general
education, if the information given by one of its most
active members can be relied on, for in February last,
we are assured, there were about 700 less children at
school than there were before the Education Act was
passed or the School Board elected. To my mind, this
was quite to be expected, and for the reason which I
have given above.

Cobden was one of the earliest advocates of a system
of national education in the true sense of the word.
In a speech which he made at Manchester on the subject, and on which I shall comment at length, on January
22, 1851, he speaks of himself as having striven for
fifteen years on behalf of a system of national education, and having always associated his hopes for this
end, 'with the idea of coupling the education of this
country with the religious communities which exist.
But I have found,' he continues, 'after trying it, as I

think, in every possible shape, such insuperable difficulties in consequence of the religious discordances of this country, that I have taken refuge in this, which has been called the remote haven of the Educationists, —the secular system,—in despair of carrying out any system in connexion with religion. I should therefore be a hypocrite, if I were to say that I have any particular repugnance to a system of education coupled with religious instruction. But there is no one in this room, or in the country, that can have a stronger conviction than I have of the utter hopelessness of ever attempting to unite the religious bodies of this country in any system of education; so that I can hardly bring myself even to give a serious consideration to the plan which has been now brought forward by gentlemen in this city, and who have brought it forward, no doubt, with the best possible intentions, and who have only to persevere in order to find what I have found, for the last fifteen years, the hopelessness of the task.'* And he proceeds to comment on a rival scheme, closely analogous to that which has received the support of the Anglican clergy, and which was then ventilated in Manchester. 'This,' he says, 'is in fact a proposal by which everybody shall be called upon to pay for the religious training of everybody else. Now this is precisely what has been objected to by a great portion of this community, and which has prevented the present system, administered through the Minutes of Council, from being successful.' The speaker then adverts to one novelty in the proposal to which he refers, the fact, namely, that now for the first time the members

* Speeches, vol. ii. p. 568 sqq.

of the Church of England have recommended that all religious denominations shall be allowed to receive public money for the teaching of their catechisms and creeds.' 'This scheme,' he adds, 'is based upon the principle of voting public money for the teaching of the religious creeds of every religious denomination in the country. If it does not recognise that principle, it is an unjust proposal. *There are but two principles on which you can carry on an education system in this country. The one is, if you will have a religion, to form your plan so as to pay for the teaching of all religions; the other is, to adopt the secular system, and leave religion to voluntary effort.*' He then goes on to discuss the difficulties connected with the education of the Roman Catholic population.

'I remember,' he states, 'so long ago as 1836, when Mr. Wyse, himself a Roman Catholic, and Mr. Simpson of Edinburgh, and others, came down here to enlighten us on the subject of education—I remember having in my counting house, in Moseley-street, the ministers of religion of every denomination, and trying to bring them to some sort of agreement on the system of education we were then anxious to advocate. I believe the insuperable difficulties which then existed have even increased now, and have not been in the slightest degree modified; and I believe those gentlemen, who with the best intentions, have brought forward this plan now, will find, before they have pursued it to the one-twentieth part of the time and trouble people have here given to the education question, that they have attempted an impossibility, and will be compelled to turn aside from what they are attempting to do. And if they view education at all as of that paramount importance I trust they do, the effect of this well-meant effort will be to bring many of those gentlemen into our ranks, if, as I sincerely hope and trust will be the case, we do nothing in the meantime to repel them from joining us.' The speaker then proceeds to refer to the history of the American school system, and to point out the process by which the advocates of a primary or national system in the United States were constrained to get rid of dogmatic teaching, and observes that the same difficulties arose in Holland, and that the same solution was found for them. There is not a word in this speech which is not a perpetual comment on Mr. Forster's measure, and which does not anticipate its failure.

'If ever there was a time,' says Cobden, 'in which it was desirable, more than in another, to try and separate religious from secular instruction, it is the present time. And why? Because we have arrived at that period when all the world is agreed that secular instruction is a good thing for society. There are no dissentients now, or if there be, they dare not avow themselves. . . . But while we are all united on that, can any one who moves in society conceal from himself that we are also arrived at a time when we have probably more religious discord impending over us than in any period of our history? I do not allude to the dissensions between Roman Catholics and Protestants,—but I think that there is, at the present moment, looming in the distance, and not in the very remote distance, a schism of the Church of England itself.'

After commenting on the inevitable rivalry, bitterness, and failure which will ensue from the struggles of the various religious bodies, and predicting the end that as in America and Holland, Englishmen will be obliged after a great waste of time to adopt the secular system which has been adopted in those countries, the speaker points out the process by which existing institutions can be utilised. As an advocate of free rate-supported schools he has little doubt that these schools will supersede those which owe their maintenance to religious zeal, and depend in part on the school-fees paid by parents, both from their general attractiveness, and for the effective way in which they will impart instruction. 'But,' he adds, 'I have never considered that the school-rooms in connexion with existing places of worship, or otherwise, would be rendered useless, for I have always considered that they might be rented or purchased in precisely the same way as Mr. Schwabe (a friend of Mr. Cobden, and an active advocate during his life of national education) has suggested, they might be rented for the week-time and left on Sunday in the hands of the congregations. This is merely a matter of detail; but we should be taking a rash leap if we had contemplated closing all existing schools, and wasting the vast capital invested in bricks and mortar for the erection of them.'

No one can doubt that it is within the power of Parliament to appropriate real estate of any kind whatever to public, or indeed to any purpose, due compensation being made to existing interests. Private property exists by the protection of the State, and by this only. It cannot therefore be allowed to exist to the detriment of the State, or in antagonism to recognised public interests. This is true even of personal property, that is—avoiding the jargon of law—portable material upon which human labour has induced a market value. Except under very peculiar circumstances, such property, being capable of indefinite production, is not rendered liable to any restrictive operations on the part of the State, or to involuntary alienation from the immediate owner. But if such property loses the quality of indefinite extension, it may come within the purview of restrictive enactments, or be made subject to involuntary alienation. Thus, for example, the inhabitants of a besieged town would not respect the ownership of corn granaries, or permit the possessor of quantities of food to withhold them from the public, or exact the fullest price which the market of want might enable him to demand. The reason is obvious. In the case quoted, society is within risk of dissolution, and private property must be sacrificed when the safety of all is imperilled, just as life is in the process of defence, and the possessions of individuals are for the funds necessary in order to meet the expense of defence. Besides, the owner of property who might exact the fullest terms which his situation permitted him, would virtually be playing into the hands of the enemy against whom the defence was carried on. Again, it may be doubted whether a State might not and ought not to interfere in order to arrest the wanton waste of any important kind of wealth, or to prevent any practice which either renders labour unproductive, or squanders the products of labour on idlers or profligates.

But if there are occasions on which the State can assert its rights against personal or moveable estate, it never abandons its discretion over land or immovable estate. The forcible alienation of land, an article of value which is not capable of indefinite extension, indeed of any extension whatever, when public interests require such an alienation, and due compensation is made for its market value, is a matter of common occurrence. A railway is a public convenience, and the State has not hesitated to direct that the private owners of real estate must be ejected from their property, should the law permit the construction of a public road. There have been occasions on which the Legislature has interfered with the rights of proprietors in order to satisfy the necessities of voluntary associations. After the schism in the Scotch Establishment, and the secession of the Free Church Ministers, and their congregations, the proprietors of Scotch estates refused to allow these congregations sites for building places of worship. But the Legislature interfered, and notwithstanding the reclamations of those who insisted, as usual, on the peculiar sacredness of landed property, gave the congregations the power of compulsory purchase, and *e converso* subjected the landowners to a compulsory sale.

But the rights of the State over corporate property, i.e. land assigned in propetuity to any given object, are still stronger, more permanent, more discretionary. By the principles of English law, the dedication of land in mortmain is a bestowal of such land on the public, subject it is true to certain trusts, but without power of reversion to the original grantor. There have been, or there seem to have been, occasions on which the law has winked at the creation of bodies of trustees whose action might secure the objects of the dedication, while the property was itself exempted from the operation of the Mortmain Law. But such colourable evasions would probably break down if the Courts of Law were appealed to in order to determine their real legal status. The property granted to such uses is national property. If the objects to which it is dedicated are mischievous or immoral, the grant, though otherwise legal, may be avoided. If the object for which the grant was made is no longer in existence or no longer possible, the State may constitute itself the representative of those objects, or as it more frequently does, assign the fund to some analogous purpose. It is ridiculous to talk of the discretionary exercise of its legal rights on the part of the State as confiscation, for when the grant was originally made, the source from which the annual revenue comes is *ipso facto* confiscated. If there be any moral guilt in the attitude assumed by Parliament towards these corporate estates, it lies in permitting their private confiscation at the hands of persons for whom the grant could never by any stretch of reasoning have been intended. Thus the funds possessed by the great city corporations were granted as charities to artisans. The real objects of the overgrown charities possessed by such Companies as the Goldsmiths, the Merchant Tailors, the Fishmongers, and the like, are not the rich people who consume great part of the income of these charities in vulgar ostentation, and scandalous gluttony, and who are neither goldsmiths nor tailors, nor fishermen, but the artisans who work at these several callings and have been simply defrauded of their due.

This confusion between the rights of the nation, and the vested interests of those who enjoy the benefits of a particular trust, is nowhere so frequently propounded as in the case of the Church. Mr. Gladstone has latterly fallen into this error, when he painted, and in glowing colours, the difficulty of granting the compensation which must be assigned to the Church in the event of its disestablishment, and the dangers which might ensue to society if so huge an estate were given to a religious organisation. Now, in the first place, there is no process by which it can be given, in the sense of a gift to a private individual. The State has not relinquished its hold on the funds of the new Irish Church, or on the compensation which it made to Maynooth and the Ulster Presbyterians. It could not relinquish them without committing an act of political suicide. The State has taken away the precedence and rank of the Irish Establishment. It has granted compensation to life interests. It has regranted under conditions, a portion of the former estate of the Establishment, to certain trustees. But what it has granted is still its own, and must be its own, by the very conditions under which a State exists and acts. The State is the reversioner to all private property, when property has no representative. It is the absolute owner of all corporate property, however fully it may permit a dedication of the revenues derivable from corporate property to particular ends.

The property of the Anglican Church belongs to the nation. In the eye of the law, every Englishman is a member of the National Church. As the Church is a creation of the State, in so far as it has a political existence, its property, its doctrines, its discipline, are all liable to the control or modification of the Legislature in Parliament. A Dissenter is as much a Churchman as the most strenuous defender of the Establishment. The technical definition of a dissenter was—a person who was put under civil disabilities because he declined to attend the worship, or subscribe to the formularies of the Establishment. The present definition of a dissenter is—a person who is under no civil disabilities because he declines to attend a particular kind of worship, and subscribe to a particular set of formularies. Except for certain trivial purposes, the law ignores dissenters and their ministers altogether, as it would ignore all religious differences whatever, and all ministers of religion, if the Church ceased to be part of the mechanism of the State. But whatever property the Church, or any of these other sects possessed, would still remain the property of the State, and be under its control.

By an absurdity without parallel in law, the trusts of the National Church, held by the Ecclesiastical Commission, are administered by a board, consisting of the Anglican hierarchy and their nominees. There can be no greater inconsistency than a trust exercised by the *cestui que trust;* than the fact that a man is trustee for himself. The consequence might have been anticipated. The first act of this Commission was to devote large sums towards the purchase or construction of huge mansions for the bishops, under the not inappropriate name of palaces or castles. The sustentation fund for the poorer clergy has been miserably dwarfed by the extravagant expenditure on these episcopal residences, and by the swarm of harpies who have been allowed to fasten on the trust. The estates ought to have been managed by a lay commission, and one of the first reforms needed, is to reconstruct the organisation of the body, with the purpose of assuring the rights of the English people in the property of the Church; of protecting this property, in the event of disestablishment, from the rapine of the landowners, who will claim the title which was given to the Irish proprietors; of inducing some economy in the administration and, I may add, some justice in the distribution of the fund.

When we are therefore listening to harangues about the property of the Church, and the danger that its due management may involve to the peace of the nation, we are simply listening to absurdities. The property is our own, and the danger which we may run arises simply from the existence of bigoted and reactionary persons among us, along with the danger or inconvenience to which all civilised communities seem to be put at present from the arrogance of a revived sacerdotalism. To imagine that that danger arises from the possession of property, or will be increased by the fact that the laity of a given Church have an estate, instead of supporting their religious organisations by voluntary subscriptions, or by State grants,

is a silly fancy of which a few facts might easily
disabuse us. The Irish Catholic priests are probably,
as far as real estate goes, the poorest ecclesiastical
organisation in the world. They are unquestionably
the most intractable. The pittance which the French
priests receive from the French Exchequer is miserably small, but they are, or were, in formidable opposition to the existing Government. The Catholic
clergy of Northern Germany are poor enough, but
they are tasking the energies of a very effective despotism, to which a pliant Parliament is giving the
colour of popular action. As a rule, the better off a
clergy are, provided always they are made to understand that what is called Church property is the
estate of the laity, held in trust for religious worship, and theological opinion expressed in that worship,
of which worship and opinion the laity are quite
as good judges as the clergy are, or can be, the
clergy are likely to be and remain very tame. In
brief, the laity is now occupying, if it pleases, exactly
the same position which Elizabeth and her advisers
did at the close of the sixteenth century, and to use
Mr. Froude's phrase, can as thoroughly 'tune their
pulpits,' as the Virgin Queen did.

If the property of the Church, then, is the estate
of the laity, held for definite purposes, of which the
laity is the judge, what shall be said of those
numerous school houses which have been in considerable degree constructed from grants out of imperial taxation. As gifts in mortmain, they are the
property of the State; as part of the estate of the
national Church, they are the property of the State;

as erected and maintained in part by the public
taxes, they are the property of the State; as part
of a compact entered into between the State and the
religious orders, under which the operations of an imperfect education is carried on, but which must be
brought to an end, because a perfect system of education is needed, but which can never be attained
under the orginal compact, they are subject to a lien
of the State. I have often heard zealous clergymen
say, that had Mr. Forster attempted to appropriate
the schools for public instruction, and put them
under boards of regulation, who should be elected,
and therefore not necessarily clerical, though, of course,
not necessarily lay, they would have shut up their
schools; and my answer has been, Your schools? What
schools? Those schools which are called national, are
not your property as clergymen. They belong to the
parishioners, the laity, the nation, the Parliament,
to every one, yourself included, but yourself included
only as an individual. There is no title whatever,
except in your own fancies, by which you can call
them yours, or in the face of facts vindicate them to
yourselves.

The true solution of the difficulty which arose in
connexion with the Education Act, the rural districts,
the School Boards, and the exigencies of national education, was to have claimed all existing schools which
were under inspection for the State. The transfer
would have been facilitated by a perfectly legitimate
threat, and two fair and reasonable offers. The threat
was, that as Parliament had seen fit to determine
the contract between school managers and the edu-

cation department, under which contract the managers undertook to supply education, and the department to assist the results of that education by grants, and as it had resolved on a thoroughly national system of education, to be carried out under a system of Boards elected by the ratepayers, and to be examined by Government inspectors who should enquire into all departments of instruction, except that of religion, the school must either, under conditions to be specified, be given up to the Board, or all grants must cease, and in the interests of the poor, new schools must be erected out of the rates. There cannot be a doubt as to what effect the proposal of such an alternative must have had, particularly if, as in all fairness it should be, it had been coupled with the following offers.

In the first place the School Board must have purchased or paid a rent for the school premises. They belong, as I contend, on all grounds to the nation, but they belong to it under the conditions of a trust which the nation is certainly not willing to repudiate, (I mean religious instruction,) imparted to those children whose parents willingly receive it for them, and which is not examined by the State. Upon the faith that such instruction would be given, subscribers have paid their money, and though the State may fairly claim a lien on the portion which itself bestowed in building grants, and to the sustentation of the institution, it would be invidious to demand anything back in consideration of the compact which the State has thought proper to break or annul, though of course in the interest of the public.

Next, the ancient proprietors of the school should have the right of reserving the buildings for Sundays, and for certain other definite times, as may be agreed on and confirmed by the Education Department, for the purpose of giving religious instruction to such persons as voluntarily accept the instruction. Were this conceded, as Cobden suggested more than twenty-two years ago, the last argument against the general supervision of the State over national education would be taken away. The State has and can have no quarrel with any religious belief which does not violate those moral laws on which civil government is founded, or which does not claim to be above the law—the most pernicious antinomianism which can be conceived. Religious bodies may define at their own discretion the terms of communion with themselves, but they are in every well-regulated community debarred from setting up their law in antagonism to public law, or from controlling civil rights. But within intelligible limits, they may proselytise whom they will and teach what they will. Such an arrangement as I have indicated might satisfy the purposes which Lord Robert Montague had the candour to avow, in a speech which he made on Messrs. Dixon and Richard's motion of May 5, 1872, and in which he argued that religious teaching in schools is a distinct preventive to political heresy; the religious teaching and the political heresy being of course defined by the speaker.

I have dwelt at length on this topic, partly because, during his life, I have conversed over and over again with Cobden on the question of national education, and derived the advantage of learning his precise views on the subject; partly because he has left abundant evidence of his opinions. In the preceding pages I have recorded, and I hope recorded faithfully, the conclusions which I arrived at under his instruction, and in view of the great interests which the subject involves, together with the difficulties of detail to which it is exposed. But I have also dwelt at length on the question, because Mr. Forster, in a speech made on May 5, 1872, claimed in answer to Mr. Richard, the authority of Cobden for his policy in the following passage*:—

'If my hon. friend (Mr. Richard) will allow me, I will read the language of a great statesman, and one whom he himself will admit to be a very high authority indeed. Mr. Cobden said

"I will never be a party to any scheme which attempts to lay down in an Act of Parliament the monstrous, arrogant, and dictatorial doctrine that a parish or community shall not, if it pleases, introduce the Bible into its schools."'

The passage occurs in a speech made by Mr. Cobden at Manchester †, in support of a system of secular education. But when Cobden made this statement, it is plain from a previous avowal of his, that he was equally averse to a local bill in which it was proposed to insert a clause to the effect that in all schools built and maintained out of a local rate, 'the reading of the Holy Scriptures in the authorised version shall be a part of the daily instruction of the scholars.' In other words, what Cobden wished was to leave the religious question entirely out of the Act of Parliament, and Mr. Forster must have given, to say the least, a very super-

* Hansard, May 5, 1872.   † Speeches, vol. ii. p. 599.

ficial attention to Cobden's speeches on education, when he claimed him in any particular whatever as a supporter of the Government Act of 1870. I am willing to admit that men of Mr. Cobden's school have constantly the satisfaction of exclaiming, with the poet of old, *sic vos non vobis*, but it is rather too much when the materials of political action which one mind has gathered or constructed are appropriated to purposes which would have been utterly repudiated by the original collector or builder. It will not be difficult to prove my case, not only by the passages already referred to, but by others.

In the speech from which I have already made extracts, Cobden reasons as follows *:—'Another strong objection which I have heard from our dissenting friends' (it is important to note the persons with whom Cobden is arguing) 'has been that the secular system is adverse to religious teaching. I cannot tell how to account for it, but there seems to be a pertinacious resolution to maintain that the teaching people reading, writing, arithmetic, grammar, and the rest is inimical to religion. Now I have found the most curious refutation of this doctrine where I have been, in the practice of the very parties who have objected to us. I remember at Birmingham†, I found there a preparatory

* Speeches, vol. ii. p. 577.
† Cobden was no doubt alluding to the Edgbaston Proprietary School, which is founded on this principle. It is not a little remarkable that my friend Mr. Sargant is at once the founder of this school, and the Chairman of the Birmingham School Board ; in which latter capacity he has severely censured his colleagues for trying to treat national education on the principles of the Edgbaston School for the wealthy.

school built by a joint-stock association, by men of every religious denomination. I heard of a clergyman sending his son to that school. No religion is taught there; the building would never have been erected, unless by a compromise, which agreed that no religion should be taught at that school; and yet, the very parties that object to us for not proposing to give religion with secular education, send their sons to schools where secular education is separated, avowedly, from religious teaching. Again in Yorkshire, I was present at a meeting where a gentleman stoutly maintained that it was impossible to separate religious from secular instruction. It was in Huddersfield. And another gentleman said, "How can you possibly maintain that doctrine? You know the Huddersfield College here could not exist a day, unless we consented altogether and totally to separate religious from secular teaching; and you know that you send your son to the college, and that he never received any religious instruction there." I must say that gentleman was silent for the rest of the evening. But I also found that at Huddersfield they have in connection with the Mechanic's Institution a very excellent school for young children (not for adults), where they may go and enjoy the benefits of this institution for a week by subscribing 3½d. They give the smallest doses of instruction, because they see the ginshops and such places offer to their customers a twopenny or threepenny taste; and so they let the children come in for a week for 3½d., in hopes they will be tempted to repeat the dose,—I think a very wise regulation. I find there are hundreds of children in this admirable school; but that excludes all religious teaching. I do not know whether the Bible exists in the institution library, but they never touch it in the schools, and never use it as a school book for teaching religion. And this applies to the schools generally connected with the mechanics' institutions in Yorkshire, of the Union of which my friend Mr. Baines is president; in these schools there is no religion taught or professed to be taught. And therefore in my travels I have found that gentlemen offered in their own practice the best example of the success of our principle, and the best refutation of their own theories.' It is difficult in connexion with this passage, uttered deliberately, with special reference to an objection of the dissenting bodies, and illustrated by the most apposite facts, to claim Cobden as an advocate of denominational education, of the system which would give secular education by the sects, instead of giving secular education by the State.

I can find space for one more quotation only from this admirable speech*. 'Have these gentlemen,' Cobden is still addressing his dissenting opponents, 'a due appreciation of the value of the education which they are opposing, apart from religious instruction? I believe they must have an adequate idea of the value of secular knowledge. I put it to them, do they not value it in their own cases, and in those of their own families? I put it to a gentleman I met with, one of my strongest opponents, a minister of religion, and he told me, in a party of religious men, that "he valued secular knowledge so much that he would not give his secular knowledge, apart from all religion, in exchange for all the world."

* Speeches, vol. ii. p. 581.

Well, and if he would not put himself on a par with the unenlightened peasant for the whole world, is he carrying out the Christian doctrine of doing to others as he would be done by, if he lightly interposes obstacles to the acquisition of some portion of that knowledge which he values so highly, by the great mass of his poorer fellow countrymen? I want to ask the gentlemen who interpose at all times the question of religion as an obstacle to secular teaching, do they or do they not consider that knowledge is itself a good? I will say, apart from religion altogether, do they consider that Seneca or Cicero were better for their knowledge than the common gladiator or peasant of their day. But even as a matter of religious import, I would ask these gentlemen, do they not think they will have a better chance of gaining over the mass of the people of this country to some kind of religious influence, if they begin by offering to their children, and tempting their children to acquire, some kind of secular knowledge? It seems to me, that to argue otherwise would contend for this—that ignorance, barbarism, vice, drunkenness, and misery are conducive to Christianity, and that the opposite qualities are contrary to it. *I feel that we are in danger of alienating the great mass of the people in these manufacturing districts from every religious communion, and even of estranging their minds from every principle of Christianity, if we allow this unseemly exhibition to go on—of men squabbling for their distinctive tenets of religion, and making that a bone of contention and a means of depriving the mass of the people of that knowledge which is necessary for them to gain their daily bread, or preserve themselves in respectability.'*

It is unnecessary that I should make further quotations from my friend's speeches on this important and engrossing subject. It will, I think, be clear from what I have already selected that Cobden may fairly be called the author of that programme which has been assumed gradually by the Birmingham Education League, and which insists on a division of the labour of education between the minister of religion and the schoolmaster. I yield to no one, and I am here speaking Cobden's mind as well as my own convictions, in my reverence for Christianity. I believe it to be at once the foundation and the guarantee of modern civilisation, and that, rightly interpreted, its moral and social doctrines are the best corrective to those numerous barbarisms and wrongs which disfigure modern society. But the teaching of religion must be in the home, in the relation of minister and congregation, in the self-denying exertions of those who strive to reclaim the fallen, to enlighten the ignorant, to strengthen the weak, and in the consistent example of high-minded, generous, and devoted men. It cannot and will not be taught in a form, and by lesson learnt by rote.

There are yet three points in connection with this subject which I must briefly dwell upon. In the first place, it cannot be denied that the principal interest felt by politicians in the inculcation of what they call religious teaching, is the political value of the lesson. State Churches and State Churchmen advocate acquiescence in existing facts, for an Established Church is necessarily conservative, even if the watch-dog did not bark on behalf of his chain and dish. Sometimes this feeling is avowed. It is always understood. As long as the children of the poor are taught by or through the clergy of the Establishment, some guarantee is given that their minds will be influenced as far as possible in favour of existing institutions. 'I care very little,' said an old-fashioned Tory of my acquaintance to me some time ago, 'for Church opinions, or for the Church itself, apart from their political uses, but I support both, for I believe that the parson and the devil are the cheapest policemen.' How long such a scheme for State religion will be found enduring, I shall not pretend to anticipate.

Another is the question of Bible reading in schools. It is said to be a gross affront on the code of Christendom that the Legislature should be invited to exclude the Bible from the schoolmaster's routine, or that men professing respect to religion should be found to endorse such a policy, or even conceive it possible. But the objection is based on a confusion. It is not seen, perhaps will not be seen, that the Bible occupies two positions. There is one with which we cannot be too familiar. This book contains the tenderest pictures of human affection, of patience, of lofty self-abnegation. It narrates a thousand tales of the most romantic interest, all the more attractive because they deal with the life and the customs of a race which is quite unlike our general experience. It assists the minds of those who live in a temperate but chill climate, to realise the vision of the glorious East, its intense light, its deep shade, its parched deserts, its fertile valleys, the palm groves of its plains, and the cedars of its mountains. It contains the maxims of the most exalted morality conceivable, exhibited under the most winning form, in the person of a perfect but suffering Being, for it rouses thereby the keenest emotions of reverence and pity, the two most purifying passions which man's heart can entertain, because they lift him most wholly out of himself. It possesses the most gorgeous and stirring poetry, which speaks at once to the deepest sympathies of nature and to the highest flights of imagination. It contains even the wisest maxims of practical statesmanship, for, as late writers have truly affirmed, the prophets of Judah and Israel were among the greatest sages whom mankind has seen, and by whom it has profited. To repudiate Bible reading, is to shut up one of the grandest pages of that great book in which the noblest human thoughts have been enshrined, and the best, the kindliest, the most generous human actions have originated.

But there is another view of the subject. This book has been the occasion of the bitterest feuds. It has roused more malignant passions than any volume which has ever been put into the hands of man. The controversies which it has excited have been more ferocious and more bloody than any crimes which ancient civilisation witnessed, under the excitement of a concentrated political faction. It has turned men, especially Churchmen, into fiends. Under the influence of it they have invented and inflicted tortures, the atrocity of which is without parallel, have perpetrated cruelties of which savages would not have dreamed. It has ministered to the most aggressive and to the meanest human passions, to irrational intolerance, and to irrational pride. It is that to which men have appealed when they wished to inculcate some barbarous fetish: it is that to which men have appealed when they wished to defend some diabolical crime. It has originated a Torquemada, a Borgia, a Leo X. It has justified a Hobbes, a Hume, a Voltaire. It is no marvel that, foreseeing the ruin of noble institutions, and the reaction of ignoble sensuality, Selden, with more bitterness of spirit than might have been expected from so calm and indifferent an intellect, said, 'Those two words, "search the scriptures," have undone the world.' Considering the man, the times, and the subject, there is, I think, no sadder utterance to be found in the whole range of those words which have been spoken with a meaning.

There is no difficulty in explaining the apparent contradiction. It consists in the difference between the personal and the professional study of Scripture. The man who reads the Bible for its own sake wishes to inform his own mind; the man who reads it for the purposes of controversy wishes to control the minds of others. To win influence and power, to gratify ambition in secular matters, men will exhibit prodigious energies, energies at which those who pursue unselfish ends with calmer passions must wonder. But when, in aid of similar purposes, men allow themselves to insist on their own interpretation of a mysterious power, whose authority is irresistible, and whose sentence is unchangeable, and can persuade their fellow-men that they can wield the judgment of God, the self-assertions of the ancient sorcerer are not nearly so gigantic, so demoralising, and so terrible as those of the priest. Judged by the light which history affords us, the pretensions of the Roman See are the most audacious imposture ever palmed upon men, a mere farrago of improbable and impossible lies. But it is, simply as a social force, the strongest power in existence, because it plays upon illimitable fears. To those who know its origin, the Anglican Church was the timid slave of what is now an exploded system of statecraft. It is at present aping the authority, mimicking the tricks, and affecting the terrors of Rome, though many of its pretensions are checked by the scorn with which its rival and exemplar treats the claims of a rebellious pupil. It is no wonder then that they who wish for peace, and believe in Christianity, say, Leave the Bible to the home, to the individual, to the voluntary interpreter, and the voluntary pupil, and give no authority to the professional person to insist on his interpretation, and couple that interpretation with his anathemas. Let us have rest, that we may work out the great problems of social duty.

In the third place, a great public interest cannot be determined by a compromise. The prescience of Cobden insisted on a scheme of national education which differs totally from the pitiful compromise which is contained in Mr. Forster's Act, and which sciolists laud as a consummate example of political genius. The danger is imminent, and it cannot be avoided by deferring to the professional interests of an established clergy, which is eager to maintain ascendancy, which attempts to justify its *raison d'être*, and which allies itself blindly to protected interests. I do not believe that the next English revolution will be violent. The dissatisfied forces of society have been too long schooled to attempt the excesses of a Jacquerie. But the revolution will be thorough, and may be founded on social heresies as destructive as those of violence are. The risk is that stereotyped opinions may exercise hereafter a social despotism, because the folly of privilege refuses discontent a hearing. Nero, we are told, fiddled while Rome was burning, and we quote the blindness of the Claudian despot as an example of supine indifference to menace. But in our day statesmen may live in a fool's paradise, and come to the knowledge of the facts only when they and theirs are wholly ostracised.

'Incedis per ignes
Suppositos cineri doloso.'

It remains that I should say a few words on the attitude which Cobden took towards the higher culture. It is commonly supposed that he spoke and felt contemptuously about such learning as is acquired in the old Universities, and persons like Messrs. Seeley and Matthew Arnold have been pleased to comment on his supposed Philistinism. Now not to linger on the question whether minds can really be great, and competent to form a just estimate of social forces and social obligations, without some tincture of the higher culture, and thereupon a true appreciation of the place which taste and refinement have in the machinery of civilisation, nothing can be more erroneous than the opinion that Cobden looked down upon the higher education. The circumstances of his early life precluded him from obtaining that kind of culture which requires considerable outlay, and a prolonged course of teaching. He was the son of impoverished gentlefolks, who had a large family, and very scanty means, and he was therefore sent early into the world to gain his living. But if there ever was a man who could be cited as an instance of what is called self-help or self-culture—two words by the way which never should have been accepted in the English language,—by which I mean progress in abundant and various knowledge under the greatest disadvantages, no person could more fairly claim to be well educated than Cobden was. For example, few historical monographs have higher merits, both for clearness, precision, and profundity than Cobden's Tract, '1793 and 1853.' 'There has been,' Cobden said *, 'a good deal of talk about the advantages or disadvantages of classical education. I am a great advocate of culture of every kind, and I say where you can find men who in addition to profound classical learning, like (instancing some of his friends), have a vast knowledge of modern affairs, and who as well as scholars, are at the same time thinkers, these men I acknowledge to have a vast superiority over me, and I bow to these men with reverence for these superior advantages.' This is not the language of a Philistine, of a person who affects to despise the 'men of the cloister,' of one who collects all literary men under the generic term of 'prigs,'. and who holds up to the scorn of well-born and wealthy bumpkins, those who believe that culture and reason have their place in the economy of society.

What Cobden complained of, and with justice, is best expressed in his own words. 'To bring young men from college with no knowledge of the country where the great drama of modern political and national life is being worked out—who are totally ignorant

* See Speeches, vol. ii. p. 364.

of countries like America, but who for good or evil
are exercising and will exercise more influence in this
country than any other persons—to take young men,
destitute of knowledge about countries like that—their
geography, their modern history, and their resources—
and to place them in responsible positions in the
government of this country,—I say it is imperilling
your best interests, and every earnest remonstrance
that can be made against such a state of education
ought to be made by every public man who values
the future welfare of his country.'

Nothing can be more ridiculous than an education
which leaves out of its programme all knowledge of
those events and places which are marked by the
history of the last seventeen centuries, to concentrate
all attention on the fortunes of Greece and Rome, and
to have no knowledge of the affairs of modern Europe
and the New World. I am myself convinced, that as
a means of mental culture, nothing can be found which
is superior to accurate training in the grammar and
literature of the two great nations of antiquity. I
trust that the time is far distant when they will be
superseded by the gossip of physical science, or by a
superficial acquaintance with either the French or
German languages. It is something to know a little
accurately, even though the pains given to the acquisition seem disproportionately large, and the interest
in the subject treated appears remote and even anti-
quarian. But to stop at this knowledge is to mistake
the instrument of instruction for knowledge, to till
the mind without giving it the means of bearing a crop.
The value of such a training as I advise, and as far

as I can, support, lies in the general aptitude which it gives for other knowledge. No person who has had experience in examining the acquirements of a great public school, or the larger field of induction supplied by the so-called Oxford Local Examinations, can fail of concluding that the boys who show most knowledge of Latin and Greek and mathematics, the two principal instruments of mental culture, are equally proficient in modern languages, geography, and history, and that taken as an average, they beat those youths who have been stinted to what is called an English education even in their own subjects. They who get their foundation broad and solid have far greater facilities in building upon it.

Cobden of course was referring to the ordinary young gentleman who gets into Parliament, because his father is rich and has local influence, and who has gone through the course of idleness miscalled education at Eton or Harrow, and Oxford or Cambridge, leaving, in many cases, the school with far too little knowledge for the purpose of obtaining a common degree at the University. It is not that these young men know Classics and nothing else, the fact is that they very frequently know nothing whatever, and as far as acquaintance with learning goes would have been none the worse off if they had never gone to school or college at all. The authorities of these places of education are greatly to blame because they do not insist on the same conditions of general knowledge for the wealthier classes of society, which they very properly exact from those who constitute their candidates for Local Examinations. But the fault lies deeper than in the rulers of schools and colleges. It comes from the sordid worship of wealth, which is so eminently characteristic of this country, and at the present time in particular, for it seems that in this generation letters have reached their lowest degradation.

There is no country in the world where the educated classes occupy so inferior a position as they do in England. At the present time there is hardly any author of repute in the House of Commons, hardly any person who shows evidence of having gone beyond ordinary school learning. In other countries, in France, Germany, the United States, men of letters are statesmen and diplomatists. We take our administrators and our ambassadors from the Montagues and the Capulets of politics and from them only. If a man of literary reputation appears before an English constituency, it is frequently the case that what ought to have been a recommendation to him is turned to a disadvantage, or if it be in any way appreciated, it is of little value when contrasted with the fortune or equipage of some rich boor, or of some successful trader. Men of letters in England have to thank themselves in some degree for the place in which they find themselves. They either stand aloof from the great interests of social life, or canvas for some quiet office, or ally themselves with those mean interests whose pretensions they could easily strip off and expose, and to which for the highest good of society, they should constitute a counterpoise. But if there ever was a time in which men who are competent for the function, should undertake the duty of interpreting those rivalries which are always so serious, and obviating that collision of interests which is always so menacing, it is the present, when English society is gathering into two camps, the one growing every day more wealthy, more contemptuous, more harsh, more vulgar; the other becoming conscious of its power, more minatory in its language, and more convinced that it cannot get justice except by ostracising its rival.

BEDFORD STREET, COVENT GARDEN, LONDON;
May 1873.

MACMILLAN & CO.'S CATALOGUE of Works in the Departments of History, Biography, and Travels; Politics, Political and Social Economy, Law, etc.; and Works connected with Language. With some short Account or Critical Notice concerning each Book.

HISTORY, BIOGRAPHY, and TRAVELS.

Baker (Sir Samuel W.)—Works by Sir SAMUEL BAKER, M.A., F.R.G.S.:—

THE ALBERT N'YANZA Great Basin of the Nile, and Exploration of the Nile Sources. Third and Cheaper Edition. Maps and Illustrations. Crown 8vo. 6s.

"*Bruce won the source of the Blue Nile; Speke and Grant won the Victoria source of the great White Nile; and I have been permitted to succeed in completing the Nile Sources by the discovery of the great reservoir of the equatorial waters, the Albert N'yanza, from which the river issues as the entire White Nile.*"—PREFACE. "*As a Macaulay arose among the historians,*" says the READER, "*so a Baker has arisen among the explorers.*" "*Charmingly written;*" says the SPECTATOR, "*full, as might be expected, of incident, and free from that wearisome reiteration of useless facts which is the drawback to almost all books of African travel.*"

THE NILE TRIBUTARIES OF ABYSSINIA, and the Sword Hunters of the Hamran Arabs. With Maps and Illustrations. Fourth and Cheaper Edition. Crown 8vo. 6s.

Sir Samuel Baker here describes twelve months' exploration, during which he examined the rivers that are tributary to the Nile from Abyssinia, including the Atbara, Settite, Royan, Salaam, Angrab, Rahad, Dinder, and the Blue Nile. The interest attached to these portions of Africa differs entirely from that of the White Nile regions, as the whole of Upper Egypt and Abyssinia is capable of development, and is inhabited by races having some degree of civilisation; while Central Africa is peopled by a race of savages, whose future is more problematical. The TIMES says: "It solves finally a geographical riddle which hitherto had been extremely perplexing, and it adds much to our information respecting Egyptian Abyssinia and the different races that spread over it. It contains, moreover, some notable instances of English daring and enterprising skill; it abounds in animated tales of exploits dear to the heart of the British sportsman; and it will attract even the least studious reader, as the author tells a story well, and can describe nature with uncommon power."

Barante (M. De).—*See* GUIZOT.

Baring-Gould (Rev. S., M.A.)—LEGENDS OF OLD TESTAMENT CHARACTERS, from the Talmud and other sources. By the Rev. S. BARING-GOULD, M.A., Author of "Curious Myths of the Middle Ages," "The Origin and Development of Religious Belief," "In Exitu Israel," &c. In Two Vols. Crown 8vo. 16s. Vol. I. Adam to Abraham. Vol. II. Melchizedek to Zechariah.

Mr. Baring-Gould's previous contributions to the History of Mythology and the formation of a science of comparative religion are admitted to be of high importance; the present work, it is believed, will be found to be of equal value. He has collected from the Talmud and other sources, Jewish and Mohammedan, a large number of curious and interesting legends concerning the principal characters of the Old Testament, comparing them frequently with similar legends current among many of the peoples, savage and civilised, all over the world. "These volumes contain much that is very strange, and, to the ordinary English reader, very novel."—DAILY NEWS.

Barker (Lady).—*See also* BELLES LETTRES CATALOGUE.

STATION LIFE IN NEW ZEALAND. By LADY BARKER. Second and Cheaper Edition. Globe 8vo. 3s. 6d.

HISTORY, BIOGRAPHY, & TRAVELS.

These letters are the exact account of a lady's experience of the brighter and less practical side of colonization. They record the expeditions, adventures, and emergencies diversifying the daily life of the wife of a New Zealand sheep-farmer; and, as each was written while the novelty and excitement of the scenes it describes were fresh upon her, they may succeed in giving here in England an adequate impression of the delight and freedom of an existence so far removed from our own highly-wrought civilization. "We have never read a more truthful or a pleasanter little book."—
ATHENÆUM.

Bernard, St.—*See* MORISON.

Blanford (W. T.)—GEOLOGY AND ZOOLOGY OF ABYSSINIA. By W. T. BLANFORD. 8vo. 21s.

This work contains an account of the Geological and Zoological Observations made by the author in Abyssinia, when accompanying the British Army on its march to Magdala and back in 1868, and during a short journey in Northern Abyssinia, after the departure of the troops. Part I. Personal Narrative; Part II. Geology; Part III. Zoology. With Coloured Illustrations and Geological Map. "The result of his labours, the ACADEMY *says, "is an important contribution to the natural history of the country."*

Bryce.—THE HOLY ROMAN EMPIRE. By JAMES BRYCE, D.C.L., Regius Professor of Civil Law, Oxford. New and Revised Edition. Crown 8vo. 7s. 6d.

The object of this treatise is not so much to give a narrative history of the countries included in the Romano-Germanic Empire—Italy during the Middle Ages, Germany from the ninth century to the nineteenth—as to describe the Holy Empire itself as an institution or system, the wonderful offspring of a body of beliefs and traditions which have almost wholly passed away from the world. To make such a description intelligible it has appeared best to give the book the form rather of a narrative than of a dissertation; and to combine with an exposition of what may be called the theory of the Empire an outline of the political history of Germany, as well as some notice of the affairs of mediæval Italy. Nothing else so directly linked the old world to the new as the Roman Empire, which exercised over the minds of men an influence such as its material strength could never have commanded. It is of this influence, and the causes that gave it power, that the present work is designed to treat. "It exactly supplies a want: it affords a key to much which men read of in their books as isolated facts, but of which they have hitherto had no connected exposition set before them. We know of no writer who has so thoroughly grasped the real nature of the mediæval Empire, and its relations alike to earlier and to later times."—SATURDAY REVIEW.

Burke (Edmund).—*See* MORLEY (JOHN).

Cameos from English History.—*See* YONGE (MISS).

Chatterton.—*See* WILSON (DANIEL).

Cooper.—ATHENÆ CANTABRIGIENSES. By CHARLES HENRY COOPER, F.S.A., and THOMPSON COOPER, F.S.A. Vol. I. 8vo., 1500—85, 18s.; Vol. II., 1586—1609, 18s.

This elaborate work, which is dedicated by permission to Lord Macaulay, contains lives of the eminent men sent forth by Cambridge, after the fashion of Anthony à Wood, in his famous "Athenæ Oxonienses."

Cox (G. V., M.A.)—RECOLLECTIONS OF OXFORD. By G. V. Cox, M.A., New College, late Esquire Bedel and Coroner in the University of Oxford. *Cheaper Edition.* Crown 8vo. 6s.

"*An amusing farrago of anecdote, and will pleasantly recall in many a country parsonage the memory of youthful days.*"—TIMES. "*Those who wish to make acquaintance with the Oxford of their grandfathers, and to keep up the intercourse with Alma Mater during their father's time, even to the latest novelties in fashion or learning of the present day, will do well to procure this pleasant, unpretending little volume.*"—ATLAS.

"Daily News."—THE DAILY NEWS CORRESPONDENCE of the War between Germany and France, 1870—1. Edited with Notes and Comments. New Edition. Complete in One Volume. With Maps and Plans. Crown 8vo. 6s.

This Correspondence has been translated into German. In a Preface the Editor says:—

"*Among the various pictures, recitals, and descriptions which have appeared, both of our gloriously ended national war as a whole, and of its several episodes, we think that in laying before the German public, through*

HISTORY, BIOGRAPHY, & TRAVELS.

a translation, the following *War Letters* which appeared first in the DAILY NEWS, and were afterwards published collectively, we are offering them a picture of the events of the war of a quite peculiar character. These communications have the advantage of being at once entertaining and instructive, free from every romantic embellishment, and nevertheless written in a vein intelligible and not fatiguing to the general reader. The writers linger over events, and do not disdain to surround the great and heroic war-pictures with arabesques, gay and grave, taken from camp-life and the life of the inhabitants of the occupied territory. A feature which distinguishes these *Letters* from all other delineations of the war is that they do not proceed from a single pen, but were written from the camps of both belligerents." "These notes and comments," according to the SATURDAY REVIEW, "are in reality a very well executed and continuous history."

Dilke.—GREATER BRITAIN. A Record of Travel in English-speaking Countries during 1866-7. (America, Australia, India.) By Sir CHARLES WENTWORTH DILKE, M.P. Sixth Edition. Crown 8vo. 6s.

"*Mr. Dilke,*" says *the* SATURDAY REVIEW, "*has written a book which is probably as well worth reading as any book of the same aims and character that ever was written. Its merits are that it is written in a lively and agreeable style, that it implies a great deal of physical pluck, that no page of it fails to show an acute and highly intelligent observer, that it stimulates the imagination as well as the judgment of the reader, and that it is on perhaps the most interesting subject that can attract an Englishman who cares about his country.*" "*Many of the subjects discussed in these pages,*" says the DAILY NEWS, "*are of the widest interest, and such as no man who cares for the future of his race and of the world can afford to treat with indifference.*"

Dürer (Albrecht).—HISTORY OF THE LIFE OF ALBRECHT DÜRER, of Nürnberg. With a Translation of his Letters and Journal, and some account of his Works. By Mrs. CHARLES HEATON. Royal 8vo. bevelled boards, extra gilt. 31s. 6d.

This work contains about Thirty Illustrations, ten of which are productions by the Autotype (carbon) process, and are printed in permanent tints by Messrs. Cundall and Fleming, under licence from the Autotype Company, Limited; the rest are Photographs and Woodcuts.

Elliott.—LIFE OF HENRY VENN ELLIOTT, of Brighton. By JOSIAH BATEMAN, M.A., Author of "Life of Daniel Wilson, Bishop of Calcutta," &c. With Portrait, engraved by JEENS. Extra fcap. 8vo. Third and Cheaper Edition, with Appendix. 6s.

"*A very charming piece of religious biography; no one can read it without both pleasure and profit.*"—BRITISH QUARTERLY REVIEW.

European History, Narrated in a Series of Historical Selections from the best Authorities. Edited and arranged by E. M. SEWELL and C. M. YONGE. First Series, crown 8vo. 6s.; Second Series, 1088-1228, crown 8vo. 6s. Second Edition.

"*When young children have acquired the outlines of history from abridgments and catechisms, and it becomes desirable to give a more enlarged view of the subject, in order to render it really useful and interesting, a difficulty often arises as to the choice of books. Two courses are open, either to take a general and consequently dry history of facts, such as Russell's Modern Europe, or to choose some work treating of a particular period or subject, such as the works of Macaulay and Froude. The former course usually renders history uninteresting; the latter is unsatisfactory, because it is not sufficiently comprehensive. To remedy this difficulty, selections, continuous and chronological, have in the present volume been taken from the larger works of Freeman, Milman, Palgrave, Lingard, Hume, and others, which may serve as distinct landmarks of historical reading.* 'We know of scarcely anything,' says the GUARDIAN, 'of this volume, which is so likely to raise to a higher level the average standard of English education.*'"

Fairfax (Lord).—A LIFE OF THE GREAT LORD FAIRFAX, Commander-in-Chief of the Army of the Parliament of England. By CLEMENTS R. MARKHAM, F.S.A. With Portraits, Maps, Plans, and Illustrations. Demy 8vo. 16s.

No full Life of the great Parliamentary Commander has appeared; and it is here sought to produce one—based upon careful research in contemporary records and upon family and other documents. "Highly useful to the careful student of the History of the Civil War. . . . Pro-

bably as a military chronicle Mr. Markham's book is one of the most full and accurate that we possess about the Civil War."—FORTNIGHTLY REVIEW.

Faraday.—MICHAEL FARADAY. By J. H. GLADSTONE, Ph.D., F.R.S. Second Edition, with Portrait engraved by JEENS from a photograph by J. WATKINS. Crown 8vo. 4s. 6d.

CONTENTS:—I. The Story of his Life. II. Study of his Character. III. Fruits of his Experience. IV. His Method of Working. V. The Value of his Discoveries.—Supplementary Portraits. Appendices:—List of Honorary Fellowships, etc.

"Faraday needed a popular biography. A man so simple and so pure, as well as so strong in intellect, so absolutely devoted to science for its own sake alone, so utterly indifferent to wealth and social distinction, so keen in his appreciation of the hard facts of sensation, and yet so permeated with a sense of the supra-sensual and spiritual, ought to be widely and familiarly known to the world at large; and Dr. Gladstone's book is excellently adapted to this result."—GUARDIAN.

Field (E. W.)—EDWIN WILKINS FIELD. A Memorial Sketch. By THOMAS SADLER, Ph.D. With a Portrait. Crown 8vo. 4s. 6d.

Mr. Field was well known during his life-time not only as an eminent lawyer and a strenuous and successful advocate of law reform, but, both in England and America, as a man of wide and thorough culture, varied tastes, large-heartedness, and lofty aims. His sudden death was looked upon as a public loss, and it is expected that this brief Memoir will be acceptable to a large number besides the many friends at whose request it has been written.

Forbes.—LIFE AND LETTERS OF JAMES DAVID FORBES, F.R.S., late Principal of the United College in the University of St. Andrews. By J. C. SHAIRP, LL.D., Principal of the United College in the University of St. Andrews; P. G. TAIT, M.A., Professor of Natural Philosophy in the University of Edinburgh; and A. ADAMS-REILLY, F.R.G.S. 8vo. with Portraits, Map, and Illustrations, 16s.

"Not only a biography that all should read, but a scientific treatise, without which the shelves of no physicist's library can be deemed complete."—STANDARD.

Freeman.—Works by EDWARD A. FREEMAN, M.A., D.C.L.:—

"*That special power over a subject which conscientious and patient research can only achieve, a strong grasp of facts, a true mastery over detail, with a clear and manly style—all these qualities join to make the Historian of the Conquest conspicuous in the intellectual arena.*"— ACADEMY.

HISTORY OF FEDERAL GOVERNMENT, from the Foundation of the Achaian League to the Disruption of the United States. Vol. I. General Introduction. History of the Greek Federations. 8vo. 21s.

Mr. Freeman's aim, in this elaborate and valuable work, is not so much to discuss the abstract nature of Federal Government, as to exhibit its actual working in ages and countries widely removed from one another. Four Federal Commonwealths stand out, in four different ages of the world, as commanding above all others the attention of students of political history, viz. the Achaian League, the Swiss Cantons, the United Provinces, the United States. The first volume, besides containing a General Introduction, treats of the first of these. In writing this volume the author has endeavoured to combine a text which may be instructive and interesting to any thoughtful reader, whether specially learned or not, with notes which may satisfy the requirements of the most exacting scholar. "The task Mr. Freeman has undertaken," the SATURDAY REVIEW *says, "is one of great magnitude and importance. It is also a task of an almost entirely novel character. No other work professing to give the history of a political principle occurs to us, except the slight contributions to the history of representative government that is contained in a course of M. Guizot's lectures . . . . The history of the development of a principle is at least as important as the history of a dynasty, or of a race."*

OLD ENGLISH HISTORY. With *Five Coloured Maps.* Second Edition. Extra fcap. 8vo., half-bound. 6s.

"*Its object,*" *the Preface says,* "*is to show that clear, accurate, and scientific views of history, or indeed of any subject, may be easily given to children from the very first. . . . I have throughout striven to connect the history of England with the general history of civilised Europe, and I have especially tried to make the book serve as an incentive to a more accurate study of historic geography.*" *The rapid sale of the first edition and the universal approval with which the work has been received prove the correctness of the author's notions, and show that for such a book there was ample*

Freeman (E. A.)—continued.

room. *The work is suited not only for children, but will serve as an excellent text-book for older students, a clear and faithful summary of the history of the period for those who wish to revive their historical knowledge, and a book full of charms for the general reader. The work is preceded by a complete chronological Table, and appended is an exhaustive and useful Index. In the present edition the whole has been carefully revised, and such improvements as suggested themselves have been introduced. "The book indeed is full of instruction and interest to students of all ages, and he must be a well-informed man indeed who will not rise from its perusal with clearer and more accurate ideas of a too much neglected portion of English history."*—SPECTATOR.

HISTORY OF THE CATHEDRAL CHURCH OF WELLS, as Illustrating the History of the Cathedral Churches of the Old Foundation. Crown 8vo. 3s. 6d.

"I have here," the author says, "tried to treat the history of the Church of Wells as a contribution to the general history of the Church and Kingdom of England, and specially to the history of Cathedral Churches of the Old Foundation. . . . I wish to point out the general principles of the original founders as the model to which the Old Foundations should be brought back, and the New Foundations reformed after their pattern." "The history assumes in Mr. Freeman's hands a significance, and, we may add, a practical value as suggestive of what a cathedral ought to be, which make it well worthy of mention."—SPECTATOR.

HISTORICAL ESSAYS. Second Edition. 8vo. 10s. 6d.

The principle on which these Essays have been chosen is that of selecting papers which refer to comparatively modern times, or, at least, to the existing states and nations of Europe. By a sort of accident a number of the pieces chosen have thrown themselves into something like a continuous series bearing on the historical causes of the great events of 1870—71. Notes have been added whenever they seemed to be called for ; and whenever he could gain in accuracy of statement or in force or clearness of expression, the author has freely changed, added to, or left out, what he originally wrote. To many of the Essays has been added a short note of the circumstances under which they were written. It is needless to say that any product of Mr. Freeman's pen is worthy of attentive perusal ; and it is believed that the contents of this volume will throw light on several subjects of great historical importance and the widest interest.

Freeman (E. A.)—*continued.*

The following is a list of the subjects:—1. The Mythical and Romantic Elements in Early English History; 2. The Continuity of English History; 3. The Relations between the Crowns of England and Scotland; 4. Saint Thomas of Canterbury and his Biographers; 5. The Reign of Edward the Third; 6. The Holy Roman Empire; 7. The Franks and the Gauls; 8. The Early Sieges of Paris; 9. Frederick the First, King of Italy; 10. The Emperor Frederick the Second; 11. Charles the Bold; 12. Presidential Government. "*He never touches a question without adding to our comprehension of it, without leaving the impression of an ample knowledge, a righteous purpose, a clear and powerful understanding.*"—SATURDAY REVIEW.

A SECOND SERIES OF HISTORICAL ESSAYS. 8vo. 10s. 6d.

These Essays chiefly relate to earlier periods of history than those which were dealt with in the former volume—to the times commonly known as "Ancient" or "Classical." All the papers have been carefully revised, and the author has found himself able to do very much in the way of improving and simplifying the style. The Essays are:—"Ancient Greece and Mediæval Italy;" "Mr. Gladstone's Homer and the Homeric Ages;" "The Historians of Athens;" "The Athenian Democracy;" "Alexander the Great;" "Greece during the Macedonian Period;" "Mommsen's History of Rome;" "Lucius Cornelius Sulla;" "The Flavian Cæsars."

THE GROWTH OF THE ENGLISH CONSTITUTION FROM THE EARLIEST TIMES. Crown 8vo. 5s. Second Edition, revised.

The three Chapters of which this work consists are an expansion of two Lectures delivered by Mr. Freeman; appended are copious notes, the whole book forming a graphic and interesting sketch of the history of the British Constitution, from an original point of view. The author shows that the characteristic elements of the British Constitution are common to the whole of the Aryan nations. His "object has been to show that the earliest institutions of England and of other Teutonic lands are not mere matters of curious speculation, but matters closely connected with our present political being. I wish to show" he says, "that, in many things, our earliest institutions come more nearly home to us, and that they have more in common

Freeman (E. A.)—continued.

with our present political state, than the institutions of intermediate ages which at first sight seem to have much more in common with our own." He attempts to shew that "freedom is everywhere older than bondage," "toleration than intolerance."

THE UNITY OF HISTORY. The "REDE" LECTURE delivered in the Senate House, before the University of Cambridge, on Friday, May 24th, 1872. Crown 8vo. 2s.

GENERAL SKETCH OF EUROPEAN HISTORY. Being Vol. I. of a Historical Course for Schools edited by E. A. FREEMAN. 18mo. 3s. 6d. Second Edition.

The present volume is meant to be introductory to the whole course. It is intended to give, as its name implies, a general sketch of the history of the civilised world, that is, of Europe, and of the lands which have drawn their civilization from Europe. Its object is to trace out the general relations of different periods and different countries to one another, without going minutely into the affairs of any particular country. This is an object of the first importance, for, without clear notions of general history, the history of particular countries can never be rightly understood. The narrative extends from the earliest movements of the Aryan peoples, down to the latest events both on the Eastern and Western Continents. The book consists of seventeen moderately sized chapters, each chapter being divided into a number of short numbered paragraphs, each with a title prefixed clearly indicative of the subject of the paragraph. "It supplies the great want of a good foundation for historical teaching. The scheme is an excellent one, and this instalment has been executed in a way that promises much for the volumes that are yet to appear."—EDUCATIONAL TIMES.

Galileo.—THE PRIVATE LIFE OF GALILEO. Compiled principally from his Correspondence and that of his eldest daughter, Sister Maria Celeste, Nun in the Franciscan Convent of S. Matthew in Arcetri. With Portrait. Crown 8vo. 7s. 6d.

It has been the endeavour of the compiler to place before the reader a plain, unvarnished statement of facts; and, as a means to this end, to allow Galileo, his friends, and his judges to speak for themselves as far as possible. All the best authorities have been made use of, and all the materials which exist for a biography have been in this volume put into a symmetrical form. The result is a most touching picture skilfully arranged of the great heroic man of science and his devoted daughter, whose letters are full of the deepest reverential love and trust, amply repaid by the noble soul. The SATURDAY REVIEW says of the book, "It is not so much the philosopher as the man who is seen in this simple and life-like sketch, and the hand which portrays the features and actions is mainly that of one who had studied the subject the closest and the most intimately. This little volume has done much within its slender compass to prove the depth and tenderness of Galileo's heart."

Gladstone (Right Hon. W. E., M.P.)—JUVENTUS MUNDI. The Gods and Men of the Heroic Age. Crown 8vo. cloth. With Map. 10s. 6d. Second Edition.

This work of Mr. Gladstone deals especially with the historic element in Homer, expounding that element and furnishing by its aid a full account of the Homeric men and the Homeric religion. It starts, after the introductory chapter, with a discussion of the several races then existing in Hellas, including the influence of the Phœnicians and Egyptians. It contains chapters on the Olympian system, with its several deities; on the Ethics and the Polity of the Heroic age; on the Geography of Homer; on the characters of the Poems; presenting, in fine, a view of primitive life and primitive society as found in the poems of Homer. To this New Edition various additions have been made. "Seldom," says the ATHENÆUM, "out of the great poems themselves, have these Divinities looked so majestic and respectable. To read these brilliant details is like standing on the Olympian threshold and gazing at the ineffable brightness within." "There is," according to the WESTMINSTER REVIEW, "probably no other writer now living who could have done the work of this book... It would be difficult to point out a book that contains so much fulness of knowledge along with so much freshness of perception and clearness of presentation."

Goethe and Mendelssohn (1821—1831). From the German of Dr. KARL MENDELSSOHN, Son of the Composer, by M. E. VON GLEHN. From the Private Diaries and Home-Letters of Mendelssohn, with Poems and Letters of Goethe never before printed. Also with two New and Original Portraits, Facsimiles, and Appendix of Twenty Letters hitherto unpublished. Crown 8vo. 5s.

This little volume is full of interesting details about Mendelssohn from his twelfth year onwards, and especially of his intimate and frequent intercourse with Goethe. It is an episode of Weimar's golden days which we see before us—old age and fame hand in hand with youth in its aspiring efforts; the aged poet fondling the curls of the little musician and calling to him in playful and endearing accents "to make a little noise for him, and awaken the winged spirits that have so long lain slumbering." Here will be found letters and reports of conversations between the two, touching on all subjects, human and divine—Music, Æsthetics, Art, Poetry, Science, Morals, and "the profound and ancient problem of human life," as well as reminiscences of celebrated men with whom the great composer came in contact. The letters appended give, among other matters, some interesting glimpses into the private life of Her Majesty Queen Victoria and the late Prince Albert. The two well-executed engravings show Mendelssohn as a beautiful boy of twelve years.

Guizot.—M. DE BARANTE, a Memoir, Biographical and Autobiographical. By M. GUIZOT. Translated by the Author of "JOHN HALIFAX, GENTLEMAN." Crown 8vo. 6s. 6d.

"*It is scarcely necessary to write a preface to this book. Its lifelike, portrait of a true and great man, painted unconsciously by himself in his letters and autobiography, and retouched and completed by the tender hand of his surviving friend—the friend of a lifetime—is sure, I think, to be appreciated in England as it was in France, where it appeared in the Revue de Deux Mondes. Also, I believe every thoughtful mind will enjoy its clear reflections of French and European politics and history for the last seventy years, and the curious light thus thrown upon many present events and combinations of circumstances.*"—PREFACE. "*The highest purpose of both history and biography are answered by a memoir so lifelike, so faithful, and so philosophical.*"—BRITISH QUARTERLY REVIEW. "*This eloquent memoir, which for tenderness, gracefulness, and vigour, might be placed on the same shelf with Tacitus' Life of Agricola. . . . Mrs. Craik has rendered the language of Guizot in her own sweet translucent English.*"—DAILY NEWS.

Hole.—A GENEALOGICAL STEMMA OF THE KINGS OF ENGLAND AND FRANCE. By the Rev. C. HOLE, M.A., Trinity College, Cambridge. On Sheet, 1s.

The different families are printed in distinguishing colours, thus facilitating reference.

Hosier (H. M.)—Works by Captain Henry M. Hozier, late Assistant Military Secretary to Lord Napier of Magdala.

THE SEVEN WEEKS' WAR; Its Antecedents and Incidents. *New and Cheaper Edition.* With New Preface, Maps, and Plans. Crown 8vo. 6s.

This account of the brief but momentous Austro-Prussian War of 1866 claims consideration as being the product of an eye-witness of some of its most interesting incidents. The author has attempted to ascertain and to advance facts. Two maps are given, one illustrating the operations of the Army of the Maine, and the other the operations from Königgrätz. In the Prefatory Chapter to this edition, events resulting from the war of 1866 are set forth, and the current of European history traced down to the recent Franco-Prussian war, a natural consequence of the war whose history is narrated in this volume. "*Mr. Hosier added to the knowledge of military operations and of languages, which he had proved himself to possess, a ready and skilful pen, and excellent faculties of observation and description.* . . . *All that Mr. Hosier saw of the great events of the war—and he saw a large share of them—he describes in clear and vivid language.*"—SATURDAY REVIEW. "*Mr. Hosier's volume deserves to take a permanent place in the literature of the Seven Weeks' War.*"—PALL MALL GAZETTE.

THE BRITISH EXPEDITION TO ABYSSINIA. Compiled from Authentic Documents. 8vo. 9s.

Several accounts of the British Expedition have been published. They have, however, been written by those who have not had access to those authentic documents, which cannot be collected directly after the termination of a campaign. The endeavour of the author of this sketch has been to present to readers a succinct and impartial account of an enterprise which has rarely been equalled in the annals of war. "*This,*" *says the* SPECTATOR, "*will be the account of the Abyssinian Expedition for professional reference, if not for professional reading. Its literary merits are really very great.*"

THE INVASIONS OF ENGLAND. A History of the Past, with Lessons for the Future. [*In the press.*

Hughes.—MEMOIR OF A BROTHER. By THOMAS HUGHES, M.P., Author of "Tom Brown's School Days." With Portrait of GEORGE HUGHES, after WATTS. Engraved by JEENS. Crown 8vo. 5s. Fourth Edition.

"*The boy who can read this book without deriving from it some additional impulse towards honourable, manly, and independent conduct, has no good stuff in him. . . . While boys at school may be bewildered by various conflicting theories of the characters of the great Englishmen whom they have been taught to admire or to hate, here, in the guise of the simplest and the most modest of country gentlemen, they may find an exemplar which they cannot do better than copy.*"—DAILY NEWS.

"*We have read it with the deepest gratification and with real admiration.*"—STANDARD.

"*The biography throughout is replete with interest.*"—MORNING POST.

Huyshe (Captain G. L.)—THE RED RIVER EXPEDITION. By Captain G. L. HUYSHE, Rifle Brigade, late on the Staff of Colonel Sir GARNET WOLSELEY. With Maps. 8vo. 10s. 6d.

This account has been written in the hope of directing attention to the successful accomplishment of an expedition which was attended with more than ordinary difficulties. The author has had access to the official documents of the Expedition, and has also availed himself of the reports on the line of route published by Mr. Dawson, C.E., and by the Typographical Department of the War Office. The statements made may therefore be relied on as accurate and impartial. The endeavour has been made to avoid tiring the general reader with dry details of military movements, and yet not to sacrifice the character of the work as an account of a military expedition. The volume contains a portrait of President Louis Riel, and Maps of the route. The ATHENÆUM *calls it "an enduring authentic record of one of the most creditable achievements ever accomplished by the British Army."*

Irving.—THE ANNALS OF OUR TIME. A Diurnal of Events, Social and Political, Home and Foreign, from the Accession of Queen Victoria to the Peace of Versailles. By JOSEPH IRVING. Third Edition. 8vo. half-bound. 16s.

Every occurrence, metropolitan or provincial, home or foreign, which gave rise to public excitement or discussion, or became the starting point for new trains of thought affecting our social life, has been judged proper matter for this volume. In the proceedings of Parliament, an endeavour has been made to notice all those Debates which were either remarkable as affecting the fate of parties, or led to important changes in our relations with Foreign Powers. Brief notices have been given of the death of all noteworthy persons. Though the events are set down day by day in their order of occurrence, the book is, in its way, the history of an important and well-defined historic cycle. In these "Annals," the ordinary reader may make himself acquainted with the history of his own time in a way that has at least the merit of simplicity and readiness; the more cultivated student will doubtless be thankful for the opportunity given him of passing down the historic stream undisturbed by any other theoretical or party feeling than what he himself has at hand to explain the philosophy of our national story. A complete and useful Index is appended. The Table of Administrations is designed to assist the reader in following the various political changes noticed in their chronological order in the "Annals."— In the new edition all errors and omissions have been rectified, 300 pages been added, and as many as 46 occupied by an impartial exhibition of the wonderful series of events marking the latter half of 1870. "We have before us a trusty and ready guide to the events of the past thirty years, available equally for the statesman, the politician, the public writer, and the general reader. If Mr. Irving's object has been to bring before the reader all the most noteworthy occurrences which have happened since the beginning of her Majesty's reign, he may justly claim the credit of having done so most briefly, succinctly, and simply, and in such a manner, too, as to furnish him with the details necessary in each case to comprehend the event of which he is in search in an intelligent manner."
—TIMES.

Kingsley (Charles).—Works by the Rev. CHARLES KINGSLEY, M.A., Rector of Eversley and Canon of Westminster. (For other Works by the same Author, see THEOLOGICAL and BELLES LETTRES Catalogues.)

ON THE ANCIEN RÉGIME as it existed on the Continent before the FRENCH REVOLUTION. Three Lectures delivered at the Royal Institution. Crown 8vo. 6s.

Kingsley (Charles).—continued.

These three lectures discuss severally (1) Caste, (2) Centralisation, (3) The Explosive Forces by which the Revolution was superinduced. The Preface deals at some length with certain political questions of the present day.

AT LAST : A CHRISTMAS in the WEST INDIES. With nearly Fifty Illustrations. New and Cheaper Edition. Crown 8vo. 6s.

Mr. Kingsley's dream of forty years was at last fulfilled, when he started on a Christmas expedition to the West Indies, for the purpose of becoming personally acquainted with the scenes which he has so vividly described in "Westward Ho!" These two volumes are the journal of his voyage. Records of natural history, sketches of tropical landscape, chapters on education, vices of society, all find their place in a work written, so to say, under the inspiration of Sir Walter Raleigh and the other adventurous men who three hundred years ago disputed against Philip II. the possession of the Spanish Main. "We can only say that Mr. Kingsley's account of a 'Christmas in the West Indies' is in every way worthy to be classed among his happiest productions."—STANDARD.

THE ROMAN AND THE TEUTON. A Series of Lectures delivered before the University of Cambridge. 8vo. 12s.

CONTENTS :—*Inaugural Lecture ; The Forest Children ; The Dying Empire ; The Human Deluge ; The Gothic Civiliser ; Dietrich's End ; The Nemesis of the Goths ; Paulus Diaconus ; The Clergy and the Heathen ; The Monk a Civiliser ; The Lombard Laws ; The Popes and the Lombards ; The Strategy of Providence.* "He has rendered," says the NONCONFORMIST, "good service and shed a new lustre on the chair of Modern History at Cambridge .... He has thrown a charm around the work by the marvellous fascinations of his own genius, brought out in strong relief those great principles of which all history is a revelation, lighted up many dark and almost unknown spots, and stimulated the desire to understand more thoroughly one of the greatest movements in the story of humanity."

PLAYS AND PURITANS, and other Historical Essays. With Portrait of Sir WALTER RALEIGH. Crown 8vo. 5s.

Kingsley (Charles).—*continued.*

In addition to the Essay mentioned in the title, this volume contains other two—one on "Sir Walter Raleigh and his Time," and one on Froude's "History of England,"—all three contributed to the NORTH BRITISH REVIEW. *Mr. Kingsley has already shown how intimate is his knowledge of the times on which all three essays touch.*

Kingsley (Henry, F.R.G.S.)—For other Works by same Author, *see* BELLES LETTRES CATALOGUE.

TALES OF OLD TRAVEL. Re-narrated by HENRY KINGSLEY, F.R.G.S. With *Eight Illustrations* by HUARD. Fourth Edition. Crown 8vo. 6*s*.

In this volume Mr. Henry Kingsley re-narrates, at the same time preserving much of the quaintness of the original, some of the most fascinating tales of travel contained in the collections of Hakluyt and others. The CONTENTS *are—Marco Polo; The Shipwreck of Pelsart; The Wonderful Adventures of Andrew Battel; The Wanderings of a Capuchin; Peter Carder; The Preservation of the "Terra Nova;" Spitzbergen; D'Ermenonville's Acclimatisation Adventure; The Old Slave Trade; Miles Philips; The Sufferings of Robert Everard; John Fox; Alvaro Nunez; The Foundation of an Empire. "We know no better book for those who want knowledge or seek to refresh it. As for the 'sensational,' most novels are tame compared with these narratives."*—ATHENÆUM. *"Exactly the book to interest and to do good to intelligent and high-spirited boys."*—LITERARY CHURCHMAN.

Labouchere.—DIARY OF THE BESIEGED RESIDENT IN PARIS. Reprinted from the *Daily News*, with several New Letters and Preface. By HENRY LABOUCHERE. Third Edition. Crown 8vo. 6*s*.

" The 'Diary of a Besieged Resident in Paris' will certainly form one of the most remarkable records of a momentous episode in history."—SPECTATOR. *"There is an entire absence of affectation in this writer which vastly commends him to us."*—PALL MALL GAZETTE. *"On the whole, it does not seem likely that the 'besieged' will be superseded in his self-assumed function by any subsequent chronicler."*—BRITISH QUARTERLY REVIEW. *"Very smartly written."*—VANITY FAIR.

Macmillan (Rev. Hugh).—For other Works by same Author, see THEOLOGICAL and SCIENTIFIC CATALOGUES.

HOLIDAYS ON HIGH LANDS; or, Rambles and Incidents in search of Alpine Plants. Second Edition, revised. Crown 8vo. cloth. 6s.

The aim of this book is to impart a general idea of the origin, character, and distribution of those rare and beautiful Alpine plants which occur on the British hills, and which are found almost everywhere on the lofty mountain chains of Europe, Asia, Africa, and America. The information the author has to give is conveyed in untechnical language, in a setting of personal adventure, and associated with descriptions of the natural scenery and the peculiarities of the human life in the midst of which the plants were found. By this method the subject is made interesting to a very large class of readers. "*Botanical knowledge is blended with a love of nature, a pious enthusiasm, and a rich felicity of diction not to be met with in any works of kindred character, if we except those of Hugh Miller.*"—TELEGRAPH. "*Mr. M.'s glowing pictures of Scandinavian scenery.*"—SATURDAY REVIEW.

Martin (Frederick).—THE STATESMAN'S YEAR-BOOK: *See* p. 42 of this Catalogue.

Martineau.—BIOGRAPHICAL SKETCHES, 1852—1868. By HARRIET MARTINEAU. Third and Cheaper Edition, with New Preface. Crown 8vo. 6s.

A Collection of Memoirs under these several sections:—(1) *Royal*, (2) *Politicians*, (3) *Professional*, (4) *Scientific*, (5) *Social*, (6) *Literary. These Memoirs appeared originally in the columns of the* DAILY NEWS. "*Miss Martineau's large literary powers and her fine intellectual training make these little sketches more instructive, and constitute them more genuinely works of art, than many more ambitious and diffuse biographies.*"—FORTNIGHTLY REVIEW. "*Each memoir is a complete digest of a celebrated life, illuminated by the flood of searching light which streams from the gaze of an acute but liberal mind.*"—MORNING STAR.

Masson (David).—For other Works by same Author, see PHILOSOPHICAL and BELLES LETTRES CATALOGUES.

Masson (David)—*continued.*

LIFE OF JOHN MILTON. Narrated in connection with the Political, Ecclesiastical, and Literary History of his Time. By DAVID MASSON, M.A., LL.D., Professor of Rhetoric and English Literature in the University of Edinburgh. Vol. I. with Portraits. 8vo. 18s. Vol. II., 1638—1643. 8vo. 16s. Vol. III. In the press.

This work is not only a Biography, but also a continuous Political, Ecclesiastical, and Literary History of England through Milton's whole time. In order to understand Milton, his position, his motives, his thoughts by himself, his public words to his countrymen, and the probable effect of those words, it was necessary to refer largely to the History of his Time, not only as it is presented in well-known books, but as it had to be rediscovered by express and laborious investigation in original and forgotten records: thus of the Biography, a History grew: not a mere popular compilation, but a work of independent search and method from first to last, which has cost more labour by far than the Biography. The second volume is so arranged that the reader may select or omit either the History or Biography. The NORTH BRITISH REVIEW, *speaking of the first volume of this work said,* "*The Life of Milton is here written once for all.*" *The* NONCONFORMIST, *in noticing the second volume, says,* "*Its literary excellence entitles it to take its place in the first ranks of our literature, while the whole style of its execution marks it as the only book that has done anything like adequate justice to one of the great masters of our language, and one of our truest patriots, as well as our greatest epic poet.*"

Mayor (J. E. B.)—WORKS Edited By JOHN E. B. MAYOR, M.A., Kennedy Professor of Latin at Cambridge:—
CAMBRIDGE IN THE SEVENTEENTH CENTURY. Part II. Autobiography of Matthew Robinson. Fcap. 8vo. 5s. 6d.
This is the second of the Memoirs illustrative of "*Cambridge in the Seventeenth Century*" *that of Nicholas Farrar having preceded it. It gives a lively picture of England during the Civil War; the most important crisis of our national life; it supplies materials for the history of his University and our Endowed Schools, and gives us a view of country clergy at a time when they are supposed to have been, with scarce an exception, scurrilous sots. Mr. Mayor has added a collection of extracts and documents relating to the history of several other Cambridge men of note belonging to the same period, all, like Robinson, of Nonconformist leanings.*

HISTORY, BIOGRAPHY, & TRAVELS.

Mayor (J. E. B.)—*continued.*

LIFE OF BISHOP BEDELL. By his Son. Fcap. 8vo. 3s. 6d.

This is the third of the Memoirs illustrative of "Cambridge in the 17th Century." The life of the Bishop of Kilmore here printed for the first time is preserved in the Tanner MSS., and is preliminary to a larger one to be issued shortly.

Mitford (A. B.)—TALES OF OLD JAPAN. By A. B. Mitford, Second Secretary to the British Legation in Japan. With upwards of 30 Illustrations, drawn and cut on Wood by Japanese Artists. Two Vols. crown 8vo. 21s.

Under the influence of more enlightened ideas and of a liberal system of policy, the old Japanese civilization is fast disappearing, and will, in a few years, be completely extinct. It was important, therefore, to preserve as far as possible trustworthy records of a state of society which, although venerable from its antiquity, has for Europeans the dawn of novelty; hence the series of narratives and legends translated by Mr. Mitford, and in which the Japanese are very judiciously left to tell their own tale. The two volumes comprise not only stories and episodes illustrative of Asiatic superstitions, but also three sermons. The preface, appendixes, and notes explain a number of local peculiarities; the thirty-one woodcuts are the genuine work of a native artist, who, unconsciously of course, has adopted the process first introduced by the early German masters. "*These very original volumes will always be interesting as memorials of a most exceptional society, while regarded simply as tales, they are sparkling, sensational, and dramatic, and the originality of their ideas and the quaintness of their language give them a most captivating piquancy. The illustrations are extremely interesting, and for the curious in such matters have a special and particular value.*"—PALL MALL GAZETTE.

Morley (John).—EDMUND BURKE, a Historical Study. By John Morley, B.A. Oxon. Crown 8vo. 7s. 6d.

"*The style is terse and incisive, and brilliant with epigram and point. It contains pithy aphoristic sentences which Burke himself would not have disowned. Its sustained power of reasoning, its wide sweep of observation and reflection, its elevated ethical and social tone, stamp it as a work of high excellence.*"—SATURDAY REVIEW. "*A model of compact condensation. We have seldom met with a book in which so much matter was compressed into so limited a space.*"—PALL MALL GAZETTE. "*An essay of unusual effort.*"—WESTMINSTER REVIEW.

Morison.—THE LIFE AND TIMES OF SAINT BERNARD, Abbot of Clairvaux. By JAMES COTTER MORISON, M.A. Cheaper Edition. Crown 8vo. 4s. 6d.

The PALL MALL GAZETTE calls this "one of the best contributions in our literature towards a vivid, intelligent, and worthy knowledge of European interests and thoughts and feelings during the twelfth century. A delightful and instructive volume, and one of the best products of the modern historic spirit." "A work," says the NONCONFORMIST, "of great merit and value, dealing most thoroughly with one of the most interesting characters, and one of the most interesting periods, in the Church history of the Middle Ages. Mr. Morison is thoroughly master of his subject, and writes with great discrimination and fairness, and in a chaste and elegant style." The SPECTATOR says it is "not only distinguished by research and candour, it has also the great merit of never being dull."

Napoleon.—THE HISTORY OF NAPOLEON I. By P. LANFREY. A Translation with the sanction of the Author. Vols. I. and II. 8vo. price 12s. each.

The PALL MALL GAZETTE says it is "one of the most striking pieces of historical composition of which France has to boast," and the SATURDAY REVIEW calls it "an excellent translation of a work on every ground deserving to be translated. It is unquestionably and immeasurably the best that has been produced. It is in fact the only work to which we can turn for an accurate and trustworthy narrative of that extraordinary career. . . . The book is the best and indeed the only trustworthy history of Napoleon which has been written."

Palgrave (Sir F.)—HISTORY OF NORMANDY AND OF ENGLAND. By Sir FRANCIS PALGRAVE, Deputy Keeper of Her Majesty's Public Records. Completing the History to the Death of William Rufus. Vols. II.—IV. 21s. each.

Volume I. General Relations of Mediæval Europe—The Carlovingian Empire—The Danish Expeditions in the Gauls—And the Establishment of Rollo. Volume II. The Three First Dukes of Normandy; Rollo, Guillaume Longue-Épée, and Richard Sans-Peur—The Carlovingian line supplanted by the Capets. Volume III. Richard Sans-Peur—Richard Le-Bon—Richard III.—Robert Le Diable—William the Conqueror. Volume IV. William Rufus—Accession of Henry Beauclerc.

It is useless to say anything to recommend this work of a lifetime to all students of history; it is, as the SPECTATOR says, "perhaps the greatest single contribution yet made to the authentic annals of this country," and "must," says the NONCONFORMIST, "always rank among our standard authorities."

Palgrave (W. G.)—A NARRATIVE OF A YEAR'S JOURNEY THROUGH CENTRAL AND EASTERN ARABIA, 1862-3. By WILLIAM GIFFORD PALGRAVE, late of the Eighth Regiment Bombay N. I. Sixth Edition. With Maps, Plans, and Portrait of Author, engraved on steel by Jeens. Crown 8vo. 6s.

"The work is a model of what its class should be; the style restrained, the narrative clear, telling us all we wish to know of the country and people visited, and enough of the author and his feelings to enable us to trust ourselves to his guidance in a tract hitherto untrodden, and dangerous in more ways than one... He has not only written one of the best books on the Arabs and one of the best books on Arabia, but he has done so in a manner that must command the respect no less than the admiration of his fellow countrymen."—FORTNIGHTLY REVIEW. "Considering the extent of our previous ignorance, the amount of his achievements, and the importance of his contributions to our knowledge, we cannot say less of him than was once said of a far greater discoverer—Mr. Palgrave has indeed given a new world to Europe."—PALL MALL GAZETTE.

Prichard.—THE ADMINISTRATION OF INDIA. From 1859 to 1868. The First Ten Years of Administration under the Crown. By ILTUDUS THOMAS PRICHARD, Barrister-at-Law. Two Vols. Demy 8vo. With Map. 21s.

In these volumes the author has aimed to supply a full, impartial, and independent account of British India between 1859 and 1868—which is in many respects the most important epoch in the history of that country that the present century has seen. "It has the great merit that it is not exclusively devoted, as are too many histories, to military and political details, but enters thoroughly into the more important questions of social history. We find in these volumes a well-arranged and compendious reference to almost all that has been done in India during the last ten years; and the most important official documents and historical pieces are well selected and duly set forth."—SCOTSMAN. "It is a work which every Englishman in India ought to add to his library."—STAR OF INDIA.

Robinson (H. Crabb).—THE DIARY, REMINISCENCES, AND CORRESPONDENCE, OF HENRY CRABB ROBINSON, Barrister-at-Law. Selected and Edited by THOMAS SADLER, Ph.D. With Portrait. Third and Cheaper Edition. Two Vols. Crown 8vo. 16s.

The DAILY NEWS *says: "The two books which are most likely to survive change of literary taste, and to charm while instructing generation after generation, are the 'Diary' of Pepys and Boswell's 'Life of Johnson.' The day will come when to these many will add the 'Diary of Henry Crabb Robinson.' Excellences like those which render the personal revelations of Pepys and the observations of Boswell such pleasant reading abound in this work .... In it is to be found something to suit every taste and inform every mind. For the general reader it contains much light and amusing matter. To the lover of literature it conveys information which he will prize highly on account of its accuracy and rarity. The student of social life will gather from it many valuable hints wherein to base theories as to the effects on English society of the progress of civilization. For these and other reasons this 'Diary' is a work to which a hearty welcome should be accorded."*

Rogers (James E. Thorold).—HISTORICAL GLEANINGS: A Series of Sketches. Montague, Walpole, Adam Smith, Cobbett. By Prof. ROGERS. Crown 8vo. 4s. 6d. Second Series. Wiklif, Laud, Wilkes, and Horne Tooke. Crown 8vo. 6s.

Professor Rogers's object in these sketches, which are in the form of Lectures, is to present a set of historical facts, grouped round a principal figure. The author has aimed to state the social facts of the time in which the individual whose history is handled took part in public business. It is from sketches like these of the great men who took a prominent and influential part in the affairs of their time that a clear conception of the social and economical condition of our ancestors can be obtained. History learned in this way is both instructive and agreeable. "His Essays," the PALL MALL GAZETTE *says, "are full of interest, pregnant, thoughtful and readable." "They rank far above the average of similar performances," says the* WESTMINSTER REVIEW.

Raphael.—RAPHAEL OF URBINO AND HIS FATHER GIOVANNI SANTI. By J. D. PASSAVANT, formerly Director of the Museum at Frankfort. With Twenty Permanent Photographs. Royal 8vo. Handsomely bound. 31s. 6d.

HISTORY, BIOGRAPHY, & TRAVELS. 25

To the enlarged French edition of Passavant's Life of Raphael, that painter's admirers have turned whenever they have sought information, and it will doubtless remain for many years the best book of reference on all questions pertaining to the great painter. The present work consists of a translation of those parts of Passavant's volumes which are most likely to interest the general reader. Besides a complete life of Raphael, it contains the valuable descriptions of all his known paintings, and the Chronological Index, which is of so much service to amateurs who wish to study the progressive character of his works. The Illustrations by Woodbury's new permanent process of photography, are taken from the finest engravings that could be procured, and have been chosen with the intention of giving examples of Raphael's various styles of painting. The SATURDAY REVIEW *says of them,* "*We have seen not a few elegant specimens of Mr. Woodbury's new process, but we have seen none that equal these.*"

Somers (Robert).—THE SOUTHERN STATES SINCE THE WAR. By ROBERT SOMERS. With Map. 8vo. 9s.

This work is the result of inquiries made by the author of all authorities competent to afford him information, and of his own observation during a lengthened sojourn in the Southern States, to which writers on America to seldom direct their steps. The author's object is to give some account of the condition of the Southern States under the new social and political system introduced by the civil war. He has here collected such notes of the progress of their cotton plantations, of the state of their labouring population and of their industrial enterprises, as may help the reader to a safe opinion of their means and prospects of development. He also gives such information of their natural resources, railways, and other public works, as may tend to show to what extent they are fitted to become a profitable field of enlarged immigration, settlement, and foreign trade. The volume contains many valuable and reliable details as to the condition of the Negro population, the state of Education and Religion, of Cotton, Sugar, and Tobacco Cultivation, of Agriculture generally, of Coal and Iron Mining, Manufactures, Trade, Means of Locomotion, and the condition of Towns and of Society. A large map of the Southern States by Messrs. W. and A. K. Johnston is appended, which shows with great clearness the Cotton, Coal, and Iron districts, the railways completed and projected, the State boundaries, and other important details. "*Full of interesting and valuable information.*"—SATURDAY REVIEW.

Smith (Professor Goldwin).—THREE ENGLISH STATESMEN. *See* p. 43 of this Catalogue.

Tacitus.—THE HISTORY OF TACITUS, translated into English. By A. J. CHURCH, M.A. and W. J. BRODRIBB, M.A. With a Map and Notes. New and Cheaper Edition, revised, crown 8vo. 6s.

The translators have endeavoured to adhere as closely to the original as was thought consistent with a proper observance of English idiom. At the same time it has been their aim to reproduce the precise expressions of the author. This work is characterised by the SPECTATOR *as "a scholarly and faithful translation." Several improvements have been made in this Edition, and the Notes have been enlarged, with the view of rendering the work more intelligible and useful to the general reader.*

THE AGRICOLA AND GERMANIA. Translated into English by A. J. CHURCH, M.A. and W. J. BRODRIBB, M.A. With Maps and Notes. Extra fcap. 8vo. 2s. 6d.

The translators have sought to produce such a version as may satisfy scholars who demand a faithful rendering of the original, and English readers who are offended by the boldness and frigidity which commonly disfigure translations. The treatises are accompanied by Introductions, Notes, Maps, and a chronological Summary. The ATHENÆUM *says of this work that it is "a version at once readable and exact, which may be perused with pleasure by all, and consulted with advantage by the classical student;" and the* PALL MALL GAZETTE *says, "What the editors have attempted to do, it is not, we think probable, that any living scholars could have done better."*

Taylor (Rev. Isaac).—WORDS AND PLACES. *See* p. 51 of this Catalogue.

Thomas.—THE LIFE OF JOHN THOMAS, Surgeon of the "Earl of Oxford" East Indiaman, and First Baptist Missionary to Bengal. By C. B. LEWIS, Baptist Missionary. 8vo. 10s. 6d.

This biography, founded on the most trustworthy materials attainable, will be found interesting, not only to all who take an interest in mission work and the spread of Christianity, but to all who care to read the life of an earnest man striving to benefit others.

Trench (Archbishop).—For other Works by the same Author, see THEOLOGICAL and BELLES LETTRES CATALOGUES, and p. 51 of this Catalogue.

GUSTAVUS ADOLPHUS IN GERMANY, and other Lectures on the Thirty Years' War. By R. CHENEVIX TRENCH, D.D., Archbishop of Dublin. Second Edition, revised and enlarged. Fcap. 8vo. 4s.

The lectures contained in this volume form rather a new book than a new edition, for on the two lectures published by the Author several years ago, so many changes and additions have been made, as to make the work virtually a new one. Besides three lectures of the career of Gustavus in Germany and during the Thirty Years' War, there are other two, one on "Germany during the Thirty Years' War," and another on Germany after that War. The work will be found not only interesting and instructive in itself, but will be found to have some bearing on events connected with the recent European War.

Trench (Mrs. R.)—REMAINS OF THE LATE MRS. RICHARD TRENCH. Being Selections from her Journals, Letters, and other Papers. Edited by ARCHBISHOP TRENCH. New and Cheaper Issue, with Portrait. 8vo. 6s.

Contains Notices and Anecdotes illustrating the social life of the period—extending over a quarter of a century (1799—1827). It includes also Poems and other miscellaneous pieces by Mrs. Trench.

Wallace.—Works by ALFRED RUSSEL WALLACE. For other Works by same Author, see SCIENTIFIC CATALOGUE.

Dr. Hooker, in his address to the British Association, spoke thus of the author:—"Of Mr. Wallace and his many contributions to philosophical biology it is not easy to speak without enthusiasm ; for, putting aside their great merits, &c., throughout his writings, with a modesty as rare as I believe it to be unconscious, forgets his own unquestional claim to the honour of having originated, independently of Mr. Darwin, the theories which he so ably defends."

A NARRATIVE OF TRAVELS ON THE AMAZON AND RIO NEGRO, with an Account of the Native Tribes, and Observations on the Climate, Geology, and Natural History of the Amazon Valley. With a Map and Illustrations. 8vo. 12s.

Wallace (A. R.)—*continued.*

Mr. Wallace is acknowledged as one of the first of modern travellers and naturalists. This, his earliest work, will be found to possess many charms for the general reader, and to be full of interest to the student of natural history.

THE MALAY ARCHIPELAGO: the Land of the Orang Utan and the Bird of Paradise. A Narrative of Travel with Studies of Man and Nature. With Maps and Illustrations. Third and Cheaper Edition. Crown 8vo. 7s. 6d.

"*The result is a vivid picture of tropical life, which may be read with unflagging interest, and a sufficient account of his scientific conclusions to stimulate our appetite without wearying us by detail. In short, we may safely say that we have never read a more agreeable book of its kind.*"—SATURDAY REVIEW. "*His descriptions of scenery, of the people and their manners and customs, enlivened by occasional amusing anecdotes, constitute the most interesting reading we have taken up for some time.*"—STANDARD.

Ward (Professor).—THE HOUSE OF AUSTRIA IN THE THIRTY YEARS' WAR. Two Lectures, with Notes and Illustrations. By ADOLPHUS W. WARD, M.A., Professor of History in Owens College, Manchester. Extra fcap. 8vo. 2s. 6d.

These two Lectures were delivered in February, 1869, at the Philosophical Institution, Edinburgh, and are now published with Notes and Illustrations. "We have never read," says the SATURDAY REVIEW, "*any lectures which bear more thoroughly the impress of one who has a true and vigorous grasp of the subject in hand.*" "*They are,*" *the* SCOTSMAN *says*, "*the fruit of much labour and learning, and it would be difficult to compress into a hundred pages more information.*"

Ward (J.)—EXPERIENCES OF A DIPLOMATIST. Being recollections of Germany founded on Diaries kept during the years 1840—1870. By JOHN WARD, C.B., late H.M. Minister-Resident to the Hanse Towns. 8vo. 10s. 6d.

Mr. Ward's recollections extend back even to 1830. From his official position as well as from other circumstances he had many opportunities of coming in contact with eminent men of all ranks and all professions on the

Continent. His book, while it contains much that throws light on the history of the long and important period with which it is concerned, is full of reminiscences of such men as Arnisobene, King Leopold, Frederick William IV., his Court and Ministers, Humboldt, Bunsen, Raumer, Ranke, Grimm, Palmerston, Sir de Lacy Evans, Cobden, Mendelssohn, Cardinal Wiseman, Prince Albert, the Prince and Princess of Wales, Lord Russell, Bismarck, Mdlle. Tietjens, and many other eminent Englishmen and foreigners.

Warren.—AN ESSAY ON GREEK FEDERAL COINAGE. By the Hon. J. LEICESTER WARREN, M.A. 8vo. 2s. 6d.

The present essay is an attempt to illustrate Mr. Freeman's Federal Government by evidence deduced from the coinage of the times and countries therein treated of.

Wedgwood.—JOHN WESLEY AND THE EVANGELICAL REACTION of the Eighteenth Century. By JULIA WEDGWOOD. Crown 8vo. 8s. 6d.

This book is an attempt to delineate the influence of a particular man upon his age. The background to the central figure is treated with considerable minuteness, the object of representation being not the vicissitude of a particular life, but that element in the life which impressed itself on the life of a nation,—an element which cannot be understood without a study of aspects of national thought which on a superficial view might appear wholly unconnected with it. "In style and intellectual power, in breadth of view and clearness of insight, Miss Wedgwood's book far surpasses all rivals."—ATHENÆUM. "As a short account of the most remarkable movement in the eighteenth century, it must fairly be described as excellent."—PALL MALL GAZETTE.

Wilson.—A MEMOIR OF GEORGE WILSON, M.D., F.R.S.E., Regius Professor of Technology in the University of Edinburgh. By his SISTER. New Edition. Crown 8vo. 6s.

"An exquisite and touching portrait of a rare and beautiful spirit."—GUARDIAN. "He more than most men of whom we have lately read deserved a minute and careful biography, and by such alone could he be understood, and become loveable and influential to his fellow-men. Such a biography his sister has written, in which letters reach almost to the extent of a complete autobiography, with all the additional charm of being unconsciously such. We revere and admire the heart, and earnestly praise the patient tender hand, by which such a worthy record of the earth-story of one of God's true angel-men has been constructed for our delight and profit."—NONCONFORMIST.

Wilson (Daniel, LL.D.)—Works by DANIEL WILSON, LL.D., Professor of History and English Literature in University College, Toronto:—

PREHISTORIC ANNALS OF SCOTLAND. New Edition, with numerous Illustrations. Two Vols. demy 8vo. 36s.

"One object aimed at when the book first appeared was to rescue archaeological research from that limited range to which a too exclusive devotion to classical studies had given rise, and, especially in relation to Scotland, to prove how greatly more comprehensive and important are its native antiquities than all the traces of intruded art. The aim has been to a large extent effectually accomplished, and such an impulse given to archaeological research, that in this new edition the whole of the work has had to be remodelled. Fully a third of it has been entirely re-written; and the remaining portions have undergone so minute a revision as to render it in many respects a new work. The number of pictorial illustrations has been greatly increased, and several of the former plates and woodcuts have been re-engraved from new drawings. This is divided into four Parts. Part I. deals with The Primeval or Stone Period: Aboriginal Traces, Sepulchral Memorials, Dwellings, and Catacombs, Temples, Weapons, &c. &c.; Part II. The Bronze Period: The Metallurgic Transition, Primitive Bronze, Personal Ornaments, Religion, Arts, and Domestic Habits, with other topics; Part III. The Iron Period: The Introduction of Iron, The Roman Invasion, Strongholds, &c. &c.; Part IV. The Christian Period: Historical Data, the Norrie's Law Relics, Primitive and Mediæval Ecclesiology, Ecclesiastical and Miscellaneous Antiquities. The work is furnished with an elaborate Index. "One of the most interesting, learned, and elegant works we have seen for a long time."—WESTMINSTER REVIEW. "The interest connected with this beautiful volume is not limited to that part of the kingdom to which it is chiefly devoted; it will be consulted with advantage and gratification by all who have a regard for National Antiquities and for the advancement of scientific Archæology."—ARCHÆOLOGICAL JOURNAL.

Wilson (Daniel, LL.D.)—*continued.*

PREHISTORIC MAN. New Edition, revised and partly re-written, with numerous Illustrations. One vol. 8vo. 21s.

This work, which carries out the principle of the preceding one, but with a wider scope, aims to "view Man, as far as possible, unaffected by those modifying influences which accompany the development of nations and the maturity of a true historic period, in order thereby to ascertain the sources from whence such development and maturity proceed. These researches into the origin of civilisation have accordingly been pursued under the belief which influenced the author in previous inquiries that the investigations of the archæologist, when carried on in an enlightened spirit, are replete with interest in relation to some of the most important problems of modern science. To reject the aid of archæology in the progress of science, and especially of ethnological science, is to extinguish the lamp of the student when most dependent on its borrowed rays." A prolonged residence on some of the newest sites of the New World has afforded the author many opportunities of investigating the antiquities of the American Aborigines, and of bringing to light many facts of high importance in reference to primeval man. The changes in the new edition, necessitated by the great advance in Archæology since the first, include both reconstruction and condensation, along with considerable additions alike in illustration and in argument. "We find," says the ATHENÆUM, *"the main idea of his treatise to be a pre-eminently scientific one,—namely, by archæological research to obtain a definite conception of the origin and nature of man's earliest efforts at civilisation in the New World, and to endeavour to discover, as if by analogy, the necessary conditions, phases, and epochs through which man in the prehistoric stage in the Old World also must necessarily have passed." The* NORTH BRITISH REVIEW *calls it "a mature and mellow work of an able man; free alike from crotchets and from dogmatism, and exhibiting on every page the caution and moderation of a well-balanced judgment."*

CHATTERTON: A Biographical Study. By DANIEL WILSON, LL.D., Professor of History and English Literature in University College, Toronto. Crown 8vo. 6s. 6d.

The author here regards Chatterton as a poet, not as a "mere vendor and defacer of stolen literary treasures." Reviewed in this light, he has found much in the old materials capable of being turned to new account:

and to these materials research in various directions has enabled him to make some additions. He believes that the boy-poet has been misjudged, and that the biographies hitherto written of him are not only imperfect but untrue. While dealing tenderly, the author has sought to deal truthfully with the failings as well as the virtues of the boy: bearing always in remembrance, what has been too frequently lost sight of, that he was but a boy;—a boy, and yet a poet of rare power. The EXAMINER thinks this "the most complete and the purest biography of the poet which has yet appeared." The LITERARY CHURCHMAN calls it "a most charming literary biography."

Yonge (Charlotte M.)—Works by CHARLOTTE M. YONGE, Author of "The Heir of Redclyffe," &c. &c. :—

A PARALLEL HISTORY OF FRANCE AND ENGLAND: consisting of Outlines and Dates. Oblong 4to. 3s. 6d.

This tabular history has been drawn up to supply a want felt by many teachers of some means of making their pupils realize what events in the two countries were contemporary. A skeleton narrative has been constructed of the chief transactions in either country, having a column between for what affected both alike, by which means it is hoped that young people may be assisted in grasping the mutual relation of events.

CAMEOS FROM ENGLISH HISTORY. From Rollo to Edward II. Extra fcap. 8vo. Second Edition, enlarged. 5s.

A SECOND SERIES, THE WARS IN FRANCE. Extra fcap. 8vo. 5s. Second Edition.

The endeavour has not been to chronicle facts, but to put together a series of pictures of persons and events, so as to arrest the attention, and give some individuality and distinctness to the recollection, by gathering together details of the most memorable moments. The "Cameos" are intended as a book for young people just beyond the elementary histories of England, and able to enter in some degree into the real spirit of events, and to be struck with characters and scenes presented in some relief. "Instead of dry details," says the NONCONFORMIST, *"we have living pictures, faithful, vivid, and striking."*

Young (Julian Charles, M.A.)—A MEMOIR OF CHARLES MAYNE YOUNG, Tragedian, with Extracts from his Son's Journal. By JULIAN CHARLES YOUNG, M.A. Rector of Ilmington. With Portraits and Sketches. *New and Cheaper Edition.* Crown 8vo. 7s. 6d.

Round this memoir of one who held no mean place in public estimation as a tragedian, and who, as a man, by the unobtrusive simplicity and moral purity of his private life, won golden opinions from all sorts of men, are clustered extracts from the author's Journals, containing many curious and interesting reminiscences of his father's and his own eminent and famous contemporaries and acquaintances, somewhat after the manner of H. Crabb Robinson's Diary. Every page will be found full both of entertainment and instruction. It contains four portraits of the tragedian, and a few other curious sketches. "*In this budget of anecdotes, fables, and gossip, old and new, relative to Scott, Marr, Chalmers, Coleridge, Wordsworth, Croker, Mathews, the third and fourth Georges, Bowles, Beckford, Lockhart, Wellington, Peel, Louis Napoleon, D'Orsay, Dickens, Thackeray, Louis Blanc, Gibson, Constable, and Stanfield, etc. etc. the reader must be hard indeed to please who cannot find entertainment.*"—PALL MALL GAZETTE.

POLITICS, POLITICAL AND SOCIAL ECONOMY, LAW, AND KINDRED SUBJECTS.

Baxter.—NATIONAL INCOME: The United Kingdom. By R. DUDLEY BAXTER, M.A. 8vo. 3s. 6d.

The present work endeavours to answer systematically such questions as the following:—What are the means and aggregate wages of our labouring population; what are the numbers and aggregate profits of the middle classes; what the revenues of our great proprietors and capitalists; and what the pecuniary strength of the nation to bear the burdens annually falling upon us? What capital in land and goods and money is stored up for our subsistence, and for carrying out our enterprises? The author has collected his facts from every quarter and tested them in various ways, in order to make his statements and deductions valuable and trustworthy. Part I. of the work deals with the Classification of the Population *into—Chap. I.* The Income Classes; *Chap. II.* The Upper and Middle and Manual Labour Classes. *Part II. treats of the Income of the United Kingdom, divided into—Chap. III.* Upper and Middle Incomes; *Chap. IV.* Wages of the Manual Labour Classes—England and Wales; *Chap. V.* Income of Scotland; *Chap. VI.* Income of Ireland; *Chap. VII.* Income of the United Kingdom. *In the Appendix will be found many valuable and carefully compiled tables, illustrating in detail the subjects discussed in the text.*

Bernard.—FOUR LECTURES ON SUBJECTS CONNECTED WITH DIPLOMACY. By MONTAGUE BERNARD, M.A., Chichele Professor of International Law and Diplomacy, Oxford. 8vo. 9s.

These four Lectures deal with—I. "The Congress of Westphalia;" II. "Systems of Policy;" III. "Diplomacy, Past and Present;" IV. "The Obligations of Treaties."—"*Singularly interesting lectures, so able, clear, and attractive.*"—SPECTATOR. "*The author of these lectures is full of the knowledge which belongs to his subject, and has that power of clear and vigorous expression which results from clear and vigorous thought.*"—SCOTSMAN.

Bright (John, M.P.)—SPEECHES ON QUESTIONS OF PUBLIC POLICY. By the Right Hon. JOHN BRIGHT, M.P. Edited by Professor THOROLD ROGERS. Author's Popular Edition. Globe 8vo. 3s. 6d.

The speeches which have been selected for publication in these volumes possess a value, as examples of the art of public speaking, which no person will be likely to underrate. The speeches have been selected with a view of supplying the public with the evidence on which Mr. Bright's friends assert his right to a place in the front rank of English statesmen. They are divided into groups, according to their subjects. The editor has naturally given prominence to those subjects with which Mr. Bright has been specially identified, as, for example, India, America, Ireland, and Parliamentary Reform. But nearly every topic of great public interest on which Mr. Bright has spoken is represented in these volumes. "Mr. Bright's speeches will always deserve to be studied, as an apprenticeship to popular and parliamentary oratory; they will form materials for the history of our time, and many brilliant passages, perhaps some entire speeches, will really become a part of the living literature of England."—DAILY NEWS.

LIBRARY EDITION. Two Vols. 8vo. With Portrait. 25s.

Cairnes.—ESSAYS IN POLITICAL ECONOMY, THEORETICAL and APPLIED. By J. E. CAIRNES, M.A., Professor of Political Economy in University College, London. 8vo. 10s. 6d.

CONTENTS.—*Essays towards a Solution of the Gold Question—The Australian Episode—The Course of Depreciation—International Results—Summary of the Movement—M. Chevalier's Views—Co-Operation in the Slate Quarries of North Wales—Political Eco-*

nomy and Land—*Political Economy and Laissez-Faire—M. Comte and Political Economy—Bastiat.*

"*The production of one of the ablest of living economists.*"—ATHENÆUM.

Christie.—THE BALLOT AND CORRUPTION AND EXPENDITURE AT ELECTIONS, a Collection of Essays and Addresses of different dates. By W. D. CHRISTIE, C.B., formerly Her Majesty's Minister to the Argentine Confederation and to Brazil; Author of "Life of the First Earl of Shaftesbury." Crown 8vo. 4s. 6d.

Mr. Christie has been well known for upwards of thirty years as a strenuous and able advocate for the Ballot, both in his place in Parliament and elsewhere. The papers and speeches here collected are six in number, exclusive of the Preface and Dedication to Professor Maurice, which contains many interesting historical details concerning the Ballot. "*You have thought to greater purpose on the means of preventing electoral corruption, and are likely to be of more service in passing measures for that highly important end, than any other person that I could name.*"—J. S. MILL, in a published letter to the Author, May 1868.

Clarke.—EARLY ROMAN LAW. THE REGAL PERIOD. By E. C. CLARKE, M.A., of Lincoln's Inn, Barrister-at-Law, Lecturer in Law and Regius Professor of Civil Law at Cambridge.

The beginnings of Roman Law are only noticed incidentally by Gaius or his paraphrasers under Justinian. They are, however, so important, that this attempt to set forth what is known or may be inferred about them, it is expected, will be found of much value. The method adopted by the author has been to furnish in the text of each section a continuous account of the subject in hand, ample quotations and references being appended in the form of notes. Most of the passages cited have been arrived at by independent reading of the original authority, the few others having been carefully verified. "*Mr. Clarke has brought together a great mass of valuable matter in an accessible form.*"—SATURDAY REVIEW.

Corfield (Professor W. H.)—A DIGEST OF FACTS RELATING TO THE TREATMENT AND UTILIZATION OF SEWAGE. By W. H. CORFIELD, M.A., B.A., Professor of Hygiene and Public Health at University College, London. 8vo. 10s. 6d. Second Edition, corrected and enlarged.

In this edition the author has revised and corrected the entire work, and made many important additions. The headings of the eleven chapters are as follow:—I. "Early Systems; Midden-Heaps and Cesspools." II. "Filth and Disease—Cause and Effect." III. "Improved Midden-Pits and Cesspools; Midden-Closets, Pail-Closets, etc." IV. "The Dry-Closet Systems." V. "Water-Closets." VI. "Sewerage." VII. "Sanitary Aspects of the Water-Carrying System." VIII. "Value of Sewage; Injury to Rivers." IX. Town Sewage; Attempts at Utilisation." X. "Filtration and Irrigation." XI. "Influence of Sewage Farming on the Public Health." An abridged account of the more recently published researches on the subject will be found in the Appendices, while the Summary contains a concise statement of the views which the author himself has been led to adopt; references have been inserted throughout to show from what sources the numerous quotations have been derived, and an Index has been added. "Mr. Corfield's work is entitled to rank as a standard authority, no less than a convenient handbook, in all matters relating to sewage."—ATHENÆUM.

Fawcett.—Works by HENRY FAWCETT, M.A., M.P., Fellow of Trinity Hall, and Professor of Political Economy in the University of Cambridge :—

THE ECONOMIC POSITION OF THE BRITISH LABOURER. Extra fcp. 8vo. 5s.

This work formed a portion of a course of Lectures delivered by the author in the University of Cambridge, and he has deemed it advisable to retain many of the expositions of the elementary principles of Economic Science. In the Introductory Chapter the author points out the scope of the work and shows the vast importance of the subject in relation to the commercial prosperity and even the national existence of Britain. Then follow five chapters on " The Land Tenure of England," " Co-operation," " The Causes which regulate Wages," " Trade Unions and Strikes," and

Fawcett (H.)—*continued.*

"*Emigration.*" *The* EXAMINER *calls the work* "*a very scholarly exposition on some of the most essential questions of Political Economy;*" *and the* NONCONFORMIST *says* "*it is written with charming freshness, ease, and lucidity.*"

MANUAL OF POLITICAL ECONOMY. Third and Cheaper Edition, with Two New Chapters. Crown 8vo. 10s. 6d.

In this treatise no important branch of the subject has been omitted, and the author believes that the principles which are therein explained will enable the reader to obtain a tolerably complete view of the whole science. Mr. Fawcett has endeavoured to show how intimately Political Economy is connected with the practical questions of life. For the convenience of the ordinary reader, and especially for those who may use the book to prepare themselves for examinations, he has prefixed a very detailed summary of Contents, which may be regarded as an analysis of the work. The new edition has been so carefully revised that there is scarcely a page in which some improvement has not been introduced. The DAILY NEWS *says:* "*It forms one of the best introductions to the principles of the science, and to its practical applications in the problems of modern, and especially of English, government and society.*" "*The book is written throughout,*" *says the* EXAMINER, "*with admirable force, clearness, and brevity, every important part of the subject being duly considered.*"

PAUPERISM: ITS CAUSES AND REMEDIES. Crown 8vo. 5s. 6d.

In its number for March 11th, 1871, the SPECTATOR *said:* "*We wish Professor Fawcett would devote a little more of his time and energy to the practical consideration of that monster problem of Pauperism, for the treatment of which his economic knowledge and popular sympathies so eminently fit him.*" *The volume now published may be regarded as an answer to the above challenge. The seven chapters it comprises discuss the following subjects:—I. "Pauperism and the old Poor Law." II. "The present Poor Law System." III. "The Increase of Population." IV. "National Education; its Economic and Social Effects." V. "Co-partnership and Co-*

Fawcett (H.)—*continued.*

operation." VI. "The English System of Land Tenure." VII. "The Inclosure of Commons." The ATHENÆUM *calls the work "a repertory of interesting and well-digested information."*

ESSAYS ON POLITICAL AND SOCIAL SUBJECTS. By PROFESSOR FAWCETT, M.P., and MILLICENT GARRETT FAWCETT. 8vo. 10s. 6d.

This volume contains fourteen papers, some of which have appeared in various journals and periodicals; others have not before been published. They are all on subjects of great importance and universal interest, and the names of the two authors are a sufficient guarantee that each topic is discussed with full knowledge, great ability, clearness, and earnestness. The following are some of the titles:—"Modern Socialism;" "Free Education in its Economic Aspects;" "Pauperism, Charity, and the Poor Law;" "National Debt and National Prosperity;" "What can be done for the Agricultural Labourers;" "The Education of Women;" "The Electoral Disabilities of Women;" "The House of Lords." Each article is signed with the initials of its author. "In every respect a work of note and value. . . They will all repay the perusal of the thinking reader."—DAILY NEWS.

Fawcett (Mrs.)—POLITICAL ECONOMY FOR BEGINNERS. WITH QUESTIONS. By MILLICENT GARRETT FAWCETT. New Edition. 18mo. 2s. 6d.

In this little work are explained as briefly as possible the most important principles of Political Economy, in the hope that it will be useful to beginners, and perhaps be an assistance to those who are desirous of introducing the study of Political Economy to schools. In order to adapt the book especially for school use, questions have been added at the end of each chapter. In the new edition each page has been carefully revised, and at the end of each chapter, after the questions, a few little puzzles have been added, which will give interest to the book, and teach the learner to think for himself. The DAILY NEWS *calls it "clear, compact, and comprehensive;"* and the SPECTATOR *says, "Mrs. Fawcett's treatise is perfectly suited to its purpose."*

Freeman (E. A., M.A., D.C.L.)—HISTORY OF FEDERAL GOVERNMENT. *See* p. 8 of preceding Historical Catalogue.

Godkin (James).—THE LAND WAR IN IRELAND. A History for the Times. By JAMES GODKIN, Author of "Ireland and her Churches," late Irish Correspondent of the *Times*. 8vo. 12*s*.

A History of the Irish Land Question. "There is probably no other account so compendious and so complete."—FORTNIGHTLY REVIEW.

Goschen.—REPORTS AND SPEECHES ON LOCAL TAXATION. By GEORGE J. GOSCHEN, M.P. Royal 8vo. 5*s*.

Mr. Goschen, from the position he has held and the attention he has given to the subject of Local Taxation, is well qualified to deal with it. "The volume contains a vast mass of information of the highest value."—ATHENÆUM.

Guide to the Unprotected, in Every Day Matters Relating to Property and Income. By a BANKER'S DAUGHTER. Third Edition. Extra fcap. 8vo. 3*s*. 6*d*.

Many widows and single ladies, and all young people, on first possessing money of their own, are in want of advice when they have commonplace business matters to transact. The author of this work writes for those who know nothing. Her aim throughout is to avoid all technicalities; to give plain and practical directions, not only as to what ought to be done, but how to do it. "Many an unprotected female will bless the head which planned and the hand which compiled this admirable little manual. . . . This book was very much wanted, and it could not have been better done."—MORNING STAR.

Hill.—CHILDREN OF THE STATE. THE TRAINING OF JUVENILE PAUPERS. By FLORENCE HILL. Extra fcap. 8vo. cloth. 5*s*.

In this work the author discusses the various systems adopted in this and other countries in the treatment of pauper children. The BIRMINGHAM DAILY GAZETTE *calls it "a valuable contribution to the great and important social question which it so ably and thoroughly discusses; and it must materially aid in producing a wise method of dealing with the Children of the State."*

Historicus.—LETTERS ON SOME QUESTIONS OF INTERNATIONAL LAW. Reprinted from the *Times*, with considerable Additions. 8vo. 7s. 6d. Also, ADDITIONAL LETTERS. 8vo. 2s. 6d.

The author's intention in these Letters was to illustrate in a popular form clearly-established principles of law, or to refute, as occasion required, errors which had obtained a mischievous currency. He has endeavoured to establish, by sufficient authority, propositions which have been inconsiderately impugned, and to point out the various methods of reasoning which have led some modern writers to erroneous conclusions. The volume contains: Letters on "Recognition;" "On the Perils of Intervention;" "The Rights and Duties of Neutral Nations;" "On the Law of Blockade;" "On Neutral Trade in Contraband of War;" "On Belligerent Violation of Neutral Rights;" "The Foreign Enlistment Act;" "The Right of Search;" extracts from letters on the Affair of the Trent; and a paper on the "Territoriality of the Merchant Vessel."—"It is seldom that the doctrines of International Law on debateable points have been stated with more vigour, precision, and certainty."—SATURDAY REVIEW.

Jevons.—Works by W. STANLEY JEVONS, M.A., Professor of Logic and Political Economy in Owens College, Manchester. (For other Works by the same Author, *see* EDUCATIONAL and PHILOSOPHICAL CATALOGUES.)

THE COAL QUESTION: An Inquiry Concerning the Progress of the Nation, and the Probable Exhaustion of our Coal Mines. Second Edition, revised. 8vo. 10s. 6d.

"Day by day," the author says, "it becomes more evident that the coal we happily possess in excellent quality and abundance is the mainspring of modern material civilisation." Geologists and other competent authorities have of late been hinting that the supply of coal is by no means inexhaustible, and as it is of vast importance to the country and the world generally to know the real state of the case, Professor Jevons in this work has endeavoured to

Jevons (Prof.)—*continued.*

solve the question as far as the data at command admit. He believes that should the consumption multiply for rather more than a century at its present rate, the average depth of our coal mines would be so reduced that we could not long continue our present rate of progress. "We have to make the momentous choice," he believes, "between brief greatness and long-continued prosperity."—"The question of our supply of coal," says the PALL MALL GAZETTE, *"becomes a question obviously of life or death. . . . The whole case is stated with admirable clearness and cogency. . . . We may regard his statements as unanswered and practically established."*

THE THEORY OF POLITICAL ECONOMY. 8vo. 9s.

*In this work Professor Jevons endeavours to construct a theory of Political Economy on a mathematical or quantitative basis, believing that many of the commonly received theories in this science are perniciously erroneous. The author here attempts to treat Economy as the Calculus of Pleasure and Pain, and has sketched out, almost irrespective of previous opinions, the form which the science, as it seems to him, must ultimately take. The theory consists in applying the differential calculus to the familiar notions of Wealth, Utility, Value, Demand, Supply, Capital, Interest, Labour, and all the other notions belonging to the daily operations of industry. As the complete theory of almost every other science involves the use of that calculus, so, the author thinks, we cannot have a true theory of Political Economy without its aid. "Professor Jevons has done invaluable service by courageously claiming political economy to be strictly a branch of Applied Mathematics."—*WESTMINSTER REVIEW.

Macdonell.—THE LAND QUESTION, WITH SPECIAL REFERENCE TO ENGLAND AND SCOTLAND. By JOHN MACDONELL, Barrister-at-Law. 8vo. 10s. 6d.

Martin.—THE STATESMAN'S YEAR-BOOK: A Statistical and Historical Annual of the States of the Civilised World. Handbook for Politicians and Merchants for the year 1873. By FREDERICK MARTIN. Tenth Annual Publication. Revised after Official Returns. Crown 8vo. 10s. 6d.

The Statesman's Year-Book is the only work in the English language which furnishes a clear and concise account of the actual condition of all the States of Europe, the civilized countries of America, Asia, and Africa, and the British Colonies and Dependencies in all parts of the world. The new issue of the work has been revised and corrected, on the basis of official reports received direct from the hands of the leading Governments of the world, in reply to letters sent to them by the Editor. Through the valuable assistance thus given, it has been possible to collect an amount of information, political, statistical, and commercial, of the latest date, and of unimpeachable trustworthiness, such as no publication of the same kind has ever been able to furnish. "As indispensable as Bradshaw."—TIMES.

Phillimore.—PRIVATE LAW AMONG THE ROMANS, from the Pandects. By JOHN GEORGE PHILLIMORE, Q.C. 8vo. 16s.

The author's belief that some knowledge of the Roman System of Municipal Law will contribute to improve our own, has induced him to prepare the present work. His endeavour has been to select those parts of the Digest which would best show the grand manner in which the Roman jurist dealt with his subject, as well as those which most illustrate the principles by which he was guided in establishing the great lines and propositions of jurisprudence, which every lawyer must have frequent occasion to employ. "Mr. Phillimore has done good service towards the study of jurisprudence in this country by the production of this volume. The work is one which should be in the hands of every student."—ATHENÆUM.

Smith.—Works by Professor GOLDWIN SMITH :—

A LETTER TO A WHIG MEMBER OF THE SOUTHERN INDEPENDENCE ASSOCIATION. Extra fcap. 8vo. 2s.

This is a Letter, written in 1864, to a member of an Association formed in this country, the purpose of which was "to lend assistance to the Slave-owners of the Southern States in their attempt to effect a disruption of the American Commonwealth, and to establish an Independent Power, having, as they declare, Slavery for its cornerstone." Mr. Smith endeavours to show that in doing so they would have committed a great folly and a still greater crime. Throughout the Letter many points of general and permanent importance are discussed.

Smith (Prof. G.)—*continued.*

THREE ENGLISH STATESMEN: PYM, CROMWELL, PITT. A Course of Lectures on the Political History of England. Extra fcap. 8vo. New and Cheaper Edition. 5s.

> "*A work which neither historian nor politician can safely afford to neglect.*"—SATURDAY REVIEW. "*There are outlines, clearly and boldly sketched, if mere outlines, of the three Statesmen who gave the titles to his lectures, which is here well deserving of study.*"—SPECTATOR.

Social Duties Considered with Reference to the ORGANIZATION OF EFFORT IN WORKS OF BENEVOLENCE AND PUBLIC UTILITY. By a MAN OF BUSINESS. (WILLIAM RATHBONE.) Fcap. 8vo. 4s. 6d.

> *The contents of this valuable little book are*—*I. "Social Disintegration." II. "Our Charities—Done and Undone." III. "Organization and Individual Benevolence—their Achievements and Shortcomings." IV. "Organization and Individualism—their Co-operation Indispensable." V. "Instances and Experiments." VI. "The Sphere of Government." "Conclusion." The views urged are no sentimental theories, but have grown out of the practical experience acquired in actual work. "Mr. Rathbone's earnest and large-hearted little book will help to generate both a larger and wiser charity.*"—BRITISH QUARTERLY.

Stephen (C. E.)—THE SERVICE OF THE POOR; Being an Inquiry into the Reasons for and against the Establishment of Religious Sisterhoods for Charitable Purposes. By CAROLINE EMILIA STEPHEN. Crown 8vo. 6s. 6d.

> *Miss Stephen defines Religious Sisterhoods as "associations, the organisation of which is based upon the assumption that works of charity are either acts of worship in themselves, or means to an end, that end being the spiritual welfare of the objects or the performers of those works." Arguing from that point of view, she devotes the first part of her volume to a brief history of religious associations, taking as specimens—I. The Deaconesses of the Primitive Church. II. The Béguines. III. The Third Order of S. Francis. IV. The Sisters of Charity of S. Vincent de Paul. V. The Deaconesses of Modern Germany. In the second part, Miss Stephen attempts to*

show what are the real wants met by Sisterhoods, to what extent the same wants may be effectually met by the organisation of corresponding institutions on a secular basis, and what are the reasons for endeavouring to do so. "*The ablest advocate of a better line of work in this direction than we have ever seen.*"—EXAMINER.

Stephen (J. F.)—Works by JAMES FITZJAMES STEPHEN, Q.C. :—

A GENERAL VIEW OF THE CRIMINAL LAW OF ENGLAND. 8vo. 18s.

The object of this work is to give an account of the general scope, tendency, and design of an important part of our institutions, of which surely none can have a greater moral significance, or be more closely connected with broad principles of morality and politics, than those by which men rightfully, deliberately, and in cold blood, kill, enslave, and otherwise torment their fellow-creatures. The author believes it possible to explain the principles of such a system in a manner both intelligible and interesting. The Contents are—I. "The Province of the Criminal Law." II. "Historical Sketch of English Criminal Law." III. "Definition of Crime in General." IV. "Classification and Definition of Particular Crimes." V. "Criminal Procedure in General." VI. "English Criminal Procedure." VII. "The Principles of Evidence in Relation to the Criminal Law." VIII. "English Rules of Evidence." IX. "English Criminal Legislation." The last 150 pages are occupied with the discussion of a number of important cases. "Readers feel in his book the confidence which attaches to the writings of a man who has a great practical acquaintance with the matter of which he writes, and lawyers will agree that it fully satisfies the standard of professional accuracy."—SATURDAY REVIEW. "*His style is forcible and perspicuous, and singularly free from the unnecessary use of professional terms.*"—SPECTATOR.

THE INDIAN EVIDENCE ACT (I. of 1872). With an Introduction on the Principles of Judicial Evidence. 8vo. 12s. 6d.

No one is more competent than Mr. Fitzjames Stephen to write on the subject of which he here treats. The Introduction, indeed, may be regarded as a short treatise on the theory of evidence, and, in connection with the appended Act of 1872, the author hopes it may prove useful to civil servants who are preparing in England for their Indian career, and to the law students in Indian Universities. The subject is one which reaches far beyond law. The law of evidence is nothing unless it is founded upon a rational conception of the manner in which truth as to all matters of fact whatever ought to be investigated. The four Chapters of the Introduction are—I. General Distribution of the Subject; II. A Statement of the Principles of Induction and Deduction, and a Comparison of their Application to Scientific and Judicial Inquiries; III. The Theory of Relevancy, with Illustration; IV. General Observations on the Indian Evidence Act.

Thornton.—ON LABOUR; Its Wrongful Claims and Rightful Dues; Its Actual Present State and Possible Future. By WILLIAM THOMAS THORNTON, C.B., Author of "A Plea for Peasant Proprietors," etc. Second Edition, revised. 8vo. 14s.

The object of this volume is to endeavour to find "a cure for human destitution," the search after which has been the passion and the work of the author's life. The work is divided into four books, and each book into a number of chapters. Book I. "Labour's Causes of Discontent." II. "Labour and Capital in Debate." III. "Labour and Capital in Antagonism." IV. "Labour and Capital in Alliance." All the highly important problems in Social and Political Economy connected with Labour and Capital are here discussed with knowledge, vigour, and originality, and for a noble purpose. The new edition has been thoroughly revised and considerably enlarged. "We cannot fail to recognise in his work the result of independent thought, high moral aim, and generous intrepidity in a noble cause. . . . . A really valuable contribution. The number of facts accumulated, both historical and statistical, make an especially valuable portion of the work."—WESTMINSTER REVIEW.

WORKS CONNECTED WITH THE SCIENCE OR THE HISTORY OF LANGUAGE.

(*For Editions of Greek and Latin Classical Authors, Grammars, and other School works, see* EDUCATIONAL CATALOGUE.)

Abbott.—A SHAKESPERIAN GRAMMAR: An Attempt to Illustrate some of the Differences between Elizabethan and Modern English. By the Rev. E. A. ABBOTT, M.A., Head Master of the City of London School. For the Use of Schools. New and Enlarged Edition. Extra fcap. 8vo. 6s.

> The object of this work is to furnish students of Shakespeare and Bacon with a short systematic account of some points of difference between Elizabethan Syntax and our own. The demand for a third edition within a year of the publication of the first, has encouraged the author to endeavour to make the work somewhat more useful, and to render it, as far as possible, a complete book of reference for all difficulties of Shaksperian Syntax or Prosody. For this purpose the whole of Shakespeare has been re-read, and an attempt has been made to include within this edition the explanation of every idiomatic difficulty (where the text is not confessedly corrupt) that comes within the province of a grammar as distinct from a glossary. The great object being to make a useful book of reference for students and for classes in schools, several Plays have been indexed so fully, that with the aid of a glossary and historical notes the references will serve for a complete commentary. "*A critical inquiry, conducted with great skill and knowledge, and with all the appliances of modern philology.*"—PALL MALL GAZETTE. "*Valuable not only as an aid to the critical study of Shakespeare, but as tending to familiarize the reader with Elizabethan English in general.*"—ATHENÆUM.

Besant.—STUDIES IN EARLY FRENCH POETRY. By WALTER BESANT, M.A. Crown 8vo. 8s. 6d.

> *A sort of impression rests on most minds that French literature begins with the "siècle de Louis Quatorze;" any previous literature being for the most part unknown or ignored. Few know anything of the enormous literary activity that began in the thirteenth century, was carried on by Rutebeuf, Marie de France, Gaston de Foix, Thibault de Champagne, and Lorris; was fostered by Charles of Orleans, by Margaret of Valois, by Francis the First; that gave a crowd of versifiers to France, enriched, strengthened, developed, and fixed the French language, and prepared the way for Corneille and for Racine. The present work aims to afford information and direction touching these early efforts of France in poetical literature. "In one moderately sized volume he has contrived to introduce us to the very best, if not to all of the early French poets."*—ATHENÆUM. *"Industry, the insight of a scholar, and a genuine enthusiasm for his subject, combine to make it of very considerable value."*—SPECTATOR.

Hales.—LONGER ENGLISH POEMS. With Notes, Philological and Explanatory, and an Introduction on the Teaching of English. Chiefly for use in Schools. Edited by J. W. HALES, M.A., late Fellow and Assistant Tutor of Christ's College, Cambridge; Lecturer in English Literature and Classical Composition at King's College School, London; &c. &c. Extra fcap. 8vo. 4s. 6d.

> *This work has been in preparation for some years, and part of it has been used as a class-book by the Editor for the last two years. It is intended as an aid to the Critical study of English Literature, and contains one or more of the larger poems, each complete, of prominent English Authors from Spenser to Shelley, including Burns' Saturday Night and Twa Dogs. In all cases the original spelling and the text of the best editions have been given; only in one or two poems has it been deemed necessary to make slight omissions and changes, that the "reverence due to boys might be well observed." The latter half of the volume is occupied with copious notes, critical, etymological, and explanatory, calculated to give the learner much insight in the structure and connection of the English tongue. An Index to the notes is appended.*

Helfenstein (James).—A COMPARATIVE GRAMMAR OF THE TEUTONIC LANGUAGES: Being at the same time a Historical Grammar of the English Language, and comprising Gothic, Anglo-Saxon, Early English, Modern English, Icelandic (Old Norse), Danish, Swedish, Old High German, Middle High German, Modern German, Old Saxon, Old Frisian, and Dutch. By JAMES HELFENSTEIN, Ph.D. 8vo. 18s.

This work traces the different stages of development through which the various Teutonic languages have passed, and the laws which have regulated their growth. The reader is thus enabled to study the relation which these languages bear to one another, and to the English language in particular, to which special attention is devoted throughout. In the chapters on Ancient and Middle Teutonic languages no grammatical form is omitted the knowledge of which is required for the study of ancient literature, whether Gothic or Anglo-Saxon or Early English. To each chapter is prefixed a sketch showing the relation of the Teutonic to the cognate languages, Greek, Latin, and Sanskrit. Those who have mastered the book will be in a position to proceed with intelligence to the more elaborate works of Grimm, Bopp, Pott, Schleicher, and others.

Morris.—HISTORICAL OUTLINES OF ENGLISH ACCIDENCE, comprising Chapters on the History and Development of the Language, and on Word-formation. By the Rev. RICHARD MORRIS, LL.D., Member of the Council of the Philol. Soc., Lecturer on English Language and Literature in King's College School, Editor of "Specimens of Early English," etc., etc. Third Edition. Fcap. 8vo. 6s.

Dr. Morris has endeavoured to write a work which can be profitably used by students and by the upper forms in our public schools. His almost unequalled knowledge of early English Literature renders him peculiarly qualified to write a work of this kind; and English Grammar, he believes, without a reference to the older forms, must appear altogether anomalous, inconsistent, and unintelligible. In the writing of this volume, moreover, he has taken advantage of the researches into our language made by all the most eminent scholars in England, America, and on the Continent. The author shows the place of English among the languages of the world, expounds clearly and with great minuteness "Grimm's Law," gives a brief history of the English language and an account of the various dialects, investigates the history and principles of Phonology, Orthography, Accent, and Etymology, and devotes several chapters to the consideration of the various Parts of Speech, and the final one to Derivation and Word-formation.

Peile (John, M.A.)—AN INTRODUCTION TO GREEK AND LATIN ETYMOLOGY. By JOHN PEILE, M.A., Fellow and Assistant Tutor of Christ's College, Cambridge, formerly Teacher of Sanskrit in the University of Cambridge New and revised Edition. Crown 8vo. 10s. 6d.

These Philological Lectures are the result of Notes made during the author's reading for some years previous to their publication. These Notes were put into the shape of lectures, delivered at Christ's College, as one set in the "Intercollegiate" list. They have been printed with some additions and modifications, but substantially as they were delivered. "The book may be accepted as a very valuable contribution to the science of language."—SATURDAY REVIEW.

Philology.—THE JOURNAL OF SACRED AND CLASSICAL PHILOLOGY. Four Vols. 8vo. 12s. 6d.

THE JOURNAL OF PHILOLOGY. New Series. Edited by W. G. CLARK, M.A., JOHN E. B. MAYOR, M.A., and W. ALDIS WRIGHT, M.A. Nos. I., II., III., and IV. 8vo. 4s. 6d. each. (Half-yearly.)

Roby (H. J.)—A GRAMMAR OF THE LATIN LANGUAGE, FROM PLAUTUS TO SUETONIUS. By HENRY JOHN ROBY, M.A., late Fellow of St. John's College, Cambridge. Part I. containing:—Book I. Sounds. Book II. Inflexions. Book III. Word Formation. Appendices. Second Edition. Crown 8vo. 8s. 6d.

This work is the result of an independent and careful study of the writers of the strictly Classical period, the period embraced between the time of Plautus and that of Suetonius. The author's aim has been to give the facts of the language in as few words as possible. It will be found that the arrangement of the book and the treatment of the various divisions differ in many respects from those of previous grammars. Mr. Roby has given special prominence to the treatment of Sounds and Word-formation; and in the First Book he has done much towards settling a discussion which is at present largely engaging the attention of scholars, viz., the Pronunciation of the Classical languages. In the full Appendices will be found various valuable details still further illustrating the subjects discussed in the text. The author's reputation as a scholar and critic is already well known, and the publishers are encouraged to believe that his present work will take its place as perhaps the most original, exhaustive, and scientific grammar of the Latin language that has ever issued from the British press. "The book is marked by the clear and practical insight of a master in his art. It is a book which would do honour to any country."—ATHENÆUM. "Brings before the student in a methodical form the best results of modern philology bearing on the Latin language."—SCOTSMAN.

Taylor (Rev. Isaac).—WORDS AND PLACES; or, Etymological Illustrations of History, Ethnology, and Geography. By the Rev. ISAAC TAYLOR. Third Edition, revised and compressed. With Maps. Globe 8vo. 6s.

"In this edition the work has been recast with the intention of fitting it for the use of students and general readers, rather than, as before, to appeal to the judgment of philologers. The book has already been adopted by many teachers, and is prescribed as a text-book in the Cambridge Higher Examinations for Women: and it is hoped that the reduced size and price, and the other changes now introduced, may make it more generally useful than heretofore for Educational purposes.

Trench.—Works by R. CHENEVIX TRENCH, D.D., Archbishop of Dublin. (For other Works by the same Author, see THEOLOGICAL CATALOGUE.)

Archbishop Trench has done much to spread an interest in the history of our English tongue. He is acknowledged to possess an uncommon power of presenting, in a clear, instructive, and interesting manner, the fruits of his own extensive research, as well as the results of the labours of other scientific and historical students of language; while, as the ATHENÆUM says, "his sober judgment and sound sense are barriers against the misleading influence of arbitrary hypotheses."

Trench (R. C.)—*continued.*

SYNONYMS OF THE NEW TESTAMENT. New Edition, enlarged. 8vo. cloth. 12s.

The study of synonyms in any language is valuable as a discipline for training the mind to close and accurate habits of thought; more especially is this the case in Greek—"a language spoken by a people of the finest and subtlest intellect; who saw distinctions where others saw none; who divided out to different words what others often were content to huddle confusedly under a common term." This work is recognised as a valuable companion to every student of the New Testament in the original. This, the Seventh Edition, has been carefully revised, and a considerable number of new synonyms added. Appended is an Index to the synonyms, and an Index to many other words alluded to or explained throughout the work. "He is," the ATHENÆUM *says, "a guide in this department of knowledge to whom his readers may entrust themselves with confidence."*

ON THE STUDY OF WORDS. Lectures Addressed (originally) to the Pupils at the Diocesan Training School, Winchester. Fourteenth Edition, revised and enlarged. Fcap. 8vo. 4s. 6d.

This, it is believed, was probably the first work which drew general attention in this country to the importance and interest of the critical and historical study of English. It still retains its place as one of the most successful if not the only exponent of those aspects of Words of which it treats. The subjects of the several Lectures are—I. "Introductory." II. "On the Poetry of Words." III. "On the Morality of Words." IV. "On the History of Words." V. "On the Rise of New Words." VI. "On the Distinction of Words." VII. "The Schoolmaster's Use of Words."

ENGLISH PAST AND PRESENT. Seventh Edition, revised and improved. Fcap. 8vo. 4s. 6d.

This is a series of eight Lectures, in the first of which Archbishop Trench considers the English language as it now is, decomposes some specimens of it, and thus discovers of what elements it is compact. In the second Lecture he considers what the language might have been

Trench (R. C.)—*continued.*

If the Norman Conquest had never taken place. In the following six Lectures he institutes from various points of view a comparison between the present language and the past, points out gains which it has made, losses which it has endured, and generally calls attention to some of the more important changes through which it has passed, or is at present passing.

A SELECT GLOSSARY OF ENGLISH WORDS USED FORMERLY IN SENSES DIFFERENT FROM THEIR PRESENT. Fourth Edition, Enlarged. Fcap. 8vo. 4s.

This alphabetically arranged Glossary contains many of the most important of those English words which in the course of time have gradually changed their meanings. The author's object is to point out some of these changes, to suggest how many more there may be, to show how slight and subtle, while, yet most real, these changes have often been, to trace here and there the progressive steps by which the old meaning has been put off and the new put on—the exact road which a word has travelled. The author thus hopes t render some assistance to those who regard this as a serviceable discipline in the training of their own minds or the minds of others. Although the book is in the form of a Glossary, it will be found as interesting as a series of brief well-told biographies.

ON SOME DEFICIENCIES IN OUR ENGLISH DICTIONARIES: Being the substance of Two Papers read before the Philological Society. Second Edition, revised and enlarged. 8vo. 3s.

Wood.—Works by H. T. W. Wood, B.A., Clare College, Cambridge:—

THE RECIPROCAL INFLUENCE OF ENGLISH AND FRENCH LITERATURE IN THE EIGHTEENTH CENTURY. Crown 8vo. 2s 6d.

CHANGES IN THE ENGLISH LANGUAGE BETWEEN THE PUBLICATION OF WICLIF'S BIBLE AND THAT OF THE AUTHORIZED VERSION; A.D. 1400 to A.D. 1600. Crown 8vo. 2s. 6d.

This Essay gained the Le Bas Prize for the year 1870. Besides the Introductory Section explaining the aim and scope of the Essay, there are other three Sections and three Appendices. Section II. treats of "English before Chaucer." III. "Chaucer to Caxton." IV. "From Caxton to the Authorised Version."—Appendix: I. "Table of English Literature," A.D. 1300—A.D. 1611. II. "Early English Bible." III. "Inflectional Changes of the Verb." This will be found a most valuable help in the study of our language during the period embraced in the Essay. "As we go with him," the ATHENÆUM says, "we learn something new at every step."

Yonge.—HISTORY OF CHRISTIAN NAMES. By CHARLOTTE M. YONGE, Author of "The Heir of Redclyffe." Two Vols. Crown 8vo. 1l. 1s.

Miss Yonge's work is acknowledged to be the authority on the interesting subject of which it treats. Until she wrote on the subject, the history of names—especially Christian Names as distinguished from Surnames—had been but little examined; nor why one should be popular and another forgotten—why one should flourish throughout Europe, another in one country alone, another around some petty district. In each case she has tried to find out whence the name came, whether it had a patron, and whether the patron took it from the myths or heroes of his own country, or from the meaning of the words. She has then tried to classify the names, as to treat them merely alphabetically would destroy all their interest and connection. They are classified first by language, beginning with Hebrew and coming down through Greek and Latin to Celtic, Teutonic, Slavonic, and other sources, ancient and modern; then by meaning or spirit. "An almost exhaustive treatment of the subject . . . The painstaking toil of a thoughtful and cultured mind on a most interesting theme."—LONDON QUARTERLY.

www.ingramcontent.com/pod-product-compliance
Lightning Source LLC
Chambersburg PA
CBHW030323020526
44117CB00030B/895